THE NEXT MONEY CRASH—
and How to Avoid It

To Steve

thanks for your participation

THE NEXT MONEY CRASH—
and How to Avoid It

*Proceedings from a Conference at the Federal
Reserve Bank of Philadelphia Building*

WILLIAM C. DUNKELBERG, ULI KORTSCH,
LAURENCE KOTLIKOFF, DAVID KOTOK, MICHAEL KUMHOF,
WILLIAM POOLE, JEFFREY SACHS, AND ADAIR TURNER

OPEN BOOK
EDITIONS
A Berrett-Koehler Partner

iUniverse®

THE NEXT MONEY CRASH— AND HOW TO AVOID IT
Proceedings from a Conference at the Federal
Reserve Bank of Philadelphia Building

iUniverse books may be ordered through booksellers or by contacting:

iUniverse
1663 Liberty Drive
Bloomington, IN 47403
www.iuniverse.com
1-800-Authors (1-800-288-4677)

ISBN: 978-1-4917-3950-1 (sc)
ISBN: 978-1-4917-3949-5 (hc)
ISBN: 978-1-4917-3951-8 (e)

Library of Congress Control Number: 2014912032

Printed in the United States of America.

iUniverse rev. date: 07/11/2014

To those who know the times and have
the courage to take action

Contents

Foreword

By this time we all know how close we came to a complete global meltdown in the financial world during the Great Recession, especially after the bankruptcy of Lehman Brothers on September 15, 2008. Here is a partial list of what we saw:

» The longest and deepest US recession in the post-WWII period[1]

» A near doubling of the US unemployment rate

» Negative home equity for 22 percent of all US home owners as late as October 2012[2]

» Massive increase in mortgage foreclosures

» Significant decrease in retirement savings

» US **Real**[3] Gross Domestic Product (real GDP) having fallen at its fastest rate since the 1950s

---

1   Federal Reserve Bank of Minneapolis, "The Recession and Recovery in Perspective," https://www.minneapolisfed.org/publications_papers/studies/recession_perspective/index.cfm.

2   Ingrid Gould Ellen and Samuel Dastrup, "Housing and the Great Recession," Ellen, Ingrid Gould and Samual Dastrup, October. 2012, http://furmancenter.org/files/publications/HousingandtheGreatRecession.pdf.

3   See Glossary under "nominal versus real". The first use of a glossary term is always in bold.

- » Civil unrest in Greece due to economic distress
- » Major **sovereign debt**[4] increases in most **OECD**[5] countries, especially the weaker members of the **eurozone**
- » A virtual paralysis of interbank lending
- » Social consequences, such as a decrease in the birthrate as well as the marriage rate, an increase in divorces, increased child malnutrition, etc.[6]

Innumerable articles and many books have been written on the supposed causes of this series of events, many of them very factual with respect to the decisions and actions of governments, banks, and companies. The premise of this book is that by far the majority of these were analyzing symptoms and not going to the very root of the matter that created those conditions in the first place.

Since those years, we have greatly increased the regulatory complexity of our financial system through the **Dodd-Frank** bill in the United States, as well as the establishment of Federal Reserve Bank oversight on systemically important financial institutions (**SIFIs**). This ongoing burden is all in the name of strengthening our financial system so that the government, through its capacity to tax its citizens, need not do that again by being forced to ride to the rescue. Many believe that the untold billions in regulatory costs this engenders are all for the sake of safety. This book argues that, again, these actions are only dealing with symptoms and not the root causes and that, in actual fact, we are not now any safer than we were before the Great Recession. And no, this cannot be laid at the feet of greedy bankers or politicians, even though they may have lent a helping hand. It is a systemic issue.

---

4 See Glossary. The first use of a glossary term is always in bold.

5 See Glossary. The first use of a glossary term is always in bold.

6 Stephen Simpson, "5 Long-Term Consequences of the Recession," *Forbes*, November 12, 2010.

Since the establishment of the Federal Reserve Bank in 1913 and especially as a result of the Great Depression of the 1930s, we have most certainly created a plethora of stabilizing forces in our financial system. Yet Mark Buchanan in his book *Ubiquity: Why Catastrophes Happen*[7] explains how we as humans—as well as most natural systems—have a tendency to organize ourselves into "critical states." As we continue to increase the complexity of our stabilizing efforts, we actually end up doing the opposite in the long term and end up creating what he calls a "knife-edge of instability." At the point of this knife-edge, it takes only a random and often seemingly minor and unrelated event to topple the whole system into a collapse. This collapse then decreases the level of complexity or tension in the system so that a new level of stability is created. This begs the question as to whether the stabilizing steps taken over the last few decades, and especially the recent ones, have actually increased our level of macro stability or simply sharpened the knife-edge.

In analyzing the root causes, we recognize that the Great Recession was not an isolated event, but we view it as a continuum in the context of historical factors. In the "olden days," if you needed money and the bank was closed (which was often, remember "banker's hours"?) life could be difficult. Technology and the demand for convenience and more complex banking services have eliminated most of those old inconveniences. But the importance of a properly functioning banking and payments system has not diminished; indeed it has become more and more important. When it fails to work properly, the cost is very high, as our most recent experience has shown.

At the core of these failures is the system's demand for leveraged risk. The guardians of our "money," the providers of "liquidity,"

---

7   Buchanan, Mark. *Ubiquity: Why Catastrophes Happen*. New York: Broadway
     Books, 2002.

have invariably mismanaged the funds that we entrusted to them in exchange for a "safe" and accordingly "low" return. In short, these institutions took risks with our money (and others' money, with leverage) that we would not have taken ourselves and did so without our knowledge. When markets took these institutions to task for their inappropriate behavior, the punishment fell on the innocent citizens (major recessions) who simply wanted a safe place to hold their liquidity. When interest rates on government bonds go negative, meaning savers don't trust financial institutions and they pay our government for safety, it is clear that the financial system has failed.[8]

What is "money"? The economics textbook will usually start with a functional definition, such as "anything widely accepted as a means of payment". Historically, gold coins have served widely as money. Certificates issued with guaranteed gold backing were more convenient. This created the opportunity to issue more claims (as "loans") than actual gold held, knowing (under normal circumstances) that not everyone would ask for their gold at the same time.

But once "Guttenberg invented the printing press," new troubles arose. In the "olden days," we defined money as currency in circulation plus deposits in checking accounts (deposits that paid no interest so were held for transactions purposes). Technology blurred this distinction, making it possible to quickly move funds from interest-earning deposits to checking accounts, eliminating the "pass book savings" and a trip to the bank to move funds.

---

8   This occurred during the Depression when bank failures were widespread and savers did not want to risk losing their deposits. Holding huge amounts of cash was expensive, risky, and impractical. Today, the FDIC guarantees deposits, but the negative return on TIPS reflected the markets' expectation of much higher future inflation because of the fragility of the banking system and the policies the Fed pursued to preserve liquidity.

Backing currencies with precious metals has become a relic of the past, as it made providing a proper quantity of the means of exchange too difficult. Now, the value of a unit of currency is determined by the quantity of goods and services it will command.

Financial institutions remain the custodians of our purchasing power, our liquidity. Consumers' deposits are protected by government insurance, and funds are quickly made available when a bank fails. (Dodd-Frank did provide unlimited insurance during the crisis, which expired December 31, 2012). When contracts cannot be honored or obligations met because financial institutions cannot keep their promises, businesses can fail. And this cost falls, ultimately, on the citizens who rely on the financial system to provide their means of payment.

So, how can we separate the two functions of providing a riskless means of deposits/payments and still allow savers who want a return that comes with some risk, to do so? The answer is simple—create insured institutions that simply hold deposits and create transaction services in exchange for fees and establish other types of institutions (many in existence today) who take some risk to get a higher return for the depositor (and their shareholders). Institutions providing transactions funds will be boring but totally safe. There will never be a concern that deposits cannot be retrieved at the demand of the depositor, no "runs" on these banks. Other institutions could accept "deposits," but these would not be federally insured. Institutions would have to disclose how they were investing the "deposits" (more like equity investments in this structure) and the historic and expected returns for the depositor. Private insurers would emerge that could provide insurance to institutions based on the risks they were taking with depositor funds if the institution wanted to pay for it. For institutions like stock brokers, it is understood that it is "caveat emptor[9]."

---

9   Meaning that the risk resides with the investor or literally, "Let the buyer beware"

This only solves one part of the problem—confidence in the currency, its liquidity, and its accessibility to its owners. Banks that provide money can't fail. But this does not eliminate "risk" in the economic system; it simply segregates it and allows other "mutual fund institutions" to provide the higher returns that risk taking can produce. These institutions may provide private insurance but have no taxpayer backing. The key here is that these mutual fund institutions must provide transparency. People who put their money in these institutions will demand it, insist on knowing the risks they are taking since there will be no government insurance. This contrasts to putting your money in an account at, say, JP Morgan today, unaware of how the bank is "investing" its money or of the risks it is taking. If it "fails," your deposit will be made good by taxpayers, but the failure will impose great costs on the citizenry, as the Great Recession illustrated. Had you known what risks these institutions were taking, you might never have lent them your money (deposited it). The social costs of this lack of transparency (and appropriate regulation) are immense. The banking system we all depend on cannot continue to be the source of such instability and costs.

What follows is based on a conference, "Fixing the Banking System for Good," organized by the Global Interdependence Center (GIC). The Federal Reserve Bank of Philadelphia provided the forum, as it does for many GIC events, but this was not an endorsement of any of the views expressed at the conference. Although several differing views are presented, they all have a common goal—to moderate the financial disruptions that the current system allows, even amplifies; to provide a sound, stable currency; to compel, through market forces, more transparency in the activities of financial institutions; and to take taxpayers off the hook. In all the plans, more capital (based on risk in the assets) and more transparency are key elements, along with the end to government guarantees, which provide advantages to large, opaque financial institutions. Dodd-Frank and the "**Volcker Rule**" tip a hat in the needed directions, but much more needs to be done, as the participants in this conference will discuss. Stay tuned.

WILLIAM C. DUNKELBERG

WILLIAM C. DUNKELBERG

Former dean and professor of economics at the School of Business and Management, Temple University, William C. Dunkelberg's prior appointments were at the Krannert Graduate School of Management, Purdue University; the Graduate School of Business, Stanford University; and the Survey Research Center at the University of Michigan. He has served as the Chief Economist for the National Federation of Independent Business (350,000 member firms) since 1971. He has BA, MA, and PhD degrees in economics from the University of Michigan.

Dr. Dunkelberg is a nationally known authority on small business, entrepreneurship, consumer behavior, and consumer credit and government policy. He was one of four final candidates for vice chairman of the board of governors of the Federal Reserve System in 1981, served as an advisor to the Secretary of Commerce, and was appointed to the Consumer Advisory Council of the Federal Reserve System in 1989 (two terms). He is a past president and a Fellow of the National Association for Business Economics (NABE). He was appointed to the Census Advisory Committee representing the American Economic Association in 1992 and again in 1995 (serving as chair) and served on the board of the National Bureau of Economic Research from 1996 to 1999. He is an elected member of the Conference of Business Economists (and chairman in 2003) and the National Business Economic Issues Council and the first recipient of the Small Business Administration's Research Advocate of the Year award.

Dr. Dunkelberg has presented expert testimony before the US House and Senate on consumer credit, inflation, tax reform, the minimum wage, small business, electronic funds transfer systems, energy efficiency standards, health care, and **monetary and fiscal policy**. He has appeared on Bloomberg; Fox Business Network; CNN; CNBC; the ABC, CBS, and NBC evening news programs; *Good Morning America*; and numerous local news and business TV and radio shows. He is frequently quoted in major news publications, including *The Wall Street Journal, Businessweek, The New York Times, U.S. News & World Report, Grant's Interest Rate Observer, USA Today, Time, The Washington Post*, and *Newsweek* and serves on the economic forecasting panels for *USA Today* and Bloomberg. He has authored and coauthored numerous books and articles and writes a monthly small business economic report for the National Federation of Independent Business. He had his own radio show on WPHT 1210 AM Philadelphia every Sunday for two years, and his editorials were carried by KYW News Radio for fourteen years.

His board service includes NCO Group, ADVANTA Corp. (1989–2001), Liberty Bell Bank (chair), Active-e Solutions (sold to Neoware), Penn Fishing Tackle Mfg. (sold December 2002), Made4me.com (a founder, dba Intellifit.com), Ensoniq Corporation (sold to Creative Labs), the Global Interdependence Center (chair), the Credit Research Center (Georgetown University), the Commonwealth Foundation, the International Visitors Council, the Ben Franklin Innovation Investment Advisory Committee, the National Economist Club (2001), the Javie Foundation for Charity, the Laboratory for Student Success, Consumer Credit Counseling

Services of Delaware Valley, and the Pennsylvania Council on Economic Education. Dr. Dunkelberg served as a regional judge for the Ernst & Young Entrepreneur of the Year program for fourteen years, as a national judge in 2001 and 2003, and as a member of the board of the Greater Philadelphia Chamber of Commerce. He served as a member of the Quality of Markets Committee for the Philadelphia Stock Exchange.

Preface

MAY 2014

I was recently asked to explain what had led me into a deep involvement with our monetary system, and I totally surprised myself by blurting out one word—anger. I had never thought of my anger as a personal root cause before but decided to find some deeper understanding of my own motivations. We usually think of anger as a negative emotion, but it can also be the hot starting point for a creative force. For a while, I moved my family to Hawaii and realized that all its beauty was spawned by hot magma flows, which had created these islands of paradise. It was my deep unconscious anger that created the heat needed for the magma that became my interest in understanding the monetary system. Ultimately that magma was to surface and start flowing.

I have spent a fair amount of time in the developing world, having worked in over fifty countries—my wife quit counting when she got to forty-five—and so have seen extremes of wealth and poverty with the attendant health and service provision disparities. I remember an event that made quite an impression on me. I was invited to a party in a major African country attended by senior government officials, investment managers, and heads of major corporations. Obviously, security was tight, but that was understandable. What struck me and became unforgettable was the level of glitz and glamor, the cost that had obviously been paid, and yet all this within a short distance from a world of squalor. Now, I am not anywhere close to being a communist or believing in total equality—rather I am a fervent believer in the free market system—but the degree of wealth and life differentiation I experienced left me deeply struggling internally.

This unease stayed with me for years, as I began to try and understand what some of the underlying factors creating such an unequal playing field could be. I have met many entrepreneurs who are intelligent, very hard working, and honorable in their dealings and yet struggle daily to make ends meet. I asked myself, are there structural impediments to which we are blind that are major causes? I started speaking out, yet always without answers.

I started working on national microenterprise loan systems, initiating the creation of secondary financial markets for these, using rudimentary securitization techniques by marrying the sophistication of a global finance system to the smallest borrower on the street. In the process, I had meetings with about fifteen heads of state and ministers of finance. The first person I hired was Romeo Horton, the founder of the African Development Bank and former Minister of Industry and Commerce of Liberia. Romeo and I crisscrossed Africa with constant interactions with the World Bank, IMF, and African Development Bank. We analyzed national credit ratings and looked at amounts and valuations of sovereign debt, capital flows, and legal structures helping or hindering business development. I believe that we were able to create some real change for good, but during the entire time, usually only subconsciously, hot magma was flowing under the crust of conscious work on our business. What are the real issues? What are the real causes? Was there a causal linking between currency fluctuations, wealth discrepancies, increasing private and government debt levels, and the general economic instability I kept seeing in so many countries? I had to find out.

I changed continents and started a securitization company in Peru. For about two years, I commuted on a weekly basis from my home in the suburbs of Philadelphia to Lima, Peru. People thought I was crazy, but with no time zone change, and normally taking all-night flights so that I could sleep comfortably on the plane, I thought it was better than a daily commute to Center City, Philadelphia. The cabin crews now recognized me as a regular, and once, the airline even pulled a plane back to let me on as I was a few minutes late; I am sure the other passengers did not appreciate that. Then we got hit by the collapse of the Asian Tigers in 1997, and instantly, all securities issued and backed by assets from the developing world were considered worthless. The economic instability was outside my control and that of those working with me, but the effect was a punch in the face for the company. I will never forget the conference call we had with all staff online from our offices when I shut the company down. I did not want to declare the company bankrupt and so personally picked up all the debts from the company, a decision that later almost caused my personal bankruptcy. Talk about heating magma!

The economic instability I witnessed created political pressures with attendant changes and often accompanied by riots on the streets from angry and impoverished people. Was there a link between the economic instability and my prior observations in Africa? Technically, I could list the reasons for the Asian Tiger malaise, but were these only symptoms of deeper problems? It reminds me of situations where, medically, the cause of death is pneumonia, but what was the underlying condition which allowed the body to succumb? Was it AIDS or cancer or a prior history of smoking? In our world of instant sound bites, we must have answers immediately or we are not heard. We tend not to have time for deep reflection.

My involvements with securitization led me naturally into the world of structured investment vehicles (SIVs), bank off balance sheet operations, and jurisdictional variations of bank leverages depending on contingent liabilities. This is the murkier world of finance but one in which those in the know or with the connections can make untold wealth—or lose all. The more I learned, the hotter that subconscious magma rumbled.

The volcano finally blew during an extended Christmas family holiday in 2012. My family and I were all together in a large chalet in the mountains of Colorado, surrounded by sun, snow, and kids with grandkids. It would appear that the mind and spirit need to be fully at rest for us to gather the insight needed for creating a unified thought field—the integration of what we did not even know that we knew. Revelation!

I had understood for some time that money is created in our fractional reserve banking system by the formation of debt. I hear people complain that our money is not backed by anything, but it is—100 percent of it is backed by debt. I had struggled with that concept ethically for some time. I don't know if, in my economics classes, we ever studied Irving Fisher or the Chicago Plan or if I had just totally forgotten about it, but during that time in the Colorado chalet, I built a monetary system in my mind that would not need the use of debt to create new stocks of money.

I spent January 2013 building out the framework of "my" new monetary system and ended with about four pages of point form notes. The more I thought about it, the larger and better the implications became economically; socially; and, yes, ethically. By the beginning of February, I realized that it must be time to come out of hibernation and see if any of this made any sense to anyone else. I called a monetary economist, Omar Borla, who had been extensively involved in monetary re-workings in South America, and he agreed to come to my home during his next visit to Philadelphia. We spent about an hour and a half together, and I went through my pages of notes with him. I will not forget his final words: "You are a really nice guy, Uli, and I really like you, but you are totally out of your mind!" I thought, *Good ideas, bad ideas; I guess this was a bad idea.* He called me back two days later and said that he had not been able to get the plan I had presented out of his mind, was sure it would work, and where do we go from here?

That encouraged me to become serious about this. Shortly afterward, I met with Dr. William Dunkelberg, who was most encouraging and has continued to be so. He is a major force in this endeavor. I then met with John Mauldin, whom I had known for a couple of decades. He led me on to Dr. Lacy Hunt, who then gave me source materials on the Chicago Plan and Irving Fisher. Today, I realize that my thoughts are by no means original—that is actually a source of great tranquility to me—and that many economists through multiple decades have proposed the same or similar measures. Evolving from this came the request to organize a conference at the Federal Reserve Bank of Philadelphia building, the proceedings of which constitute the contents of this book.

The journey for me is very personal and continues. Our proposals are not perfect—nor will they ever be—but as we are open to change, improvements will continue to be made and come from many quarters. I have made new friends through this endeavor and find increasing interest both in the topic generally and more specifically in the proposals expounded in this book. We all want a world of greater stability and an increasingly level playing field. The proposals in this book provide both.

CHAPTER ONE

Conference Summary

AS THE ORGANIZER AND CONVENER of the conference presented in *The Next Money Crash—and How to Avoid It*, I realized the need for an overall outline to aid readers' understanding. Hence, I created this summary chapter (and a similar video[10]) to ensure that readers (and viewers) can see the forest without getting lost in the trees.

There are times in the presentations when the authors need to present extensive data or exhaustive arguments in order to make a point real or prove that conclusions that may be counterintuitive are, in fact, true. At times like that, all of us have a tendency to glaze over and lose track of the logical flow of the presentation. This summary, with quotes from each author, is meant to create that flow without going into the extensive background given by the various authors. If the reader were to read nothing but this chapter, it would give him or her the gist of what this book is all about.

---

10   The video summary is available at http://www.youtube.com/
     watch?v=ZaC1VxQPqtc

In April 2013, the United States Federal Reserve Bank in Philadelphia hosted a seven-hour conference sponsored by the Global Interdependence Center.

World renowned economists offered their important analyses and solutions to help guide us through our current turbulent economic times.

Together, we asked the questions on the minds and in the hearts of many people around the world:

» Why does it appear that everywhere governments are making great promises, cutting spending, and yet we have an ever increasing debt load?

» Why does it feel like your taxes are increasing but government services are deteriorating?

» Why did the real estate bubble occur, and why is it still so difficult to get out of it?

» Why does it appear that social inequality continues to increase?

» Why is Japan experiencing what we commonly call "the lost two decades"?

» Why does Europe appear to be coming apart at the seams over the euro?

» Why do we keep on seeing ethical lapses on Wall Street?

» Why are there bank lines in Cyprus?

» Why are there riots in Greece?

» Why, why, why …

Is it possible that what appear to be disparate elements are, in effect, connected by a common theme? Yes. That common theme is what our conference dealt with.

I was pleased to be asked to organize the conference and even more so when we were able to bring together world-class leaders and thinkers in economics to look at these issues and what can be done with them—to consider radical solutions to the economic conundrum we are currently facing worldwide.

Our dignitary speakers included Professor Jeffrey Sachs of Columbia University, twice listed by *Time* magazine as one of the one hundred most influential people in the world; Larry Kotlikoff, economics professor at Boston University and formerly on the president's Council of Economic Advisers; Lord Adair Turner, former chairman of the British Financial Services Authority; David Kotok, the CIO and CEO of Cumberland Advisors; Bill Poole, former president of the St. Louis Fed; Michael Kumhof of the International Monetary Fund; and me as a wrap-up speaker.

All of those speeches are online in full at http://www.interdependence.org/resource/ and then filter for the desired author from this book for the year 2013. I trust that this short summary will give you an idea of what we went through.

The theme was our fractional reserve banking system; how money really works, not only in our country but in the whole world; and some radical solutions toward solving the debt and instability problems we regularly face.

I want to start off by looking at banking as it actually works.

Here's an excerpt from the presentation given by Michael Kumhof of the International Monetary Fund, in which he discusses deposit creation.

MICHAEL KUMHOF:

The key function of banks is money creation and not **intermediation**[11]. If you tell that even to a mainstream economist, it's provocative. But it is 100

> The key function of banks is money creation and not intermediation

percent correct. What banks do is create a new loan on the asset side of the balance sheet and, when that is done, create a new deposit of exactly the same amount that is credited to the guy who has just borrowed the money. I was a banker at Barclays Bank for five years; I made loans, and I know exactly what the entries are that you need to create when you make a loan.

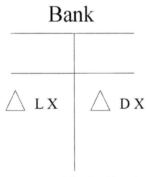

Bank

Figure 1.1, Loans and the Bank's Balance Sheet

When the bank makes a loan, the balance sheet is like this. (See figure 1.1, "Loans and the Bank's Balance Sheet") When it creates a loan, it creates an additional loan entry, delta-L, on the asset side, for the customer. Let's call him customer "X". The bank then creates an additional deposit entry on the debit side, delta-D, and that is also in the name of the same person, X. The bank at that moment creates new money out of thin air, and I will go into more detail about that now.

---

11   See Glossary. The first use of a glossary term is always in bold.

Now, how about intermediation? A common definition of intermediation is that the banks—or the banking system as a whole, and it's important to make that distinction—accept nonbank deposits of savings, somebody's savings, and then lend them out to somebody else who needs them. Under this definition, banks are not intermediaries. They never, ever do that! Because what they do is what I have just shown with my little drawing. And this is not intermediation, because this customer, X, is the same on both sides of the balance sheet. In terms of causation, the critical issue here is that loans come before deposits. Loans create deposits, and not vice versa. What the intermediation story misses completely is the monetary nature of financing.

So, let's go into more detail now. What story would I have to tell in order to tell the intermediation story? Let's look at the scenario, where A wants to buy goods or assets and B wants to sell. Now B dumps the goods at the bank and the deposit is recorded, and then the bank gives the goods to A and the loan is recorded. That story is, of course, complete nonsense, because that never happens. But that's how you have to argue if you say that banks intermediate funds, that is, intermediate savings from some customer to some other customer because that implies that deposits come before loans.

What you have to ignore for this is, of course, if somebody comes into bank one and brings in a check that is drawn on bank two. That is a micro-phenomenon. That doesn't change the overall amount of loans and deposits in the economy; it just reshuffles them between different banks. That's not relevant for this argument. Cash deposits are also not relevant. First of all, cash is a tiny item in terms of the overall bank business, and secondly, banks never lend out cash directly. You only draw out cash against an existing deposit.

The intermediation story is a completely impossible story, yet it dominates in today's debate. It is also known as the "loanable funds story."

For the "money creation story," we start with the exact same scenario. A wants to buy goods, and B wants to sell goods. Now, A goes to the bank to get financing, and B stays at home. He has nothing at all to do with this. A gets a new loan of $1 million and a new deposit of $1 million. What the bank has done is to create its own funds, deposits, in the act of lending. It has not had to wait for anybody to deposit something first in order to make the loan. It created its own funding. That, of course, is an absolutely extraordinary privilege that is not enjoyed by any other kind of business.

We've now learned that it takes debt to create money. Every time you take a loan out, part of that money is created out of thin air, or of what we call "ex nihilo," a fancy word. But what's

> It takes debt to create money

even harder to understand is the opposite. What happens when you pay part of that debt back; when you make a mortgage payment, when you pay your car off, what happens? You are actually destroying money; it's not just that you do not have the proceeds of your loan anymore. You are actually taking money out of circulation. That's a difficult concept. Just as the loan which the bank authorized by creating a deposit into your account out of nothing, so the repayment of that loan goes back to where it came from: nothing. The bank only gains by the interest it is allowed to charge in the meantime while you are paying it off.

Well, what happens when millions of people, when most of society, is trying to do that because we've taken too many loans? We call it a de-leveraging economy, and that's what creates the difficulties that we are currently facing.

Since the Great Recession at the beginning of 2008, the Federal Reserve Bank has been printing; you know, we use that word, but it's not like the printing presses are running all the time, it's only a small portion that is physically printed. The rest is just electronic money; you understand that. We call it "quantitative easing." Let me keep on using the word *printing* just because it's easy in all of our minds. The Federal Reserve has been printing a steady stream of new money in order to compensate for the money that we are destroying by getting rid of the leverage, the debt, that we have taken on. Currently, they're printing $85 billion a month. Back to the Great Recession, since that time, the assets of the Federal Reserve Bank have increased from about $900 billion to $3.3 trillion. Here's a short clip by David Kotok going through this process. Remember, David's from Cumberland Advisors, and he's an expert on this subject.

DAVID KOTOK:

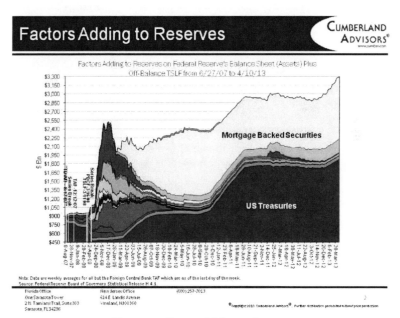

Figure 1.2: Factors Adding to Reserve

This is the Federal Reserve's asset side of its balance sheet. (See figure 1.2, "Factors Adding to Reserve") We see this all the time. We call this a rainbow chart, something we put on our Web site at Cumberland Advisors. You're all welcome to come look at it. We now have twenty thousand to thirty thousand visitors a week who look at the series of central bank charts. The data's available to anybody, but I guess we make it convenient for them.

As you can see, before the 2007/2008 financial crisis, we see a total of about $900 billion in assets, most of it treasuries. Then we had a little excitement called Lehman, AIG, a few other things. We had this big rainbow of Fed programs they're running off, and by early 2013 we're at about $3 trillion and climbing every month. You can see that a big part of it is mortgage-backed securities; the rest of it is in treasuries, and the treasuries are now with mixed maturities, long, intermediate, and short. They're no longer just short.

David goes on in his speech to show how the four largest central banks in the world—what we tend to call the G4—have been on a tear printing. There is that word again. And they've gone from about $3.5 trillion into $11.5 trillion. This is a global experiment; we have never, ever done this before—not in the whole world. Did we ever think this was going to happen? Here's another short excerpt from David on this subject.

DAVID KOTOK:

The growth rate of the size of the central banks' balance sheets is accelerating. Think about that. If we had had this meeting six years ago and somebody were to stand here and say, "Six years from now, we're going to come together at a conference. We're going to have the central banks' balance sheets of the world go triple the size, accelerate the growth rate, and when we do it, we'll have a large negative output, high unemployment worldwide, next to zero inflation, the short-term interest rate will be near zero, the long-term interest rate of high-grade sovereign debt throughout the world will be somewhere between 1 and 2 percent," everybody in this room would have said, "Hmm, he's a nut; we should lock him up." But that's exactly where we are today.

Let's look at our system in a bit more detail. We have what we call a fractional reserve banking system. What does that mean? It means that banks only hold a fraction of the deposits. How big is that fraction? In the United States as an average, it's just under 10 percent, give or take.

What is a reserve of the fractional reserve banking system? It's what banks have in their vault, plus any deposit with the Federal Reserve

> Central banks are on a global experiment

Bank. This system works just fine as long as we all leave our money in the banks—as long as we trust what the bank is doing. You see, when you deposit, say, a hundred dollars into what you think is your bank account—well, it is your bank account—it's not your money anymore. You have now traded your hundred dollars that you've deposited in the bank for an IOU from the bank that simply says, "When you want it, we promise to pay it back to you." You understand, if the bank only has a small portion of that hundred dollars, how does it pay it back if everyone wants it at the same time? It can't. We have what we call a bank run; the bank may be in a good position from its net asset value; the problem is liquidity. The bank cannot liquidate its assets—loans and investments that it has—fast enough in order to pay everybody back, and then we get a bank run.

Here is Larry Kotlikoff of Boston University to explain to us some of these issues that we are currently experiencing.

LARRY KOTLIKOFF:

> I want to first of all summarize where we are. I think the big thing to say is that Wall Street, broadly defined, has become a very dangerous place for **Main Street**. We have had two global financial crises in the last five or six years and devastating impacts on hundreds of millions of workers and retirees. One was centered in the United States and one was centered in Europe. I believe it's fair to say, they are still ongoing in both places. The next one might be centered in China.

Or

Bad Regulators?

Bad Financial Rules?

Bad Governance?

Bad Politicians?

Bad Bankers?

Bad Disclosure?

Bad Leverage?

Bad Luck?

Figure 1.3: Possible Bank Crisis Causes

So, what is really going on? Well, some people think it is bad assets, and here are a couple of examples—sovereign debt, **subprime real estate mortgages**, definitely bad assets. Other people think it is just bad banks. The bankers are the bad people here, and we've got all these banks. I should have added a couple of Cypriot banks at the end here, such as the Bank of Cyprus and Laiki. So it's about twenty-nine bad banks we could list right away.

Or Bad Banks?

Bear Stearns, Country Wide, Lehman Brothers, Northern Rock, Royal Bank of Scotland, HBOS, BNP Paribas, UBS, Anglo-Irish Bank, MBIA, Citigroup, Merrill Lynch, Fannie Mae, Freddie Mac, Washington Mutual, Glitnir, Allied Irish, Bank of Ireland, Dexia, Landsbanki, AIG, Lloyds, Barclays, Bradford and Bingley, ING, ABN AMRO, Fortis, ...

Figure 1.4: Bad Banks

Other people think it is bad regulators, bad financial rules, bad governance, bad politicians, bad bankers again, bad disclosure, bad leverage, or bad luck.

Larry's comments drew laughter from the audience. He goes on and describes how the two primary problems with our banking system come down to two words, really—

> Wall Street has become a very dangerous place for Main Street

opacity and *leverage*. Opacity simple means you can't see it; you can't see once you deposit money at the bank what the bank actually does, within the constraints of banking law. And leverage is the fact that, in order to create the debt that it lends out, the bank is leveraging funds on its own—as we've already described.

How does that work? Well, here is William Poole, former president of the St. Louis Federal Reserve Bank, dealing with this issue of opacity, because what you'll hear him say now is that even a PhD economist cannot tell whether a bank is in good shape or not.

BILL POOLE:

Investors in banks do have an information deficit, and Larry Kotlikoff emphasized that point. Suppose you're walking down the street and a well-dressed man, you know with a suit and tie, approaches you and says, "I'm a bank. Please deposit a hundred dollars with me, and I'll keep it safe. And here's a little book and we'll sign you up, and you can have it back at any time." Your reaction of course is that this guy is a nut. You don't just hand over a hundred dollars to somebody walking down the street. However, if you walk past a building that has impressive pillars, iron grates over the windows, and the word *Bank* in gold letters up there somewhere, you may be quite willing to walk in and deposit your hundred dollars without much investigation at all. And of course it's **FDIC** insured.

But the fact is that there is no possibility—no possibility—that the average PhD economist, even I think, the way up in the upper tail, trained PhD economist, trained in finance, can determine the safety of a bank. Of course the reason is that the publicly available information just doesn't tell you what you really need to know about the quality of the assets.

Dr. Poole goes on and deals with the second issue that Larry has already brought up, which is the whole aspect of leverage. And what he's saying is that regulation, even though we have a lot of it, is no substitute for good capital. Once again, here's Dr. Poole.

BILL POOLE:

Given regulatory experience in the United States and elsewhere, regulation of bank activities is not an adequate substitute for capital. Regulators, and apparently banks' senior management as well, can have the same difficulty private investors do in understanding what a bank is doing.

And finally, as I've already empha-sized, regulators are subject to po-litical constraints to encourage cer-tain activities, such as housing. The actual record of regulation and the

> Even a Ph.D. economist cannot determine the safety of a bank

constraints we understand through the public choice literature destroy—and I don't think that's too wild a word—destroy the case for regulation as a substitute for adequate capital.

You can now see that there's general agreement on the banking issues that we face within our current system. You now have two totally separate speakers addressing the same two issues in very different ways. They were not asked to do that; they came up with this on their own, because that is the truth.

Allow me to make a few more points before we get to solutions. Here's a portion of my speech dealing with banking instability.

ULI KORTSCH:

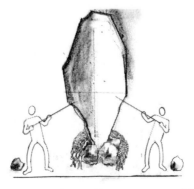

Figure 1.5: The Banking System Monolith

Here in figure 1.5 you see the instability of our monetary system, our banking system. So what it is, is this huge monolith or menhir, and it's standing on a point. It's very unstable. Now you will notice that we've created some really nice rocks here at the bottom; these are stability systems that are part of what it is that we've created. That's the FDIC; that's all sorts of regulatory constructions that we've created that helped us stabilize this block. But we've got these big guys, and they are the Federal Reserve Bank here in the United States, working to stabilize a highly unstable system.

I am in a Fed building, and I want to praise the governors and presidents of the Federal Reserve System. I think they've done a phenomenal job for a system that I would consider as inherently unstable, and essentially everybody has said that today. We may disagree on different policies, systemic issues, whatever, but I don't think anybody has not agreed with that. We've all agreed that the system is highly unstable. So we've got these guys in the figure and they've done a good job. This is the hundredth anniversary, as the Fed was created in 1913. It's not that we haven't had any problems, but by and large, I can't believe how few problems we've had, considering the essential nature of what the system looks like.

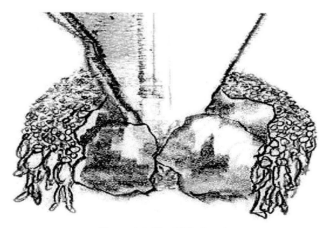

Figure 1.6: The Little People

Let me show you another thing about this picture. You see those little people in figure 1.6? Those are all human beings; those are little people down there. They actually cover everything, but then of course the whole picture wouldn't make any sense. When that big monolith falls down, it crushes those people—and that's what we're talking about today. It's a very important subject!

I also speak to social inequality, a very serious issue in our society. Here, I point out that the very banking system that we have in place is a significant part of this social problem that we do need to deal with.

ULI KORTSCH:

Let's talk about social inequality. Remember, I'm zipping through this really fast. Here is a paper[12] (*shows front page of the academic paper with photos taken from the Occupy Wall Street movement*) written by one of our very own, a member of the Global Interdependence Center, John Silvia, chief economist of Wells Fargo. So we don't have to go very far to look at discussions of social inequality. Here's the abstract (*displays the paper's abstract*). I know we can read English, but let me read it to you:

We study the effects and historical contribution of monetary policy shocks to consumption and income inequality in the United States.

> The banking system itself creates inequality

Though Silvia said "United States," the study's findings on monetary policy and how it effects consumption and income

---

12   John Silvia, Olivier Coibion and Yuriy Gorodnichenko, *Monetary Policy and Economic Inequality in the United States,* (Global Interdependence Center's Society of Fellows, 2012, Banque de France, Paris), http://RealMoneyEcon. org/lev2/images/pdfs/monetary_policy.pdf.

inequality can be extended to the entire world. We continue with the abstract from the paper.

Contractionary monetary policy actions systematically increase inequality in labor earnings, total income, consumption and total expenditures.

Now let's see what part of the economy is missing from the list given; there must be something missing. No there isn't anything missing. You can clearly see that Silvia says that every part of our economy is effected, giving rise to increases in inequality throughout.

Furthermore, monetary shocks can account for a significant component of the historical cyclical variation in income and consumption inequality. Using detailed micro level data on income and consumption, we document the different channels by which monetary policy shocks affect inequality as well as how these channels depend on the nature of the change in monetary policy.

What this says is—pardon, John, I'm about to tell what it is you said in that abstract—what it says is, when people are doing everything correctly, the system *inherently* (the system itself) creates inequality.

And now I need to make a short clarification of what I just said in that excerpt, because at first glance is sounds like I am saying that all inequality is the result of our monetary and banking structure.

ULI KORTSCH:

Now this is a conference on banking; it's not a conference on social equality. And I'm not going to stand here and tell you that the banking system creates all that inequality; I think that would be patently wrong. All I'm saying is that—as I have already said—even our very own [Dr. John Silvia] agrees that the very banking system that we have is a significant part of a social problem that we do need to deal with.

Finally, in reviewing our banking and monetary system, here is a short excerpt from Professor Jeffrey Sachs of Columbia University talking about how the very regulatory environment that we have created, tends to lead toward ethical lapses.

JEFFREY SACHS:

This is where I would start actually. I think the macroeconomics is important, but I think that the lawlessness and the sense of impunity of the system is absolutely massive. Wherever we look, we see the same thing continuing till today; and that is massive bonuses at the top of the financial markets, massive civil fines being paid for really incredible behavior, and massive campaign contributions going from this financial leadership to the political class.

Perhaps in the United States we are allowed to make these kinds of mistakes. On the other hand, perhaps not. I think we tend to forget that, as the world's largest economy, we tend to be the elephant in the room, and when we catch a cold, the rest of the world can easily get pneumonia. Here, again, is Dr. Jeffrey Sachs on the global implications of the structure and elements of our monetary system.

JEFFREY SACHS:

Maybe it's useful to just share with you a sense that I received a few days ago when meeting with about a hundred UN ambassadors who are discussing the global economy and global policy framework for the period from 2015 to 2030, which is very much the United Nations' agenda. What was palpable in the room was a very, very deep sense of anger and grievance at the American financial system.

I think this is important to state because we have our debates as if we're sometimes operating in a cocoon, and the rest of world, especially the developing world, feels that they have been the victims of the United States and its mismanagement over the last few years. I think it's a geopolitical reality that is very real and very justified. In other words, the sense of the 2008 crisis is, "You did this to us." And the failures of regulation in the United States have contributed markedly to instability and economic stresses in other places.

As several of the ambassadors reflected, the US and the IMF more or less treat the policy discussions as if nothing really has happened, and what several ambassadors said is, "Why is it we're taking advice from the people who have mismanaged the financial system so badly?" This is not an insignificant context; it's hard for the key currency and the center of the world financial system maybe to hear this very well and to take it as seriously as it should be taken. But the backdrop from the world's point of view is that the United States has failed badly in financial management and the implications of that are felt around the world.

My feeling about this is similar, and I think it is worth speaking outside of the monetary and macroeconomic framework for just a moment. And that is to reflect on the Fed's role as regulator and on the real lessons of the financial crisis since 2008. The angle that I would emphasize again—I think it's not typical for us as economists—is the massive illegality that has been exposed in the system.

Now let's get to some solutions. What was presented at the Federal Reserve Bank on that day in April were two elegantly simple points—first of all, to replace the fractional reserve banking system and, second, to

> Massive illegality has been exposed in the system

create a new way of printing (if I may use that word) money in order to have continuing price stability. That's it; it's really that simple—only those two points.

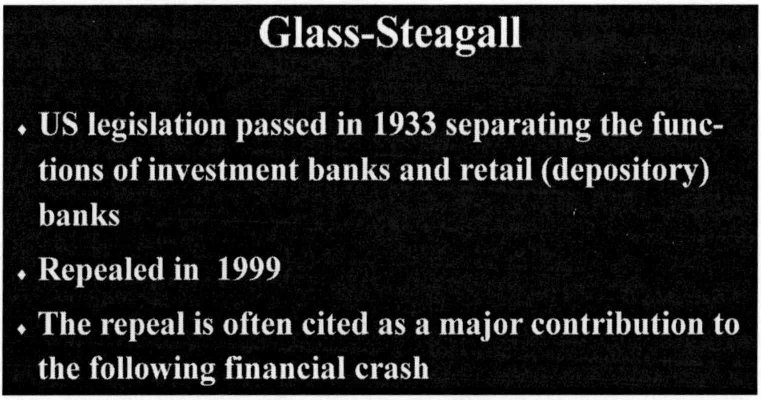

Glass-Steagall

+ **US legislation passed in 1933 separating the functions of investment banks and retail (depository) banks**
+ **Repealed in 1999**
+ **The repeal is often cited as a major contribution to the following financial crash**

Figure 1.7: The Glass-Steagall Act

Let's look at those in more detail. As for the replacement of the fractional reserve banking system, we would go onto what I would call **Glass-Steagall** on steroids. That means that the payment portion of the system would be a trust banking system. What does that mean? When you deposit the hundred dollars that I was talking about earlier into your bank account, it is still yours. The bank does not have free choice anymore of what to do with that money. It can only do what it is you tell it to do with the money. Well, what's that? If you write a check, the check will be good. If you spend money on a credit card, the bank will pay your credit card, obviously only to the amount that's in your bank account.

On the investment side, we would have a series of mutual funds represented by the risk, etc., of what it is that you desire. We're going to go into more detail on that later as we talk about this issue, which was presented by Dr. Larry Kotlikoff. What does this do? This means that it would be impossible for bank runs to exist anymore. We would stabilize Europe in a heartbeat, at least for several years with some of the issues that they're facing.

Let's look at point number two; how do we create new money? We would need to have a new entity; let's call it a "Monetary Commission." It doesn't really matter what we call it. My suggestion is that we have it controlled by the Federal Reserve Bank but owned by the citizens. This means that, as new money is created, the seigniorage for that money would actually go to us as citizens. What is **seigniorage**? Seigniorage is the difference between the cost of producing money and the value of that money. Let me give you an example. Let's talk about a physical one dollar bill. Let's say it costs one cent to print that bill, but of course, we know it's worth a dollar. So the difference between the dollar and the one penny is the $.99. That seigniorage would go to the government. What would that do? Instantly, your taxes would be lowered and your services would increase; we would live in a different world from a governmental perspective.

The concept embodied by these two points is not some new crazy thinking; this initially came out in the 1930s at the end of the Great Depression and is routinely today referred to as the Chicago Plan. It was vetted by the top economists of that day. Over 230 of them signed off on it, which represented about the whole economic establishment at that time.

In the next excerpt, Michael Kumhof of the International Monetary Fund lays out the advantages of this plan.

MICHAEL KUMHOF:

Having set the stage, here are the six advantages of the Chicago Plan. Fisher identified four advantages. We found two more, and this summarizes them:

1. Dramatic reduction of public and private debts
2. Complete elimination of bank runs
3. Much better control of credit cycles
4. Output gains
5. Elimination of **liquidity traps**
6. Therefore, the possibility of zero, steady state inflation

So how do we get from the current fractional reserve banking system to this new state—what I call a Trust Banking System? Michael Kumhof has given an excellent, lengthy overview of that process. It can all be done over a weekend, because it would be planned well in advance. But it's a very powerful process because, you see, what we need to do is top up the banks with this 90 percent that is missing, so that we do not have a fractional reserve anymore but so that the full capacity of the depository aggregates would be held by the banks.

How do we do that? Well, the Monetary Commission would print—if I may use that word—the missing 90 percent, but remember, it's already in circulation. There is absolutely no inflation involved in this whatsoever.

How do we place that 90 percent into the banks? We're not just going to give it as a present, thank you. There are a number of different ways of doing it. One of the ways is to simply have the Monetary Commission purchase the 90 percent that is already in loans. These are good loans; we run a good banking system. So what happens is, in that purchase, you roll the cash into the banks and the loan assets into the Monetary Commission. Then the Monetary Commission divides these up into the mutual fund segments and puts those up for auction.

What is the effect of this? In a heartbeat, the federal government would go from a net debtor nation to a net creditor nation. You see, what is the value of that 90 percent? It's in excess of $18 trillion. Currently, the US federal government owes about $16.5 trillion, so we would essentially have all that paid off and still have enough money left to pretty well pay off most of the state debt. That's one way of doing it.

Or we can have a citizen's dividend. There are a number of different ways of doing this. The details in this particular point aren't that important; the fact is that the government now is a net creditor nation, not the other way around.

> In a heartbeat the Federal Government would become a net creditor

Let's just look at the steady state aspect for a minute. That's where Dr. Larry Kotlikoff comes in with his "Limited Purpose Banking," which is what he calls it. These are equity-backed loan funds, and because they're equity backed, you can lose money but the banks cannot have a run. It changes the entire system.

What would this create? Here is a list of the conditions that we would have:

- » This would be true intermediation and not gambling
- » It would be transparent and provide full disclosure
- » It would never collapse or put the economy at risk
- » It would not require government guarantees or threaten taxpayers
- » It would be sufficiently well structured so as to require limited regulation

Finally, banks would do what it is that pretty well most of us think banks actually do, which is to take money from savers and get that money to the hands of those who need to borrow it or need it for investments. Here is a list of prominent people who have either publicly stated their agreement or privately in conversations have done so or who have said we need to thoroughly look into this.

Prominent Economists and Policymakers Endorsing
Serious Consideration of Limited purpose Banking

» Mervyn King, Governor of the Bank of England
» Seven Nobel Laureates in Economics (Ackerlof, Lucas, Prescott, Phelps, Fogel, Merton, Sharpe)
» Former U.S. Secretary of Treasury (George Shultz)
» Former U.S. Secretary of Labor (Robert Reich)
» Former U.S. Senator (Bill Bradley)
» Two Past Chairs, Council of Economic Advisers (Michael Boskin and Murray Weidenbaum)
» Two Former Chief Economists of the IMF (Harvard's Ken Rogoff and MIT's Simon Johnson)
» Former Chief Economist of the SEC (Susan Woodward)
» Former Deputy Comptroller of the Currency (Robert Bench)
» Former Vice Chairman of Joint Chiefs of Staff (Admiral Williams Owens)
» Jeff Sachs (Renown Macro Economist and Head of Columbia's Earth Institute)
» Jagadish Bhagwati (Renown International Economist)
» Martin Wolf (Senior Economics Columnist for the Financial Times)
» Steve Ross (MIT's Premier Financial Economist and Father of Arbitrage Pricing Theory)
» Niall Ferguson (Harvard's Distinguished Economic Historian)
» Kevin Hassett (Distinguished Economist at AEI and McCain's Former Chief Economic Adviser)
» Paul Romer (Stanford's Distinguished Growth Theorist)
» Domingo Cavallo (Former Economic Minister of Argentina)
» Wiliam Niskanen (Chairman Emeritus, The Cato Institute)
» Preston McAfee (Chief Economist, Yahoo)
» Other Very Prominent U.S. Economists

We know we're not going to create heaven on earth, so here is a portion of the speech from Lord Adair Turner giving some muted critiques of what it is I have just described.

LORD ADAIR TURNER:

There were some issues that I'm not absolutely clear that make this in total doable or necessarily desirable.

First of all, I think, that any system that involves a big write-off of existing debts, however hard you try, is going to, somewhere in the system, create winners and losers. I think it's almost impossible to do large debt write-offs without some distributional consequences. I think that's just very difficult politically, as well as creating some simply uncertain consequences that will result from distributional effects on wealth.

Secondly I think there's an open issue about how we should think about lending for **intertemporal consumption smoothing**. I think there's far too much of it, but I think there could still be an argument that some of it is valuable up to a point. The basic process of saying, "We enable younger people to borrow money to buy houses off older people rather than all houses flowing through an inheritance process or being bought by the accumulation, first, of enough cash to buy them"—I think that may have a social welfare optimality.

I think one of the most important bits of economic theory that we really haven't thought through is, what is the social optimality there? How much is socially optimal? But I think that's an unexplored bit of economic theory. Even some elements of lending from patient to impatient people may be social welfare optimal, even though it has absolutely nothing to do with creating higher growth.

I do have some concerns about the distributional issues, about how we should think about intertemporal consumption smoothing. And I do have some concerns that any attempt to create an entirely 100 percent reserve banking system would be likely to create more shadow banking systems, in other words, **near money** substitute. So I'm more doubtful than Michael [Kumhof] is about our ability to prevent the creation of near money substitutes.

In relation to Larry's [Kotlikoff] proposals, I'm not totally convinced that it [Limited Purpose Banking] would get rid of **pro-cyclicality**. Given that I think that **mark-to-market** systems in the shadow banking system were themselves a cause of pro-cyclicality, I can imagine that, if we have mutual loan funds in which you hold a mark-to-market investment, and if we can really mark-to-market those on a day by day basis, or even a week by week basis, I think we may see some pretty strong pro-cyclical behavior in response—in self-reinforcing cycles—in response to the mark-to-market of the value of such funds.

Yes, we will address those points from Lord Turner. They do need to be handled.

Back to the conference, at the end of the day, I did the final wrap-up speech and ended on a note of hope and encouragement.

ULI KORTSCH:

Ladies and gentleman, I believe it's possible, I really do.

(*Shows new slide that reads, "Change is* not *possible."*) Oops, that's the wrong thing; it says change is *not* possible. I've been told that as I've told people what this conference was all about. I had a banker say to me, "Uli, it's impossible." And every time I hear that I go, "Really?"

Bank Regulation in the United States

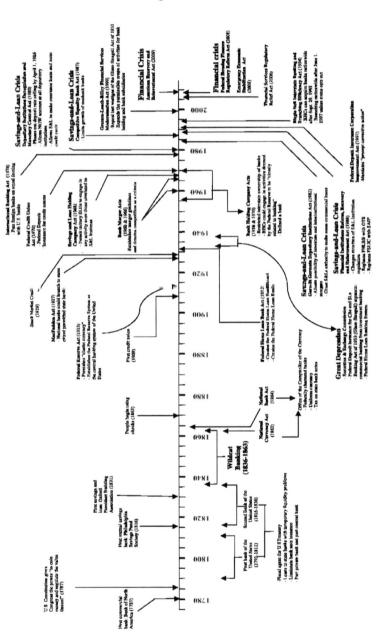

Figure 1 Historical perspective on U.S. banking structure and regulation.
Source: J. R. Barth, T. Li, and W. Lu (2009), "Bank Regulation in the United States," CESifo Economic Studies, November, doi: 10.1093/cesifu/ifp026

Figure 1.8: US Banking Regulatory Changes Since 1780

Figure 1.8, showing US banking regulatory changes since 1780, is a most interesting chart. This chart maps out the major banking regulatory changes that have occurred over the last two hundred years. It's not like we haven't created major changes before. It's not like history has not seen events that demanded significant decisions.

Why is today different? Too many people believe that changing our financial system today is impossible. But I know our financial predecessors did change the system— they did so 100 years ago with the creation of the Federal Reserve Bank and again they did so fifty years ago when we went off the gold standard. And those are only two of the many changes shown in this chart.

We could do all those things then, but why should that not be possible today? Today I guess there's something wrong with us. "Todayans" can't do these things anymore.

There is another interesting aspect to figure 1.8. If we were to draw a graph representing the number of changes over time, it would show a parabolic curve. The closer we get to today, the more changes have been created. I want to tell you we can still do it. We have a history of making good corrections. Let's keep it up.

Well, it's obvious the issues we dealt with that day at the Federal Reserve Bank are ultimately very personal. They affect each one of us deeply. It doesn't matter whether we're in the economic profession or not. All

> We have a history of making good corrections—lets keep it up

of this is very important in our lives. So, what can you do as part of the change that is needed in our system? I would suggest, simply, sign up onto the YouTube channel listed below, come onto our Web site, get involved, and learn more. http://realmoneyecon.org/ or http://www.youtube.com/ukortsch

CHAPTER TWO

Introduction

HERB TAYLOR:

My name is Herb Taylor. I am the vice president and corporate secretary here at the Federal Reserve Bank of Philadelphia, and I want to welcome you all here this morning. Today's conference is the 31st Annual Monetary and Trade Conference arranged by the Global Interdependence Center and the LeBow College of Business.

Traditionally, this conference has been held on the Drexel Campus, and we're very pleased to have it here at the Fed this year. We're particularly pleased because we recognize the importance of this year's topic, "Fixing the Banking System for Good."

As I'm sure you all know, the Fed serves as the central bank for the United States, and in that capacity, we supervise and regulate banks. We serve as a payments processor for banks, and it is through the banking system that we execute our monetary policy.

> We recognize the importance of this year's topic

So we appreciate the contribution that a good banking system makes to people's economic well-being by providing trustworthy intermediation between borrowers and lenders, by providing a reliable means of transacting the day-to-day business of buying and selling, and by providing a stabilizing flow of money and credit overall. And so we are very much interested in fixing the banking system for good.

Again, today's conference is cosponsored by the Global Interdependence Center and by Drexel's LeBow College of Business, and so there is no more appropriate person to formally open today's conference than the chairman of the Global Interdependence

Center and the Dean Emeritus and George Francis Professor of Finance at the LeBow College of Business, Dr. George Tsetsekos.

DR. TSETSEKOS:

I appreciate the introduction, and first of all, I'm George Tsetsekos, of course, chairman of the GIC. I'm very privileged to be in that spot, and I can tell you that we have a wonderful organization with so many interesting conferences, forums, and discussions, and I urge you to participate in these programs.

Our mission, of course, focuses on expanding the global dialogue to improve cooperation and understanding among citizens and nations. In the process, we have been around the world organizing conferences. Most recently, we participated in a very well-organized conference in Abu Dhabi, talking about global issues from that part of the world. And, of course, we plan to continue our efforts not only here in Philadelphia but also around the country.

I can tell you that GIC has a very good membership. We also try to expand our membership, and I urge you and your colleagues to become members of our organization. But I also urge you to consider sponsorship of some of the events that we conduct. We are very pleased to have LeBow College of Business as the major sponsor today. And, of course, we are very happy that the Philadelphia Fed has provided the necessary facilities for us to have this well-organized conference.

It's a very good topic, as Herb indicated, and I look forward to the discussions today. With this, once again, welcome, and I would like to turn it to David Kotok, chairman and chief investment officer of Cumberland Advisors and GIC Chair of the Banking Series. Thank you.

CHAPTER 3

Central Bank Actions

THIS CHAPTER REPRESENTS THE OPENING of the conference held at the Philadelphia Federal Reserve Bank building. Here, David Kotok sets the framework for the responses of the key central banks globally, that is the Federal Reserve Bank of the United States (Fed), the European Central Bank (ECB), the Bank of Japan (BOJ), and Bank of England (BOE), collectively known as the G4. Other central banks are important also, but these four control the currencies of about 85 percent of the capital markets of the world. David adds the Swiss National Bank to this list, as that institution pegs the floor of their currency to the euro.

This opening is important because, after implementation of the **zero interest rate policy (ZIRP)**,[13] central banks are left with few tools in their kit bag. Central bank balance sheet expansion through asset purchases, which is what Kotok primarily discusses, has multiple implications on the monetary and banking system. Though this topic will not be reviewed again until the end of the book, it's important to keep it in mind as one of the underlying factors upon which the rest of the edifice of our monetary system currently exists. What used to be considered highly unorthodox for central bank actions has become a global de facto state of existence.

Kotok's résumé is found at the end of this chapter.

---

13   See the glossary at the end of the book for explanations of this and many other key terms and economic concepts. The first use of a glossary term is always in bold.

DAVID KOTOK:

I'm going to talk about central banks from the point of view of the investment advisor or money manager. That's what we do in our firm. For the last dozen years at the Global Interdependence Center, we've had an organizational component called the Central Banking Series. And the Central Banking Series has become a lot of fun these days.

The size of the central banks' balance sheets in the world is of unprecedented magnitude (see figure 3.1), and I know of no period in history that we've had anything like this. Now, to create a metaphor to explain the size of the central banks' balance sheets, I want to tell a little story.

The story starts in the Middle East over a hundred years ago. The British built the first rail line, a narrow gauge rail, from Istanbul to Cairo, actually to Alexandria. And as they were building the line across the desert in what now would be the Negev in Israel or the Sinai Peninsula in Egypt, on the first completion of the line, on the first run of the maiden run of the train to go to Egypt, the engineer was taking that train across the desert.

And while he was doing so, there was a Bedouin tribesman, Muhammad, who was walking across the desert. And the Bedouin, for the first time in his life, saw a rail line. He saw the ties and the metal parallel going as far as he could see, and he never had seen that in his life. So Muhammad quickly realized that if he could walk in the direction he was going on the railroad ties instead of on the sand, it would be much easier.

He began to walk in the direction of Egypt on the ties, and, of course, the train is coming down the tracks. The engineer looks out, and he sees the Bedouin walking on the rail line. So he says, "My gosh." He blows his warning whistle, a steam whistle—*whoo*. The Bedouin's never heard a steam whistle, never seen a railroad. He keeps walking. The train gets closer. The Bedouin doesn't change his pace. The engineer blows the whistle again—*whoo*. Nothing.

Finally, the train is very close, and the engineer has no other choice. If he does not act, he will hit him and kill him. He leans on the whistle—*whoo*—and he puts the wheels on the old train in reverse to try to stop it. There's this clanking of metal, all these engines. The Bedouin turns around, hearing the whistle and looks at the train. It hits him, and it knocks him unconscious.

He wakes up that afternoon, and he's in a two-story British hospital about fifty miles away. He's in a room he's never been in; the room is entirely white. He's bathed. He's in white robes. He's in a room at the end of the hall. He doesn't know what happened, but he figures, *I must be in heaven now.*

It's 4:00 in the afternoon when he awakens in the British hospital. In the room next to him is a kitchenette. What happens in a British hospital a hundred years ago in a kitchenette at 4:00 in the afternoon? Anybody tell me? Tea. The teapot comes to a boil, and the tea kettle starts to whistle—*whoo whoo whoo*. The Bedouin jumps out of his bed, runs next door, grabs the teapot, and starts to smash it, beat it all up.

The orderlies and the doctor come in. They grab him, hold him, restrain him, and they say, "Muhammad, Muhammad, what are you doing?"

He says, "You have to kill these things when they're small."

The central bank balance sheets of the world are no longer a teapot or tea kettle. Figure 3.1 shows the asset side of the Federal Reserve Bank balance sheet. We now see similar ones all the time. We call this a rainbow chart, something we put on our Web site at Cumberland Advisors. You're all welcome to come look at it. We now have twenty thousand to thirty thousand visitors a week that look at the series of central bank charts. The data's available to anybody, but I guess we make it convenient for them.

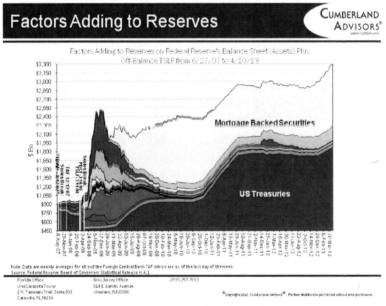

Figure 3.1: The Asset Side of the Fed Balance Sheet

Before the 2007/2008 financial crisis we were 900 billion in size, most of it treasuries. Then we had a little excitement called Lehman, AIG, a few other things. We had this big rainbow of Fed programs they're running off, and now in early 2013 we're about 3 trillion and climbing every month. A big part of it is mortgage-backed securities, and the rest of it is in treasuries, and the treasuries are now with multiple maturities, long, intermediate, short. They're no longer just short. We all know this. I'm going to go quickly.

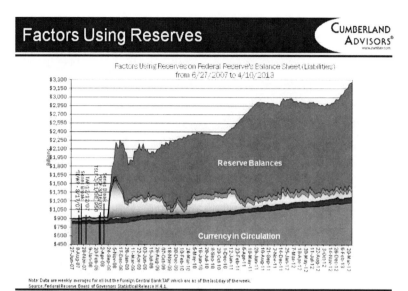

Figure 3.2: The Liabilities Side of the Fed Balance Sheet

Figure 3.2 shows the liability side of the Federal Reserve's balance sheet. We're familiar with this one, too. Essentially, here's what matters. As far as currency in circulation, we're a little over a trillion—currency with pictures of George and Ben and the others. Roughly two-thirds of it circulates outside of the United States.

It gives us a trillion dollars' worth of a free lunch in seigniorage, and the Fed now has figured out, right or wrong, that it can have long duration assets because, as a practical matter, this currency in circulation is a long, permanent, infinite duration liability, and it can match them and is doing so. Whether it's right or wrong is a subject of debate. It will be debated at this conference all day. At the end of the day, we'll conclude that we don't know. Now everybody can go home.

What's this (*pointing to "Reserve Balances" on figure 3.2*)? This is all the **excess reserves** that get created when you print money out of thin air. The New York Fed goes into the market on a Tuesday at 11:00, buys $100 million dollars in treasury bills, puts them in the portfolio, and pays the primary dealer. It [the money] goes into his [the dealer's] bank account at 2:00. So at 2:00 that afternoon, it's back on deposit at the Fed. At 1:59 that day, it had been in the bank. But they [the bank managers] had to make a decision: Do they hold it and earn zero or do they earn twenty-five **basis points** and put excess reserves at the Fed? They obviously make a business decision.

So in only three hours, the Fed has created $100 million and added a security to its assets, and that was the transaction. That's happening to the tune of $85 billion a month gross. Some of that is replacing roll-off securities, and that's the current policy of the Federal Reserve.

Now, the big question—it'll be discussed today—is how is this going to be resolved? Is there an exit strategy? When does it end? And once it ends, does it plateau? And after that, does it decline? The answer is that we don't know.

But there's a paper out. Four erudite authors wrote it. One of them was Rick Mishkin, who was a governor of the Federal Reserve. Essentially what they did is make some assumptions, all of which are wrong, but they're close, maybe. And they said, this is what it's going to look like if we have the following. We extend the policy. We peak up here somewhere [see peak on figure 3.3]. There's a distribution of the treasuries, which I'm ignoring. I've lumped them all together in this slide. And then we're going to start to taper down, and in 2020, the size of the assets of the balance sheet will be somewhere about a trillion seven.

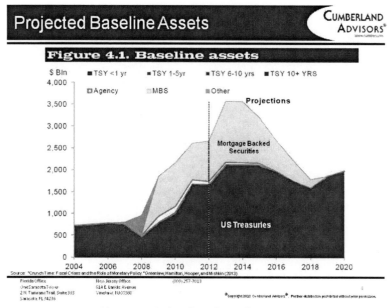

Figure 3.3: Fed Projected Baseline Assets

Now, in our view, in our firm, in our work today, we don't have a clue what the size of the balance sheet will be then. It might be a trillion seven. It might be two. It's not likely to be much smaller than a trillion seven. Okay. That's the asset side projected in the Mishkin paper.

Figure 3.4 shows the liability side, and the liability side would have said, by then, under certain growth assumptions, certain inflation assumptions, certain worldwide economic assumptions, currency will be somewhere around the trillion seven. That'll be the liability of the Fed. And the Fed will either roll off the balances or they'll sell. Will they sell or will they not? Well, in the most recent Bernanke speech, essentially Bernanke implied that it's not likely they're going to sell.

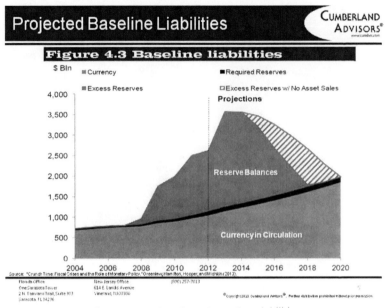

Figure 3.4: Fed Projected Baseline Liabilities

Now think about selling from a central bank. Cyprus, a little speck the size of Camden, hears from the European Finance Ministers that you've got a little gold and you may have to sell some of it. Is there a market reaction? Markets are traders, and they front run every piece of information. There are thirty people I work with every day, and they spend every single day figuring out how to be ahead of the market.

The Federal Reserve announces they're going to sell a hundred billion dollars' worth of securities. What do you think the market's going to do? Calmly sit by and do nothing or change pricing in anticipation of a large seller? All the opinions that are given here are my own, not those of the Global Interdependence Center; not the Federal Reserve; and, in some cases, not fully those of my firm, although there is an influence there.

So you think about the Fed selling, and you realize that it's not likely to happen. And Bernanke has implied that in his recent statement. So what we're saying is, if you go by the Mishkin paper, we're going to roll it off, and if everything goes perfectly, we will benignly reach some equilibrium in another five, six, seven, eight years.

What is the goal? The stated goal today is 6.5 percent unemployment according to the Evans Rule, named after Charles Evans, the president of the Chicago Fed. You will see statements saying that's too high. There's talk from different **FOMC**[14] members who talk about 5.5 percent and 6 percent. You don't hear anybody talking about 6.5 or 7. So we have a bias toward lower levels, but 6.5 is a number, and the requirement is that 6.5 be reached in the unemployment rate as long as the inflation rate remains 2.5 percent or lower. And that's a more general term, but it's assumed that inflation is directed at the Personal Consumption Expenditure [**PCE**] deflator. So that's more or less now a stated goal or target.

How Many Jobs Does the Economy Create? CUMBERLAND ADVISORS®

Assumed Quarterly % Real GDP Growth	Estimated Number of Jobs Created within the Quarter	Estimated Number of Quarters to Create 3.217 Million Jobs	Estimated Number of Jobs Created Within Quarter	Estimated Number of Quarters to Create 3.217 Million Jobs	Estimated Number of Jobs Created Within Quarter	Estimated Number of Quarters to Create 3.217 Million Jobs
	Average		Hi (95%) Interval		Low (95%) Interval	
1	161	20	188	17	134	24
2	322	10	377	9	268	12
3	483	7	565	6	402	8
4	644	5	753	4	536	6

Assumed Quarterly % Real GDP Growth	Estimated Number of Jobs Created per Month	Estimated Number of Months to Create 3.217 Million Jobs	Estimated Number of Jobs Created per Month	Estimated Number of Months to Create 3.217 Million Jobs	Estimated Number of Jobs Created Within Month	Estimated Number of Months to Create 3.217 Million Jobs
	Average		Hi (95%) Interval		Low (95%) Interval	
1	54	60	63	51	45	72
2	107	30	126	26	89	36
3	161	20	188	17	134	24
4	215	15	251	13	179	18

Source: Haver and Cumberland Advisors

Florida Office
One Sarasota Tower
2 N. Tamiami Trail, Suite 303
Sarasota, FL 34236

New Jersey Office
614 E. Landis Avenue
Vineland, NJ 08360

(800) 257-7013

Figure 3.5: Estimated Job Creation Statistics

14   Federal Reserve Bank Open Market Committee. See Glossary

We created a table, figure 3.5, as a model to show how many jobs we have to create at a certain growth rate, which we depict here. About the only thing I know about the slide is it's an estimate, and it's subject to a wide band of confidence, meaning many assumptions which may or may not be correct. Bob Eisenbeis, my partner, helped put it together.

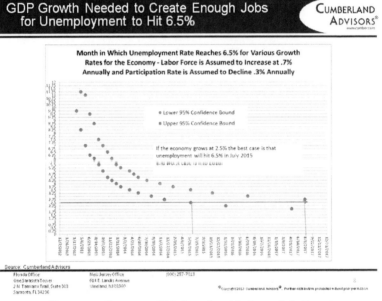

Figure 3.6: Necessary GDP Growth to Hit Evans Rule Target

Essentially what we did in creating figure 3.6 is ask what GDP growth rate do we need in order to create enough jobs to get the traditional unemployment rate to 6.5 percent? And the answer is something like what is shown in this figure. When will we hit it? Somewhere between 2015 and 2017, if you use this model. Again, the only thing we know about models when we make assumptions and forecasts is that we're wrong. It's the only thing we know.

Here is another model, as seen in figure 3.7—a different way to attack the problem. What kind of job growth do we need to hit 6.5

percent unemployment? Well, this is a simple case. If we get more job growth every month, we get there sooner. If we have 88,000 new nonfarm payroll jobs, it would take a long time. And this is a monthly indicator that everybody watches. It makes a lot of hype on television. And more importantly are the revisions of the previous two months because they really tell you something. But television can't work with a twelve-month or two-month or one-month lag. It is limited to a twelve-second lag. So we have to deal with this, but it's another model. If this model's right, we'll get there in a year or two.

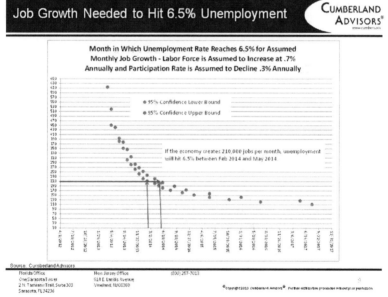

Figure 3.7: Needed Job Growth for 6.5% Unemployment

Now I have issues, these are mine, with this whole notion of a 6.5 percent unemployment rate and using the U3 traditional calculation. There are people who think it's the right way to count, and there are others who feel differently. I'm in the "count differently" category.

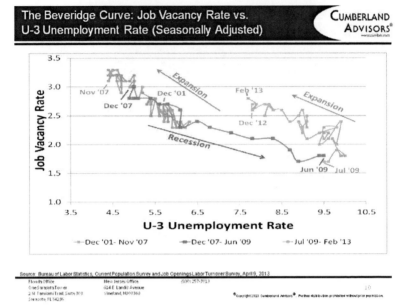

Figure 3.8: The Beveridge Curve

So what we did is put together a slide of the Beveridge Curve, which takes job openings and the unemployment rate, and tries to depict the regime change that took place pre- and post-financial crisis. So this is how we attacked it. You can see the expansion curve prior to the latest recession on the left side as labeled in figure 3.8. In the center portion of the chart are the years and the dates of this recent recession which was not only a down, tough cyclical recession, but we also had a financial crisis, restrictive credit, changed behaviors. We're still doing that. And we didn't come back from where we were at the beginning of the recession, but we came back from the end of it, and the following expansion is on the right side of the chart. So to me this asks the question, is the U3 6.5 percent unemployment rate the right target? I'm not so sure.

Let's take a look at figure 3.9. If you use a **Phillips curve** model, and I learned this from Harvey Rosenblum at the Dallas Fed, who did wonderful work on the Phillips curve by taking the issue of the unemployment rate and the inflation rate and trying to measure the trade-off between the two. When you do that with some linear constructions, Harvey showed in his work that the slope of the Phillips curve is a changing vehicle.

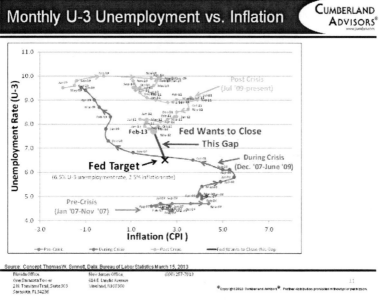

Figure 3.9: U3 Unemployment versus Inflation

What I thought we might do is look at an engineering approach to this question. We created a series of Phillips curves in figure 3.9, and here's that pre-crisis period that we had, labeled on the chart "Pre-Crisis Jan '07–Nov '07". If you were to draw the slope of the Phillips curve, it would look just like this horizontal line. Then we have this crisis indicated by the curved line shown by the arrow "During Crisis," with dates in the small subtext on the curve moving from the bottom right up toward the top left. We then began the recovery process, and now we are at the "Post-Crisis" label.

The structure here is called an underdamped oscillatory system, so my engineering friends tell me. It's underdamped because the slopes change, which means the whole notion of a 6.5 percent unemployment and a 2.5 percent inflation rate Phillips curve model as a way to set a policy decision would assume damping so that the oscillations that are reflected in that data can be consistently observed, obtained, and depended on. In our view, the answer is you cannot do that. So to the question posed in the title of this conference—can we "Fix the Banking System for Good"?—the answer is no. Now we can all go home.

In an underdamped oscillatory engineering construction, this gap shown by the label "Fed Wants to Close this Gap" is a very large gap. The Fed wants to close this gap, says it wants to hit 6.5 percent unemployment on U3, and it wants to do it within a 2.5 percent inflation rate construction.

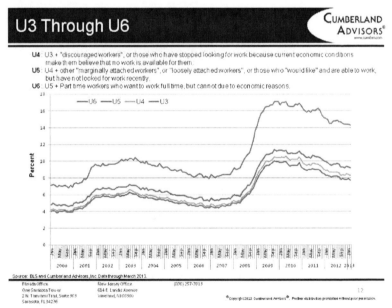

Figure 3.10: Differing Unemployment Rate Curves

In order to dissect the U3, we put figure 3.10 together. We show curves for the U3, 4, 5, and 6. They have this action of running parallel with each other because each successive measure has, in fact, all the component parts of the earlier one.

And what do we see when we disaggregate it? We see the difference between the U6 and the U3, as shown here in figure 3.11.

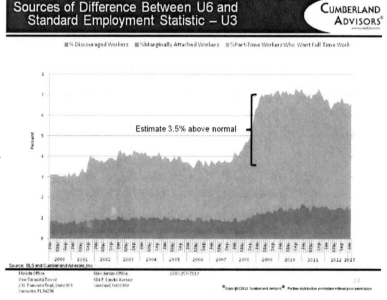

Figure 3.11: Sources of Difference Between U3 and U6

U6 is not the Fed target, but in my view it should be if there's going to be a target at all, which is a separate question from what is being debated here today. They're looking at the wrong measure. So if you say, I'm going to use the U6, what's the gap now between the U6 and the U3? Five, six million people in the labor force represented by the 3.5 percentage points shown in figure 3.11.

So we then constructed an implied underdamped oscillatory system showing the crisis with the Phillips Curve and taking a 3.5 point difference from history to look at the gap.

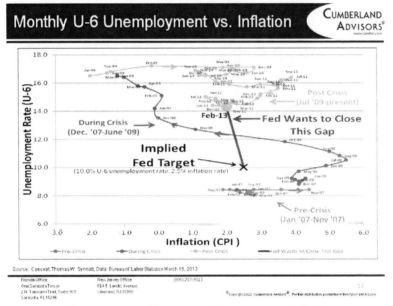

Figure 3.12: Monthly U6 Unemployment versus Inflation

It's a monster! Maybe by the year 2046, the Fed could close it because the Fed's tools are not designed to close an employment gap to start with. They have marginal impact, in our view.

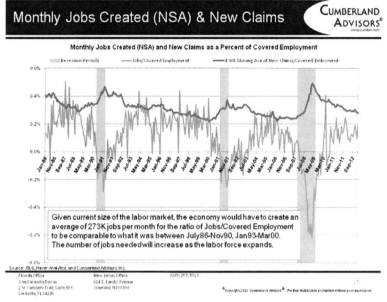

Figure 3.13: Monthly Jobs Created and New Claims

Figure 3.13 is another way to get into job creation estimates. Bob Eisenbeis helped do this. What we're trying to look at is weekly unemployment claims and jobs versus recovered labor force. What do we need to hit some equilibrium rate? Our estimate is 273,000 new nonfarm jobs per month on average at the present size of the labor force. That's our estimate. By the way, it's wrong but we hope it's close.

All right. What's happening with the central banks, the railroad across the desert, and killing things when they're small?

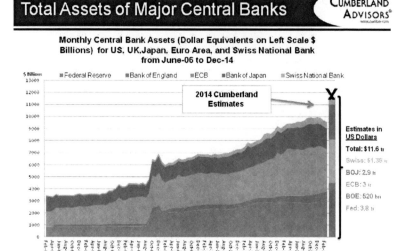

Figure 3.14: Total Assets of Major Central Banks

Figure 3.14 shows the total assets of the G4 central banks and Switzerland. We've got four currencies here—the US dollar, the pound, the euro, and the yen. The reason we added the Swiss National Bank is because Switzerland is now pegging its currency on the floor to the euro. So there are times when the Swiss National Bank grows rapidly in size because of that influence to Switzerland and its one-sided peg management; 1.2 Swiss francs to 1 pound is the current official number.

We track the collective G4, these four currencies, because when you take them and everything that connects to them, you have defined about 85 percent of the capital markets of the world. This includes all of those countries, central banks, and economic entities that peg their own currency to one of these four. For example, Bermuda runs against the US dollar, Hong Kong against the US dollar, Switzerland partially against the euro, Chile manages against the US dollar, and so on.

Now it's not that the rest are not important. I don't want to disparage Norway, Singapore, or Sweden, marvelous places to visit. But when it comes to the policy impact globally, only these big four count. One of them is going through some very unusual behavior. That's called Japan. We're going to talk about that in a minute.

But the total is what counts. And that was 3.5 trillion before the shooting started. It's 10 trillion now, and the far left column, labeled "2014 Cumberland Estimates" are our estimates for one year from now based on present policy as currently announced and converted to US dollars. And I don't know which month of 2014, but essentially we guess that the total size of the G4 plus a little bit of Switzerland will be $11.5 trillion.

In other words, the growth rate of the size of the central banks' balance sheets is accelerating. Think about that. If we had this meeting six years ago, and somebody were to stand here and say, "Six years from now, we're going to come together at a conference. We're going to have the central banks' balance sheets of the world go triple the size, accelerate the growth rate, and when we do it, we'll have a large negative output, high unemployment worldwide, next to zero inflation, the short-term interest rate will be near zero, the long-term interest rate of high-grade sovereign debt throughout the world will be somewhere between 1 and 2 percent," everybody in this room would have said, "Hmm, he's a nut; we should lock him up." But that's exactly where we are today.

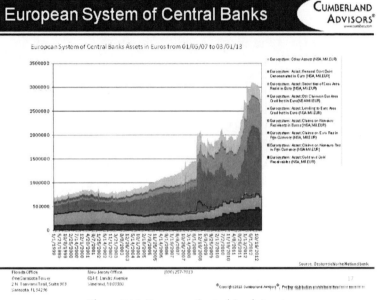

Figure 3.15: European Central Bank Assets

So let's take a look at figure 3.15. There's the central bank that we know so well. Right now, the European Central Bank is lagging behind in the horse race because of some internal constructions. There's a big debate in the ECB. Are they going to do another round? They actually did a $200 billion withdrawal of liquidity early, and there's now zero growth in the eurozone for the entire year, arguably zero growth in the entire European Union for the entire year—that's twenty-seven countries—and arguably zero growth in the European Economic Community; that's thirty-one countries. And if I missed somebody, I apologize. Zero growth. Austerity. Budgets out of balance, with debt ratios to GDP subject now to a debate depending on how you view Vince Reinhart's study.

Reinhart/Rogoff now has controversy about the study because of some questionable data in one space. Those who have nothing to do late at night can read those e-mails, look at them, and form your own conclusions. I have no opinion on the criticism.

We expect in our shop that the ECB will use the only tool it has to construct additional liquidity input, and if it doesn't, the Euro will just get stronger and stronger and stronger, in spite of all the activity that we see, because this is now relative value gain.

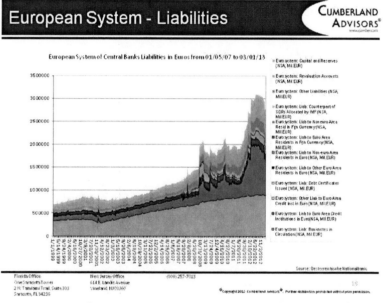

Figure 3.16: European Central Bank Liabilities

Figure 3.16 is the other side of this balance sheet. Remember, on the bottom of these balance sheets, you see currency in circulation; it's just paper. In the case of the ECB, lots of the euro circulate outside of the eurozone. It's not just the US dollar which does this. The point of the slides is it's not just us.

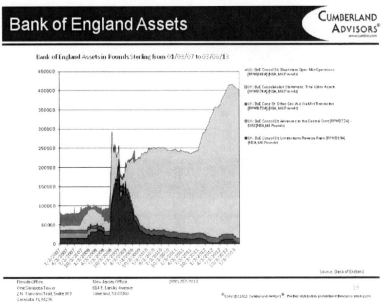

Figure 3.17: Bank of England Assets

England speaks for itself in figure 3.17.

Let's switch for a second to the other side of the balance sheet. Currency in circulation is gradually growing, all the time, as seen in figure 3.18.

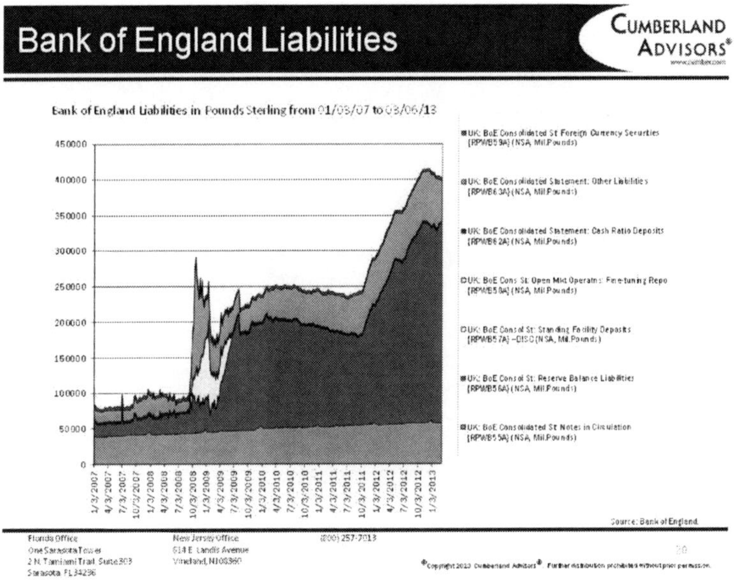

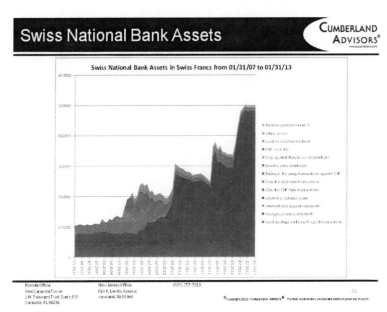

Figure 3.18: Bank of England Liabilities

Here's Switzerland. Same story, as seen in figures 3.19 and 3.20.

Figure 3.19: Swiss National Bank Assets

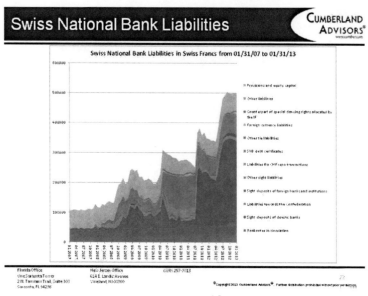

Figure 3.20. Swiss National Bank Liabilities

Now, let me get to Japan. Figure 3.21 shows the asset side of the Japanese balance sheet.

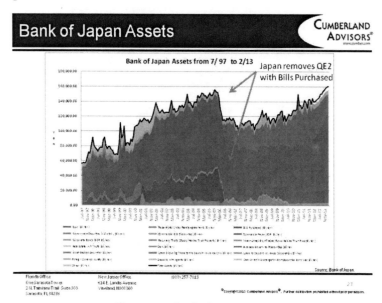

Figure 3.21: Bank of Japan Assets

Please note that I marked a key date there in 2006. The *only* instance of a major central bank withdrawing from QE in any significant way is in 2006 in Japan. There was a regime change, and the Central Bank was managing against a zero interest rate. They didn't know how much excess liquidity they had created; they had been doing it for years.

The policy shift then was to take the equilibrium interest rate that was at zero; and when you are at zero, you don't know what equilibrium is, because equilibrium is something lower than zero. So, the idea was, we'll involve ourselves in transactions. We'll sell Japanese short-term government bonds. We'll absorb liquidity and excess reserves from our system, and we will do it until we see an equilibrium rate clearing the market, above zero.

This transaction took about six weeks. It was very ordered. It was unique to only one country, one government. The policy was announced in January and then reversed because of a quirk in the way the Japanese central bank has to make a decision, where the finance minister can ask the governor of the central bank out of tradition to delay the decision. So, the markets expected something in January, and then they didn't get it. Then they got what they thought was a surprise in March when they did get it, and the reason is because of this unusual political construction in the Bank of Japan. But the policy was put in place. How much was withdrawn in US dollar terms? About $90 billion; $88 billion was an estimate I saw at the time. And figure 3.21 shows what it looked like on the asset side of the Japanese balance sheet. Essentially what they did is they took their equivalent of our treasury bills, sold them, and soaked up excess reserves.

Now, on the liability side, figure 3.222 shows the other side of the transaction.

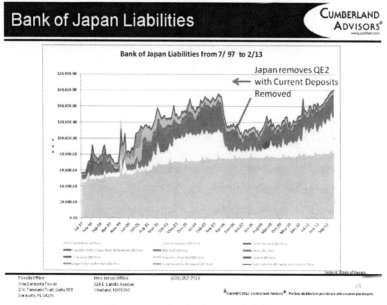

Figure 3.22: Bank of Japan Liabilities

What happened in the markets in 2006 when one country made an adjustment on a QE for about $90 billion and took about $90 billion of excess reserves? If you go back and look at the transactions at that period of time, it was a stormy session of the markets. You wouldn't have liked the volatilities in the first half of 2006 if you were on the investment side, and you would have been worried about secondary effects. That passed. There were no other actions, just a $90 billion withdrawal.

Ladies and gentleman, the excess reserves in the world are now about $6 trillion. All the central banks are in one direction only. They are either stable or enlarging QE. They have not even reached a level of stabilization globally, let alone talked about the other side.

All the short-term interest rates in the world now center somewhat between 0 and 1 percent—all of them. When you take short-term interest rates and define the cost of short-term money at 0 or half of 1 percent or one-quarter of 1 percent, regardless of the currency, you do two things. You have to move the volatility and adjustment process among and between those currencies to something other than interest rates.

In the old days, if you wanted to do a transaction in yen and you were based in euro, you could go into the market and make a decision. You could make a decision to buy or sell yen versus euro today and make the payment tomorrow, and you could place your funds in either currency at a rate of interest, and the rate of interest would **arbitrage** the difference between the currencies in terms of future price. When you take interest rates down to 0, you remove interest rates as the mechanism that has been that arbitrage for the last half century.

So, what do you do? You are shifting volatility to the currencies—to the foreign exchange markets. And we see it every day. Japan changes policy and markets take off like a rocket. If Japan continues on the policy it says it's going to take with the new government which is in office—and very strongly supported by the populace—and the new central bank, which is a product of the new government, which has made its position very clear as well, then in our view it won't be long, maybe it will be a year or two, and then we may look at a yen to US dollar exchange rate at 130 or 140.

Now, in the old days, if you really believed the yen was going to be 130 and it's 100 today, you would go into the markets and arbitrage that difference in a trade. And a lot of folks did. But, in the new days, you can't do it in interest rates. You can do it other ways, but you can't do it in interest rates. So what do you do? Is there anybody in this room who thinks in the next twelve months, the yen will strengthen against the US dollar? Raise your hand.

(*No hands are raised.*)

Is there anybody in this room who thinks that, in the next twelve months, the yen will weaken against the US dollar? Raise your hand.

(*Many hands are raised.*)

Is there anybody in this room who doesn't care what happens?

(*Laughter.*)

So, if you are in the investment community and one of the G4 central banks has broken ranks with the tradition and essentially says, don't tell us what to do. And furthermore, who are you in the United States to tell us what to do? Look at those balance sheets. We are the ones who behaved for the last five years and look at the price we had to pay in terms of deflation and no growth. Now, will Japan have structural reforms? That's a whole separate question. Will they alter their tax system and open up their economy? A whole separate question.

But, in terms of this conference, the issue is banking and central banking. And in this conference, the yen is on a tear. The only question is at what price. A G4 central bank has changed the regime. The G4 Central Bank of Japan is in this new regime and is acquiring assets through monetary creation, with no short run, inflation impact. Long run is a whole different story. That creates an upward bias on every asset class in Japan. And because of the linkages and 0 percent interest rates, it does so on every asset class in the world. And at the same time, the United States is doing it too; the UK is doing it, too. The Europeans are taking a break; it takes them a while to make decisions. They need a lot of meetings to make a decision. My view is, by the time we gather here a year from now, the ECB balance sheet will be up a couple hundred billion euro or more. It will have to be.

The second issue is that we have something new going on in the world called "**bail-in**." That's the new technique for resolving troubled banks. We used to have something called "bailout."

Now, what's the difference between the two? Bailout means, when we have trouble, when a financial institution needs resolution, we use the taxpayers' or the sovereign's credit to settle things down. In the United States, we had a financial crisis that blew up the money market fund. We had bank failures; we had a mess. What happened? We bailed out to the extreme. We took the federal government's credit through the FDIC and said, we will now insure without limits the transactional demand deposits (0 interest rate deposits) in every bank in the United States, without limits. You do not have to take your money from your operating business and try to hide it in forty different banks, and we've driven the interest rate to 0 so that the collateral is now trading at a negative interest rate if you try to park your money somewhere using repos.

So, we will create a system in which we will have the maximum bailout in the United States. If you had an insured deposit in the United States, everybody in the United States, all 325 million of us, plus all the foreigners, trust the insurance of the FDIC. How many people in this room believe that, if you put $250,000 in a bank insured by the FDIC and the bank fails, you will get your $250,000?

(All hands went up.)

Everywhere in the United States, all the hands go up. Now you think about that. The FDIC is headquartered in a town called Washington, DC. It doesn't have enough money to meet the liabilities if they all came at once. It's an insurance operation that flirted with being broke. And we all believe it. It's a good thing, by the way. So, the notion of the insured deposit is sacrosanct. It's one notch below the deity until the finance ministers in the eurozone attacked it in Cyprus—or Cyprus invited them to attack it, depending on which side is telling the story. Fortunately, there was a barrier between protection of the insured deposit and the attack, which would have confiscated a piece of an insured deposit in a eurozone bank that had passed the stress test eighteen months earlier. And that was in a political system in a country where people vote. The barrier about insured deposits in the world was held by the parliament of Cyprus. God bless them. And the shock taught the eurozone financial ministers a lesson that they had not paid attention to when they voted—sixteen of the seventeen in a meeting—to attack the insured deposit.

They all are running for cover now, but they are all politicians, and they are saying, "Well, they asked us to do it." Now, this is a finger-pointing game. We do it in our country, too. Anyway, it seems to me that, when it comes to the insured deposit in the world now, it has become safer because of these events. What about the uninsured deposit? Well, in a paper in December 2012, the FDIC and the Bank of England had a discussion about resolving troubled financial institutions using bail-in and implied in language that the uninsured deposit is a liability of the bank, just like its debt, depending on its structure and priorities. In New Zealand, the governor of the central bank says, we can't price deposit insurance accurately, and if we have to resolve one of our twenty-three banks in New Zealand, we will use bail-in, which means depositors are in a different place than they were. In the eurozone in Cyprus, the uninsured depositors took a hit, and that final hit in one of those banks will be somewhere between 40 percent and 60 percent of their deposit. We are about to see this test in a country called Slovenia.

In Canada's Economic Action Plan 2013, on page 145, there is a discussion about using bail-in techniques and the uninsured depositor. I've got a piece I haven't published yet that I'm writing about it. Remember, an uninsured depositor is a claimant on a bank, just like a bond holder or a note holder, depending on the structure. Depending on what governance you use, that uninsured depositor is ahead of a shareholder, ahead of a preferred shareholder, and either ahead of a bond holder or behind a bond holder.

Now, here's my point for the central banking question at a conference like this where you will have diverse views. In a structure which is bailout, meaning sovereigns and taxpayers are supporting the backbone of the credit and safety of a banking system—there may be a question about the strength of the sovereign—the pledge is to have the sovereign and the taxpayer support the backbone of the banking system. If you switch to a regime in which you have bail-in instead of bailout, the insured part of the deposit structure of the banking system is relieved, but the uninsured part, which is commercial enterprises, large organizations, transactional deposits, and worldwide trade, is now subject to bail-in.

Have you changed the credit multipliers, the **money multipliers** of the entire system? If the answer is no, we will have huge long-term impacts from these larger central bank balance sheets. But if the answer is yes and you have been shrinking those multipliers and the multipliers are multiples of those reserves, so that if you raise the reserve by a trillion worldwide and you shrink the monetary credit expansion, which is tenfold on that trillion, you may not be creating enough reserves.

In fact, monetary policy may be too tight. We do not know. We do not know what multipliers are in a bail-in regimen. We do not know how deeply the bail-in regime is being impacted in decisions and reflected in transactional decisions, and the only thing we know is, we have some other phenomenon going on. We have this huge mass of rising currency. Think about that. We have this huge mass of rising currency in circulation in all these regimes being created by these central banks, who are forecasting a continuing rise in currency, so that way down the road, their liabilities and assets will close at some big number out in the future—the day of electronic money growing rapidly; currency rising.

Bill Dunkleberg told me, "I want you to be provocative." I hope I was, thank you very much.

BILL POOLE. David, I have two observations and then a question. One observation, this is a room full of economists; I think that's right. Second observation, from the literature, the best model for predicting exchange rates is a random walk model[15]. So my question is, why all those hands up there when you asked the question about the direction of the yen?

KOTOK. Why all the hands up about the direction of the yen? Well, I am a markets guy, Bill, and I think there is a momentum trade in the yen. I wanted to get a sense of the room, and it looks like I'm on the right side of the trade today. My task now is to sell one day before everybody else does. Thank you.

QUESTIONER. I am not an economist. I'm just an ordinary guy. David, when you start talking and say, "I don't know," it gives you a lot of credibility. I talk to experts. They know everything; they are never wrong. So, it's good to hear that. When I hear all of this, I believe I'm clueless and this is way, way over my head. But I'm hearing that I want hard assets. I have some land in Texas,

---

15   Further information may be found at http://www.investopedia.com/terms/r/randomwalktheory.asp or http://en.wikipedia.org/wiki/Random_walk

and I'm feeling better and better about that, because it's land in an area that is growing. When I look at the cash I have invested with Merrill-Lynch, I think, well that's nice, that'll be okay, but I hear that flittering away. I hear the land and assets being real. I am wondering if you could comment as to what somebody, an ordinary investor should do.

Kotok: The question is whether assets, land in Texas particularly, have an upward bias in price. Is that good? I have no idea where the land is in Texas. I hope there is no radioactive waste buried underneath it. If you print an extra trillion dollars out of thin air in the next year and you do it in four currencies and those four currencies drive capital markets of the world, we have now created a situation in which markets want central banks to keep doing it.

We manage a few billion dollars of other people's money, and we own no land in Texas, sir, so we have no bias. Markets want central banks to keep expanding their asset bases, and as long as central banks keep doing it and say they are going to keep doing it, asset prices, such as art, collectibles, real estate, stocks, and futures will keep rising in price because the stuff that you pay for them is being cheapened. It can be created without limits.

Now, do you get inflation in consumption elements? Does the CPI start to rise? That is a much harder question. You need a **transmission mechanism**, and I don't understand the transmission mechanism.

You are going to hear from Professor Bill Poole this afternoon, who is, in my view, an authority and a good friend who has examined that transmission mechanism all of his adult life. It's not working now. Does it work later? Maybe. Maybe we have enough economic recovery in the United States. We employ ten million more people, we go back to an equilibrium rate, and we have rising labor income and the credit system heals, and we have credit multiplier. Yeah, we will get inflation. When is that going to happen? I don't know. So, good luck with the land in Texas, and the only thing I would add to the land in Texas, if it doesn't appreciate in price in Texas, pick it up and move it to Nevada.

QUESTIONER: One of the value competitions that a banking community provides to its partners is an assurance that the money will be protected and available upon demand. Having been in Africa and witnessed people paying banks for that service because it was viewed as a service that warranted investment, I am reminded of witnessing a new kind of industry, an informal industry, taking shape in the United States, where money is transacting through the Internet without a bank, without anything except a transaction.

There is a service that has taken shape in Oregon, another one that I know of in Colorado, where people are simply relaying exchanges of money, deposits paid. I have not yet seen a credit card company accept such payments, but I expect that, within a year or so, we will start to see that they will accept those. So, you don't have any relays of dollars as a service without the value proposition of real money being lent. Where do you see that going in light of these issues that have arisen with the Cyprus predicament?

KOTOK. The question is electronic transfer rapidly among parties, and what isn't clear to me, are you talking about the bitcoin phenomenon, or are you talking about dollar to dollar within a currency transfer?

QUESTIONER. I am talking about both, frankly.

KOTOK. Okay. Electronic transfer is accelerating. And it's a real question about how it's even accounted for. I don't think we even know the volume. I have money in my pocket. It looks like this (*he shows a physical one-dollar bill*). We all know what it looks like. And I have in my pocket money that looks like this (*he shows a credit card.*)

QUESTIONER. You could have a smart chip that you put into your smart phone and take payment from me for advice you gave me.

KOTOK. Well, that's right. And if it cleared, it cleared in an instant. Now, here's a question for you. Let's assume you are right; it's a growing trend—there is no question about that—so it continues. Why is currency also growing? And by the way, the most popular bill is a one hundred-dollar bill and two-thirds of them are outside the United States, which has a separate message about underground economics or things that are below the radar screen.

It's a fascinating question. I don't have an answer. I do have an answer about bitcoin. All I do know is that bitcoin is a new version of a tulip.

(*Much laughter.*)

And we will find out what bitcoin amounts to. It's kind of hard for me to visualize it, so I don't know that I could say more. Fascinating question. Five years from now, we will know a lot more about it. Last question.

QUESTIONER. From your perspective, should we, as depositors, be concerned about the FDIC?

KOTOK. I don't believe so. I think the FDIC in the United States is one of the premier federal agencies. The United States doesn't default. We flirt with it politically, but we don't default. And the

FDIC in a pinch could get as much money from the treasury as it needed, so as a practical matter, insured deposits in the United States, I believe, are very, very safe.

The eurozone is a more complicated situation. I do a little work in Europe and do some discussion with central banks there, and I will tell you that the bankers did not want to do this in Cyprus. This was a political decision driven by finance ministers who didn't listen to their central bankers who said, "Don't do this; you will create a monster." Well, they did. Now they go back to the bankers and say, "Fix it."

And you have strange politics. You have the finance minister of France, who voted yes, saying, "I didn't want to do it." And you have the governor of the central bank, Christian Noyer, who by the way is a global citizen and a member of the Global Interdependent Center, who will endorse protecting the insured deposit and will say, "We have to get to a model like the FDIC. We have to do it our way, it has to have our supervision, we have to have our rules, and we have to amend treaties, but that's where we need to get to." Why does his finance minister vote yes?

So the politics are not totally clear yet. I'm not worried about the FDIC. I think there is a different question for an uninsured deposit. In my firm—we are a small firm of thirty people run with a single-digit million balance—my CFO says, "I'm going to take money and distribute it, with $250,000 limits among banks, because electronically I can govern our payroll and payments and safety, and I'm worried because I've been listening to your speeches too much." (*Laughter.*) "What do you think?"

I said, "Do it." Excess liquidity in our firm is now in securities in safekeeping and hedged, not in an uninsured deposit.

Now, there are two reasons for that. Number one, I can get a higher interest rate than I can get from a bank. And I feel safer. So we are doing that for more and more institutional clients. That says something about shifts in uninsured deposits. It will be interesting to see what other speakers say about the cessation of protection of uninsured deposits in the United States, which took effect on December 31 when the law expired[16].

---

16   See the FDIC notice on the termination of unlimited insurance of noninterest bearing transaction accounts as of December 31,, 201 here: http://www.psboc.com/pdfs/FDIC%20unlimited%20Ins%20expires%20notice.pdf

DAVID KOTOK

Chairman and Chief Investment Officer of Cumberland Advisors and GIC Vice Chair of the Central Banking Series

David R. Kotok cofounded Cumberland Advisors in 1973 and has been its Chief Investment Officer since inception. He holds a B.S. in economics from The Wharton School of the University of Pennsylvania, an M.S. in organizational dynamics from The School of Arts and Sciences at the University of Pennsylvania, and a masters in philosophy from the University of Pennsylvania.

Mr. Kotok's articles and financial market commentary have appeared in The New York Times, The Wall Street Journal, Barron's, and other publications. He is a frequent guest on financial television including Bloomberg Television, Al Jazeera, Reuters, and Fox Business. He also contributes to radio networks such as NPR and media organizations like Bloomberg Radio, among others. He has authored two books, including the bestseller From Bear to Bull with ETFs.

Mr. Kotok currently serves as a Director and Vice Chairman of the Global Interdependence Center (GIC) (www.interdependence.org), whose mission is to encourage the expansion of global dialogue and free trade in order to improve cooperation and understanding among nation states, with the goal of reducing international conflicts and improving worldwide living standards. Mr. Kotok chairs its Central Banking Series. He organized a five-continent dialogue held in global locations including London, Philadelphia, Paris, Zambia (Livingstone), Hanoi, Singapore, Prague, Cape Town, Shanghai, Hong Kong, Rome, Milan, Tallinn, and Santiago, Chile. He has received the Global Citizen Award from GIC for his efforts.

Mr. Kotok is a member of the National Business Economics Issues Council (NBEIC) and the National Association for Business Economics (NABE). Mr. Kotok has served as a Commissioner of the Delaware River Port Authority (DRPA) and on the Treasury Transition Teams for New Jersey Governors Kean and Whitman. He has also served as a board member of the New Jersey Economic Development Authority and as Chairman of the New Jersey Casino Reinvestment Development Authority.

Mr. Kotok hosts an annual Maine fishing trip, where, it is rumored, most of the nations important financial and economic decisions are actually made.

CHAPTER 4

The Chicago Plan Revisited

MICHAEL KUMHOF IS A MEMBER of the International Monetary Fund research staff and an expert in dynamic stochastic general equilibrium (**DSGE**) mathematical modeling. He uses a DSGE model of the US economy to analyze the effects of changing the monetary system over into a modern version of the Chicago Plan as contemplated by Irving Fisher during the 1930s. Much of the remaining conference is then built on this model, plus a potential variation of it by using the techniques of Limited Purpose Banking introduced in the following chapter.

Michael starts off by giving a comprehensive explanation of our current way of creating money, because without that understanding, the following presentations are nonsensical. Step by step, he builds a theoretical model and then goes into the mechanics of what would occur on the macro level during system changeover. The positive results forecast would surprise even Irving Fisher.

His résumé is found at the end of this chapter.

MICHAEL KUMHOF:

It is important that this presentation comes with the usual IMF disclaimer: None of this, none of what I present today represents official IMF policy. It is research.

First, a very brief introduction. Then I'm going to go into how we should be thinking about banks in our models. This is not just a geeky question but is actually really important for how we think about banks in the real world. There are a lot of very misleading statements being made, including in the media, about how banks work, and I first of all want to set that straight because a realistic understanding of how banks actually work is fundamental to understanding the Chicago Plan. The insights that I'm going to discuss were insights that Irving Fisher and others had in the 1930s that have been almost completely lost today.

Then I'm going to talk about the advantages of the Chicago Plan; that's the bulk of the paper. Then there are a lot of questions that I have received since publishing this paper in August 2012, and I'm going to address the

> The level of debate was far more profound during the Great Depression than it is today

most important ones here. Then, I'm going to go through a little application of what I would call a mini-Chicago Plan, mainly another way to resolve bad debt problems in the banking system through central bank purchase of non-performing loans (NPLs) and then a summary and discussion.

The Great Recession obviously revealed very serious weaknesses in the financial system. The financial system is where everything started. It triggered significant financial system reform—that is, monetary reform. For eight years now, I've been reading about monetary history and the history of monetary thought, and I discovered that, at the time of the Great Depression, the level of the debate was actually in many ways more profound, far more profound, than what we have today. And I will explain why that is. That debate culminated eventually in the 1933 and 1935 Banking Acts, but in competition with that, was the Chicago Plan, and part of why the Banking Acts were passed was that the banking lobby was even more strongly opposed to the Chicago Plan.

The Chicago Plan was actually supported at that time by a majority of the leading macroeconomists. It was created by Frederick Soddy, who was a Nobel Prize winner in chemistry from the UK. That tells you that sometimes noneconomists have much more profound thoughts about economics than economists. Support came from Irving Fisher, as well as Henry Simons and Frank Knight, both of whom were teachers of Milton Friedman, who also supported the Chicago Plan but obviously a bit later.

What the Chicago Plan proposes is the separation of the monetary and credit functions of the banking system—that is, for the deposit or liability side of the banking system to be backed 100 percent by public reserves. Secondly, on the credit or asset side of the banking system, credit cannot be financed by the creation of bank deposits ex nihilo, or out of nothing. Because we just had a talk that said that the central bank can create money out of nothing, I wish to say that banks can do that too and on a far greater scale if they wish to do so, and I will explain how that works.

Today's talk amounts to comparing the characteristics of the world during the Chicago Plan and the world that we have today and transitioning between the two. Then we'll turn to what good that would do and what the problems would be.

> The key function of banks is money creation and not intermediation

Now for some key insights on banks. The key function of banks is money creation and not intermediation. If you tell that even to a mainstream economist, it's provocative. But it is 100 percent correct. What banks do is create a new loan on the asset side of the balance sheet and, when that is done, create a new deposit of exactly the same amount that is credited to the guy who has just borrowed the money. I was a banker at Barclays Bank for five years; I made loans, and I know exactly what the entries are that you need to create when you make a loan.

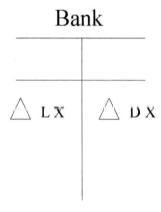

Bank

Figure 4.1: A Simple Bank Balance Sheet Representation

When the bank makes a loan, the balance sheet is like figure 4.1. When it creates a loan, it creates an additional loan entry on the asset side, delta-L for the customer, let's call him "X". The bank then creates an additional deposit entry on the debit side, delta-D, and that is also in the name of the same person, X. The bank at that moment creates new money out of thin air, and I will go into more detail about that now.

Now, how about intermediation? A common definition of intermediation is that the banks—or the banking system as a whole, and it's important to make that distinction—accept nonbank deposits of savings, somebody's savings, and then lend them out to somebody else who needs them. Under this definition, banks are not intermediaries. They never, ever do that! Because what they do is what I have just shown with my little drawing. And this is not intermediation, because this customer, X, is the same on both sides of the balance sheet. In terms of causation, the critical issue here is that loans come before deposits. Loans create deposits, and not vice versa. What the intermediation story misses completely is the monetary nature of financing.

Let's go into more detail now. What story would I have to tell in order to tell the intermediation story? Let's look at the scenario where A wants to buy goods or assets and B wants to sell them. Now B dumps the goods at the bank and the deposit is recorded, and then the bank gives the goods to A and the loan is recorded. That story is, of course, complete nonsense, because that never happens. But that's how you have to argue if you say that banks intermediate funds, that is, intermediate savings from some customer to some other customer because that implies that deposits come before loans.

What you have to ignore for this is, of course, if somebody comes into bank one and brings in a check that is drawn on bank two. That is a micro-phenomenon. That doesn't change the overall amount of loans and deposits in the economy; it just reshuffles them between different banks. That's not relevant for this argument. Cash deposits are also not relevant. First of all, cash is a tiny item in terms of the overall bank business, and secondly, banks never lend out cash directly. You only draw out cash against an existing deposit.

The intermediation story is a completely impossible story, yet it dominates in today's debate. It is also known as the "loanable funds story."

For the "money creation story," we start with the exact same scenario. A wants to buy goods, and B wants to sell goods. Now, A goes to the bank to get financing and B stays at home. He has nothing at all to do with this. A gets a new loan of $1 million and a new deposit of $1 million. What the bank has done here is to create its own funds, deposits, in the act of lending. It has not had to wait for anybody to deposit something first in order to make the loan. It created its own funding. That, of course, is an absolutely extraordinary privilege that is not enjoyed by any other kind of business.

Then, what happens is that A uses this new deposit to pay B to get the goods or the asset. So then it looks like intermediation has happened because then it's going to be somebody else on the liability side of the balance sheet, but the bank at that point does nothing active. The bank just provides check-clearing services so that people can exchange the money that has been created among themselves for their business needs. The actual work of the bank has been the creation of new money, and of course it can also destroy money. This story happens every single time a bank makes a loan, and it is completely different from the loanable funds story.

The implication is that new loans involve no intermediation; no funds are being withdrawn from previous users or savings. This is absolutely

> New loans involve no intermediation

critical, and for Irving Fisher, it was front and center, the fact that banks can easily start a lending boom. Because if they can do what I have just demonstrated, they can simply grow their balance sheets by expanding the money supply—the **broad money** supply that is, not the narrow money supply. They do not have to attract deposits of preexisting money.

I have already mentioned the next point—that if the deposit is transferred to another bank, this bank will simply have to re-borrow it in the interbank market. But for the overall banking system, once this deposit has been created, it remains in the banking system prior to either default or repayment of the underlying loan.

I will briefly explain next that reserves or cash balances impose no limits on this process. That is the "deposit multiplier story." The deposit

> Reserves impose no limits on lending

multiplier story is wrong. The only constraints on banks in this process are solvency and profitability. The bank will ask itself, "If I make this loan, am I going to get a high enough interest rate given how much capital reserves I have to put into it? And is there too high a risk that this loan will default completely and wipe me out?" That depends entirely on the bank's sentiment of how the economy is going, and this kind of optimism can be extremely volatile.

So, our regulation of the money supply, that is the broad money supply or the liability side of the banking system, depends on this sentiment of the banking system about how the economy is doing and on very little else. There is one other factor—the policy rate. I will get to that toward the end, but it is a relatively weak influence. I have quotations from various people to back up the statements I just made.

Most of them are brief, but this one I want to list in full because it is so beautiful and so insightful. It comes from Schumpeter[17] in 1954:

> But this makes it highly inadvisable to construe
> bank credit on the model of existing funds being
> withdrawn from previous users by an *entirely*

---

17   Joseph Schumpeter, considered one of the most influential economists of the 20th century, who popularized the term "creative destruction."

imaginary act of saving [emphasis by Kumhof] and then lent out by their owners. It is much more realistic to say that the banks create deposits in their act of lending than to say that they lend the deposits that have been entrusted to them. The theory to which economists cling so tenaciously, makes depositors out to be savers when they neither save nor intend to do so. It attributes to them an influence on the supply of credit which they do not have[18].

And now we go into a very interesting bit of history which is relevant to where we are today.

Nevertheless, it proved extraordinarily difficult for economists to recognize that bank loans and bank investments do create deposits. In fact, throughout the period under review, they refuse with practical unanimity to do so. And even in 1930, when a large majority had been converted ...[19]

So, where are we today? If you look around, the academic literature is in some sense back to prior to World War I. The loanable funds model again dominates. We have lost a lot of the lessons that Fisher, Knight, and Simons had learned by the 1930s, painfully learned, because, for many decades in the interim, banks have been almost completely off the radar screen of macroeconomists. We are starting again at a point that is almost pre-World War I. For Fisher and all of the people who supported the Chicago Plan, this insight was key, and it will be incorporated in our own work.

---

18   Schumpeter, Joseph *History of Economic Analysis*, Oxford University Press, New York, 1954, p1114

19   Ibid

Central banks are corroborating this multiple times. In my paper I have more complete quotes[20]. The Federal Reserve Bank of New York published a working paper which basically tells exactly this story that I have on the board here as figure 4.1. Graham Towers, former Governor of the Central Bank of Canada, "Each time new bank credit is created—new deposits—brand new money." Then there is a statement from the Bank of England and from the Bundesbank, which essentially say the same thing.

Here is a little corollary to what I just told you. It is relevant and I included it here because Professor Jeffrey Sachs is going to talk later, and this

> Investment does not require prior savings

is especially relevant to development economics. Bank-financed investment does not require prior savings. Very often among macroeconomists, you hear the story that, oh, this country needs to have more investments, so we need to generate more savings so there is enough savings available to finance the investment. This is not correct.

What happens if you finance investment—at least to the extent that investment can be financed by a banking system—before any savings or investment comes a new loan and a new deposit. This new deposit is obviously not yet savings because the net of these two things is zero. "X" has net savings of zero, but by providing new purchasing power to X, it allows investment to go ahead. X can use this now to buy a machine. Then the seller of the machine acquires the deposit, and then it becomes saving. Then, this seller has exchanged that machine against some financial asset that he is saving, and saving is equal to investment in the macro-economy, in the closed economy at least. In this way, the investment has actually happened—through the buying of the machine.

---

20   See Bibliography

However, this saving is a consequence of lending and, thereby, the creation of money and investment. So for economic development, this is an absolutely fundamental insight. Saving is not a precondition for investment; rather it is a byproduct of efficient investment finance. I will leave it there.

My next point is that the deposit multiplier is a myth. This goes back to the point earlier that reserves do not impose a constraint on banks' money creation. The deposit multiplier can always be calculated as a number, that is, broad money versus narrow money. You can calculate that number, but that number is not a transmission mechanism. The deposit multiplier story is that the central bank fixes narrow monetary aggregates first and broad monetary aggregates are the **endogenous** results, as banks lend this money in multiple stages. You have all seen this in undergraduate textbooks.

Finn Kydland and Edward Prescott, Nobel Prize winners, refer to this as a myth. Why? Because it actually turns the monetary transmission mechanism on its head. It's upside down. What they showed for the monetarist's era is that broad monetary aggregates lead the cycle and broad monetary aggregates are created by banks. Narrow monetary aggregates lag the cycle and they are under the control of the central bank. In other words, the banks decide first and narrow money follows.

These numbers, the leads and lags, are not from Kydland and Prescott; they are from Steve Keene and more recent data. In the inflation targeting era, it is even more fundamental that, if you control the price, which of course is the interest rate, then you have to let the quantities adjust; and quantities are the reserves. This means that the central bank has a duty, if it sets the interest rate at a certain level, to ensure the stability of the payment system to supply the payment system with the reserves that it needs at that interest rate. The evidence for this statement is completely overwhelming, both in institutional and empirical terms.

And here are some supporting statements, first from the vice president of the New York Fed in 1969. At the time, from what I know, he was arguing against the introduction of monetarism under a fractional reserve banking system. The statement as a whole is a very interesting statement, but I just picked the key sentence: "In the real world, banks extend credit, creating deposits in the process, and look for the reserves later[21]." That is exactly the story that I just told you. Carpenter and Demiralp, in a Federal Reserve Board working paper that was cleared for publication at the Federal Reserve Board, said, "The relationships implied by the money multiplier do not exist in the data. The textbook treatment of money in the transmission mechanism can be rejected[22]." In an ECB Monthly Bulletin, less than a year old, "The Euro system, however, always provides the banking system with the liquidity required to meet the aggregate reserve requirement[23]." *Always*. No questions asked. There are exceptions, but only at extreme times, and I will come to them right now.

So here are the conclusions. When banks ask for reserves, the central bank obliges. The transmission, therefore, starts with loan creation, which equals deposit creation, and it *ends* with reserve creation, at normal times. Of course now we have QE, and we have a lot of special things going on. This is important to emphasize, also in light of the previous talk [Chapter 3], I'm

---

21   Alan Holmes, Senior Vice President, Federal Reserve Bank of NY, 1969

22   Carpenter, Seth and Selva Demiralp *Money, Reserves, and the Transmission of Monetary Policy: Does the Money Multiplier Exist?*, Finance and Economics Discussion Series, Division of Research and Statistics and Monetary Affairs, Federal Reserve Board, Washington, DC, 2010-41

23   European Central Bank Monthly Bulletin, May 2012, page 21

talking about banking in normal times. There are a lot of special considerations right now.

Because of what I just said, banks are almost fully in control of the money creation process. The only tool the Fed has for affecting the money supply is the very blunt tool of the policy rate. How do they affect the money supply? Well, to limit it, they have to keep banks from lending the broad money supply. They have to keep banks from lending. The only way you can do that is by making their borrowers not creditworthy or borderline not creditworthy so that banks are too scared to make loans or the borrowers don't want to borrow themselves. You have to drive them into bankruptcy, literally.

When I presented this paper at the Fed two weeks ago, nobody disagreed with me on any of this. There were, however, some people in the audience who basically said there was a very short period during [Fed Chairman Paul] Volcker's tenure, right at the beginning, when he was willing to use the policy rate for this very blunt purpose. But those are extreme times.

Having set the stage, now here are the six advantages of the Chicago Plan. Fisher identified four advantages. We found two more, and this summarizes them:

> Here are the 6 advantages of the Chicago Plan

1. Dramatic reduction of public debts
2. Dramatic reduction of private debts
3. Complete elimination of bank runs
4. Much better control of credit cycles
5. Output gains

6. Elimination of liquidity traps and, therefore, the possibility of zero, steady state inflation

By the way, Fisher's book from 1936—I'm talking about the short one—*100% Money and the Public Debt*, which is only about twenty-five pages, is the most exciting piece of monetary economics I've ever read. There is not one equation in there and not one bit of econometrics. It's just super-deep thinking. I highly recommend it.

So now the six advantages of the Chicago Plan in detail.

First and second are dramatic reduction of public and private debt. We have to start going through the balance sheets here, and I've tried my best to lay this out as clearly as possible, starting with this banking system balance sheet. [See figure 4.2] I say current; it's calibrated roughly to 2006, prior to the crisis because, again, many things subsequent to that are very special. This is from the flow of funds and various other data sources. All numbers are for the United States and all numbers are in percent of GDP.

So, we have banks holding some government debt, but most of it is actually held outside the banking system and, in fact, outside the country. Then we have 80 percent of GDP as investment loans, both for corporate investments and also for housing. Then we have 100 percent of GDP as other types of loans—that is, mortgages against land (I make a distinction between houses under construction and loans against land), short-term working capital loans for firms, and short-term consumer loans for households. So we have four different loan classes here, and all of them are carefully calibrated. We did a really intensive job to try to map the financial system to a modern business cycle model.

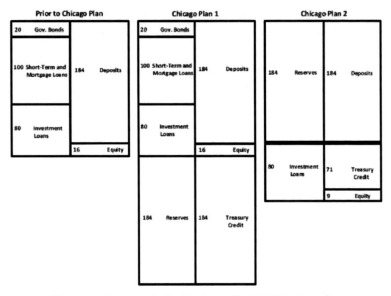

Figure 4.2: Changes in Bank Balance Sheet During Transition

On the liability side, we have deposits, and notice that there I go into less detail. This is a very broad category of deposits. Some of them are transaction balances with zero interest; some of them are much less liquid but still liquid balances. Money is a spectrum; money is not just one thing, not just cash in your wallet. Money is much broader; it's everything that can be used for transactions. And some things are used more and some things are used less; therefore, some things pay a lower interest rate, and some things pay a higher interest rate. We lump all that together. Then, we have bank equity, and this is a state-of-the-art model that manages to map the **Basel III** regulations into a modern banking system where there are penalties on having too little equity.

Now, what does the Chicago Plan amount to? The Chicago Plan basically says that the government now goes to these banks and says, "Look, you have these deposits as 184 percent of GDP, and from now on you have to back these deposits with reserves of public money, 100 percent reserve public cover. So, you need 184 percent of GDP for that, which at this point simply does not exist, right? The way you bring it into existence is by borrowing it from the government—the central bank or the treasury.

So how do I get these reserves? As a banking system, I basically issue an IOU to the government. I borrow these reserves from the government by paying a low interest rate on it. The balance sheet still balances, and now we can rearrange this. All the elements here are exactly the same; they are just in different places [see center of figure 4.2]. We rearrange this into what I call "money banks" for the bottom of the balance sheet and "credit investment trusts" for the top. The money banks are basically just a warehouse for reserves of public money. You can think of this reserve of public money as the cash in your wallet. In the real world, it will mostly take the form of electronic cash. But in legal and functional terms, it's almost the same.

I am abstracting equity from banks previously needed for certain kinds of activity, as now they are just managing a payment system—providing ATMs, providing sophisticated services, **SWIFT** facilities, etc. The credit investment trust now still has the same bank equity. They still have the same loans, but they are now entirely funded by the government. That's not the end of the story, in case that makes you nervous. There will be more. Right now, it looks like credit is financed 100 percent by government. That is, by no means, necessary, and I will show you the next steps.

So what the government now has at this point is a debt, a gross debt outstanding of 80 percent, minus the 184 percent that it has lent to the banking system. I will show the government balance sheet later. This windfall is, by the way, essentially the government reappropriating the seigniorage money creation that banks have been taking in over the decades by creating deposits out of thin air. The government is reappropriating that same thing in one step, for the benefit of everyone, as I will show you.

What it can do with that is, first of all, retire government debt that is held by banks as it comes due or prepay it. That is a question of detail, and in the model, it happens immediately. In the

> The government is re-appropriating the seigniorage

model, everything happens immediately because it's much easier to see what is going on. Then the credit investment trusts become a little smaller in terms of their balance sheet.

Now, the next step is that this treasury credit is essentially the government having a huge bank account in the banking system, being a huge depositor in the banking system. The next step of the Chicago Plan would be a citizen's dividend, where the government just says to every citizen, you get something like your annual income as a one-off citizen's dividend. I redistribute this seigniorage to you—every citizen!

In fact, the way I do it here is exactly 100 percent of GDP, so that would be an equal amount per capita and would match up with the way I have done it quantitatively here. So the government has a smaller account now in the banking system, and the citizens have a larger account. The way this would be done and the way I conceptualize it in the paper is that these citizens' accounts cannot be freely used for transactions; the first thing they have to be used for is to repay any outstanding debt that is out there in the banking system and the financial system more broadly speaking. I know this is somewhat arbitrary. I assume that this is exactly enough to repay everything except investment loans. By investment loans I mean the loans for housing construction and for commercial plants and machines.

So, in this fashion, a huge chunk of credit is going to be repaid inside these credit investment trusts, and we end up with this balance sheet. The government still looks like it finances all remaining credit, but that is still not the end of the story. First, we need an intermediate step. If you have a Basel III regulation and suddenly the size of the balance sheet shrinks so much, then the banks need less capital in order to support their activities, so they are going to pay out a one-time dividend to their shareholders, and the government is going to inject some more treasury credit to make up the difference. Nothing changes with the size of the balance sheet.

Finally, the government in this economy still has 60 percent outstanding debt outside the financial system. This is for the federal US government, so from roughly 80 percent of GDP debt in 2006, 20 percent has already been repaid here. This is not part of the model simulation. The government could essentially repay that 60 percent also and pay agents with these treasury credit balances. The only reason I am showing that is that people get nervous when they see that scenario; the government finances all private credit, and therefore, the fear is that the government is going to dictate the terms of credit.

First of all, even if the government were to be a major funder, it would not necessarily imply that it would determine terms of credit at all. The government could just set a price and let the banks get on with their business. But, as you see here, you could also end up with a situation where there is just a very small slice of treasury credit outstanding and everything else is financed either by private equity in the banking system or by nonmonetary private deposits. And by the way, instead of making this a debt-financed credit investment, the government could also convert its claims into equity and then distribute them to private agents. And then you would be in a world closer to Larry Kotlikoff's Limited Purpose Banking [see next chapter in this book], where all the credit investment transactions have to be financed by non-debt liabilities—i.e., by equity.

Now for changes in the government balance sheet see Figure 4.3. As you see on the left, prior to the Chicago Plan, we have government bonds of 80 percent of GDP outstanding and some unspecified other assets; I don't care what they are, but I just wanted this to be a balanced balance sheet. In the middle then is the first step of the Chicago Plan with 100 percent reserve backing. And so, on the asset side, the government now has this claim on the banking system, and on the liability side, they have these reserves of public money.

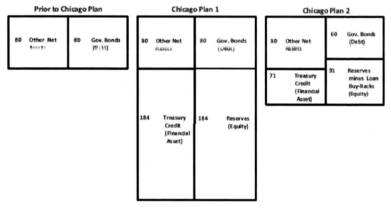

Figure 4.3: Changes if Government Balance Sheet in Transition

Now comes a very important argument. These reserves of public money are not debt. What you have on the liability side of a balance sheet is always debt and equity—that is, your own funds. Now, if you think about this, this (*he holds up a dollar bill*) is the current central bank money in the United States, and this is debt-based money. We saw that in the first presentation, [David Kotok's]. This (*he again indicates the dollar bill he's holding*) is on the liability side, and it's backed on the other side by government debt. So it's something very similar to a checking account in the bank. It's backed by debt on the other side of the balance sheet.

But this is a coin (*he holds up a coin*) issued by the Treasury, and this is treated in official US accounting conventions as equity in the common wealth of the nation. It is treated as one-off revenue when it is created. Of course, that revenue is probably negative because it costs more to make these things than it brings in. But anyway, the principle matters. This is treated as equity of the government as one-off revenue, and what the Chicago Plan essentially amounts to is to say that all money in existence should have that same status as that coin that I've just shown you.

Finally, on the right-hand side of figure 4.3 we have the final government balance sheet. Net government debt becomes negative at the end of the day.

The counterpart to this equity position that the government gets is this high treasury credit, but then some of it is written off through the citizens' dividend. And at the end of the day, the government has less equity and a smaller claim on the banking system, but it still has a net positive claim on the banking system. So the government ends up with negative debt and a positive equity position.

Third., complete elimination of bank runs is the second advantage of the Chicago Plan. That, of course, is pretty obvious. Once the money is backed by public reserves, there is no reason why there should be a run on your bank because you know the money is there. It is literally there. The government has provided the means of payment. The means of payment is provided by the government debt-free, as opposed

> The Chicago Plan provides for complete elimination of bank runs

to being dependent on the performance of a private debt liability on the other side of the balance sheet.

Also, credit assets must be funded by nonmonetary liabilities, and this is important. This could be treasury credit; this could be bank equity, as in Larry Kotlikoff's scheme and also in Henry Simons' Financial Good Society[24]. Or it could be private debt. I am listing here various provisions that could be adopted to make sure that that private debt would not lead to money substitutes, and that's one of the important points that also occupied Henry Simons a lot. I don't have enough time to talk about those provisions, but I think there are some effective provisions that would easily rule this out.

Fourth, under the Chicago Plan, there is much better control of bank-lending-driven business cycles because bank money creation becomes impossible. Now banks become the true intermediaries of our textbooks. They are no longer money creators. That makes it much easier to prevent credit cycles and what we show in our simulation is that, if you combine that with a policy of quantitative lending guidance, which is allowed for under Basel III in the form of countercyclical capital buffers[25], then you can actually lower the amplitude of business cycle fluctuations.

So in figure 4.4, the black line is a simulation of a pre-transition business cycle, where banks for three years get more optimistic about the creditworthiness of their customers and then suddenly change course after three years. Their sentiment changes dramatically, and that leads to an initial boom followed by a very deep recession. You can see that there is a drop of almost 6 percent in GDP at the end of the boom. What you can see here is that these

---

24   Simons, Henry *A Positive Program for Laissey Faire. Some Proposals for a Liberal Economic Policy*, The University of Chicago Press, 1948

25   See Glossary under pro-cyclicality

banks create their own deposits in the act of lending. This is in the simulation. Then, when the cycle crashes, both loans and deposits crash by enormous amounts—in this particular simulation, over 50 percent of GDP.

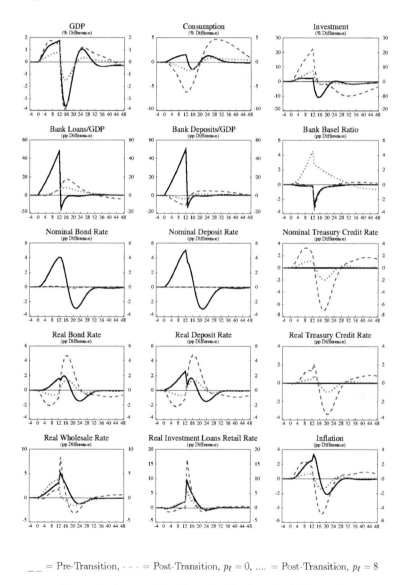

___ = Pre-Transition, - - - = Post-Transition, $p_\ell = 0$, ... = Post-Transition, $p_\ell = 8$

Figure 4.4: Pre- and Post-Transition Business Cycle Properties

Now, in the existing mainstream model of loanable funds, this is impossible. You could never have this. If banks were intermediators of saving rather than creators of money, you could not have this. Continuing with figure 4.4, the dashed line is a simulation where instead, we have the Chicago Plan economy, and what happens there is that these banks accumulate additional capital; the Basel ratio is the ratio of capital to overall assets. If they want to lend more capital in order to back their additional loans, they have to put that aside so that, when the change in sentiment happens after three years, which is the same, they have a very comfortable buffer, and there is a very gradual reduction in loans, but the amplitude of fluctuations in GDP is very, very much reduced.

Fifth we have output gains approaching 10 percent. Why do we find that? Now, this goes for the first time to our model simulations backing this talk[26], but let me describe the story just in words here. Why do we get such large output gains? First of all, under normal monetary conditions, interest rates would be much lower in a world where debt levels are much lower. It is very clear in any good model that, when the debt to equity ratio is high, there is a higher real interest rate. And if you have a higher real interest rate, you have lower investment. So, if you do a huge debt to equity swap, with the equity being the money, the equity in the commonwealth, you get lower interest rates, higher investment, higher capital, and higher output.

> The Chicago Plan greatly lowers bank monitoring costs

---

26   Jaromir Benes and Michael Kumhof, *The Chicago Plan Revisited: Revised Draft of February 12, 2013*, http://www.imf.org/external/pubs/cat/longres. aspx?sk=26178.0.

You also get lower tax rates in this world because the government has a money stock of 180 percent of GDP that has to grow at the rate of real growth of the economy, and I'm assuming real growth is 2 percent in this economy. So, you need to grow your nominal money supply at 2 percent just to keep the economy supplied with sufficient money. That gives you completely noninflationary seigniorage of between 3 percent and 4 percent of GDP. That can be used to lower distortionary taxes, including taxes on capital, which we all know would stimulate the economy.

The Chicago Plan will greatly lower monitoring costs. In the current economy, a lot of intelligent people have to sit there and monitor loans to make sure that the banks get their money back. Not all of these loans, but a good chunk of them, are there so that the economy can have an adequate money stock. That is the only way in this economy that we can provide the broad money supply— through banks getting people into debt, so that on the other side of the balance sheet, there can be money. When people can have money in a debt-free way provided by government, that part of lending is no longer necessary, and the people who are deployed in the banking system to monitor loans for that purpose can be redeployed somewhere else and switch their job from Citibank to GE and make something, some real product. We quantified the resource savings from that as well.

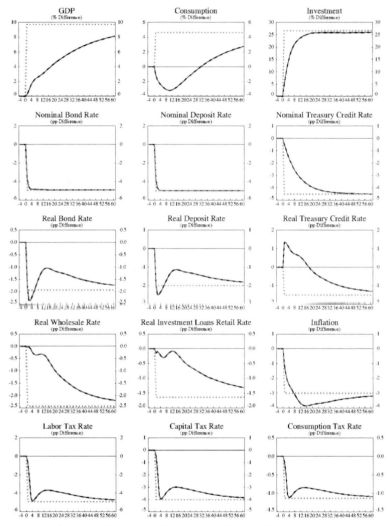

Figure 4.5: Transition to Chicago Plan

In figure 4.5 we show some impulse responses. This is a model simulation. On the horizontal axis, you have sixty quarters; on the vertical axis you have percentage point or percent differences. The dashed line in each case is where the economy jumps in the very long run, versus the dark line, which tells you how it transitions to that very long run. Essentially, we have to start looking on the right-hand side. What we have here is the lending rate dropping by over two hundred basis points because of this huge debt-equity swap over time. The labor tax rate and also the capital tax rate show the same picture, dropping by four or five percentage points. This gives a big stimulus to the economy, especially to investment, to the extent that it actually initially crowds out consumption a little bit. That is specific to this simulation, and that leads to a GDP gain in this simulation of 10 percent.

These are very specific numbers, and they can be debated, but that is why we laid out the calibration of our model in great detail—so that we can be criticized for that detail and not for the broad story. The broad story does hold together; the details we can talk about.

Finally, inflation in this simulation goes from 3 percent steady state to 0 percent steady state over that period.

Next in figure 4.6 we show the fiscal accounts. The only thing I want you to notice here, apart from the big drop in government debt and government deficit, is that here on the right-hand side, seigniorage, i.e. the revenue from money creation, increases by 3.6 percent of GDP. We have assumed that this seigniorage is mostly used to lower various distortionary taxes by 3.6 percent and, thereby, stimulate the economy.

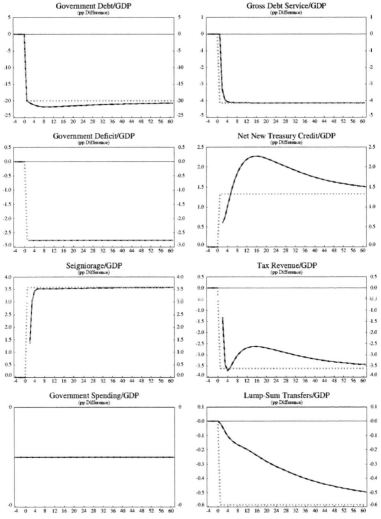

Figure 4.6: Transition to Chicago Plan: Fiscal Variables

Sixth, we have no liquidity traps. The main tools of monetary policy under the Chicago Plan are a nominal money growth rule, á la Friedman, and an interest rate rule that controls the price of treasury credit to banks as well as the Basel capital adequacy ratio. These are tools well known from the literature, with perhaps the second one not as well known.

With these rules, there can be no liquidity traps in the resultant economy. A liquidity trap is when the central bank loses its ability to stimulate the economy, either by creating more money or by lowering interest rates further. In the current economy, and this is something that came out in the first talk [see the previous chapter in this book], we now have the "pushing-on-a-string problem," in that the central bank can create as many reserves as it wishes in attempting to increase the broad money in circulation. It's still pushing on a string because it wants banks to lend in order to create broad money, which is what people actually use in order to spend on goods, services, and assets. And if the banks don't feel like it, or if their customers don't feel like it, then good luck. It's not going to happen, right?

In a Chicago Plan economy, on the other hand, the central bank would directly control the broad quantity of money by spending it into circulation or by lending it into circulation through investment trusts.

> The Chicago Plan eliminates liquidity traps

And that would directly end up in people's pockets—quantitative easing for the people, if you like. Some people have called it that. It would directly stimulate spending.

There is no zero interest rate floor in this economy because the interest rate that the central bank controls, or the government more generally controls, is the interest rate on treasury credit, which is the rate at which it lends to banks, and that can temporarily become negative. So, of course, if you don't have a zero interest rate floor, then you can have much lower steady state inflation, including zero steady state inflation, and you could therefore have a much less inflationary economy under the Chicago Plan.

Now, in the interest of time, I have answers to many common

questions, and perhaps we can come back to those this afternoon when we have time for questions [see Chapter 7: "Panel Discussion with Larry Kotlikoff and Michael Kumhof"]. However, I want to get to one of them, which is the question of inflation.

Will government control over money cause inflation? Inflation is determined by the relative quantities of money in private hands, and the supply of goods. The quantity of money in private hands remains virtually unchanged when transitioning from today's economy to a Chicago Plan economy, and therefore, this cannot be inflationary. What changes is what money represents.

Somebody at the ECB said that, in the current economy, what money represents is "destructible money" because it represents loans on the asset side of a bank's balance sheet, and banks can either call in those loans or the loans can default, and therefore the money is destructible. The money under the Chicago Plan is permanently issued by the government and indestructible money. That is what changes during a transition to a Chicago Plan, not inflation.

The quantity of money in people's bank accounts at each stage of transition to the Chicago Plan never changes. What changes is what happens on the asset side of the balance sheet. Money takes on a different nature. The quantity of money does not increase; therefore there's no inflation.

In the technical paper backing my talk [see previous footnote], there is also a very long historical section that talks about what has been the historical experience with periods of private versus public money issuance. And contrary to what many will want to tell you, it is exactly the opposite of what you tend to hear.

On the whole, the periods of public money issuance have exhibited much more stability than periods of private money issuance, and in some cases, that is hundreds of years ago. There is a very interesting section on the German hyperinflation. I'm German myself. The episode of German hyperinflation is completely misrepresented in much of the literature. If you read [Hjalmar] Schacht's book, and Schacht was the Reichsbank president in 1923, he will tell you that this was an episode of hyperinflation caused by excessive private money creation, aided and abetted at that time by what was a private central bank. When he asserted the public prerogative and reasserted it in late 1923, he killed speculation and stabilized the currency.

Here is a very brief application—a mini-Chicago Plan. I want to talk about this because I talked with [Lord] Adair Turner yesterday, and he's going to talk a little bit about this also [see Chapter 8: "Money and Debt: Radical Solutions to the Challenge of De-Leveraging"]. We now have this spectacle out there in the policy debate where various national banking systems have problems with potential insolvencies of individual institutions. What if the central bank were to just purchase those nonperforming loans? This has been done successfully in at least two historical episodes—the United Kingdom in 1914, which had made large loans to continental powers that were obviously not recoverable at that time, and also Japan in 1945, when everything was basically gone on the asset side of the balance sheet.

The central bank just bought those nonperforming loans and exchanged them for reserves. What this does, and very successfully in each case, is it simultaneously improves the balance sheet of the government, the banks, and private borrowers. It's a win-win-win situation. Understood correctly, this policy amounts to a small-scale version of the Chicago Plan, as I will show you.

And of course, it's an almost completely painless alternative to policies that resolve bank solvency issues through the destruction of part of the private money supply, the destruction of part of this (*he points to the right side of figure 4.2, in other words, the deposit side*). It's already been mentioned this morning where that is being tried. All the Chicago school economists would have been absolutely horrified by a policy that destroys your money supply or part of your money supply and makes people nervous about the remainder of the money supply.

So here is a brief simulation. We start off with an **aggregate** bank balance sheet—banks have nonperforming loans that far exceed their equity; these institutions would essentially be insolvent. Now the central bank purchases these nonperforming loans and adds these to the asset side of its balance sheet and issues reserves against these and puts those reserves into the banking system. We are assuming that these nonperforming loans are going to pay off 40 percent of their face value. The banks are now in perfect shape. The borrowers might also be, depending on what the government does with its claims against the borrowers. But the banks are in shape now.

Now what you do is raise the banks' reserve requirement to make sure that these reserves become permanent features of their balance sheet. You just say you have to keep those reserves from now on, for example, against all your checking deposits or something like that.

So the banks remain the same, but the central bank now writes off the nonperforming loans against their equity. And contrary to what you might think, the taxpayer has not lost anything. The taxpayer has actually gained something because the government has issued new money, equal to 30 percent of GDP, which is a one-off seigniorage gain. And then it has a charge against that equity of

18 percent of GDP, which is the nonperforming portion of loans (60 percent of 30 percent of GDP). The rest, the performing portion of the loans, which equals 12 percent of GDP (40 percent of 30 percent of GDP), is a net gain to the taxpayer that can actually be used to reduce the government's debt.

So the summary is that any decision on the Chicago Plan comes down to a cost-benefit analysis. The benefits we've been through, and the costs, well, the transition might be potentially a little difficult. The issue of substitute money is important. But what I hope to have demonstrated to you is that the benefits would be so large that at least a reasonable cost-benefit analysis should be done to consider this. To just reject this out of hand on the basis of transactional complexity would be just discounting very large benefits, and I don't think that would be wise. Thank you very much.

MICHAEL KUMHOF, PHD

Deputy Division Chief of the Modeling Division in the IMF Research Department

Michael Kumhof is deputy division chief of the modeling division in the International Monetary Fund research department. His main responsibility is the development of the IMF's global macroeconomic model GIMF, a DSGE model that is used heavily for IMF policy and scenario analyses in multilateral and bilateral surveillance, for the World Economic Outlook publication, and for work on G-20[27] issues.

Mr. Kumhof presently pursues three main research agendas. The first centers on the macroeconomic effects of resource constraints, specifically constraints on the physical availability of fossil fuels. The second studies the role of banks in the macroeconomic transmission mechanism and develops proposals for comprehensive monetary and financial reform. The third studies the role of income inequality in causing economic imbalances and economic crises.

---

27   The G-20 is a club of nations comprising a mix of the world's largest advanced and emerging economies, representing about two-thirds of the world's population, 85 per cent of global gross domestic product and over 75 per cent of global trade. See https://www.g20.org/

Mr. Kumhof holds a PhD in economics from the University of Maryland at College Park and was assistant professor in economics at Stanford University between September 1998 and March 2004. His work has been published by, among others, the *Journal of Monetary Economics*; *American Economic Journal: Macroeconomics*; *Journal of International Economics*; *Journal of Economic Dynamics and Control*; *Journal of Money, Credit and Banking*; *European Economic Review*; and *Journal of Macroeconomics*. Prior to returning to academia, Mr. Kumhof was a corporate account executive at Barclays Bank PLC, Singapore, from 1991 to 1993, where he managed a US$100 million corporate loan portfolio in Indonesia, Malaysia, and Singapore. Prior postings by Barclays included Portugal and the City of London. Mr. Kumhof is a citizen of Germany.

CHAPTER 5

Limited Purpose Banking

In this chapter, Dr. Laurence Kotlikoff develops the tenets of Limited Purpose Banking (LPB) and how it would stop bank runs, thereby greatly increasing economic stability. He starts by giving an overview of the factors leading to the Great Recession and how some commonly held causes of this are actually counterfactual. He goes on to describe several suggested remedies and shows how these do not, in fact, solve the underlying issues. His final analysis of the underlying root cause comes down to the fact that the fractional reserve banking system has two characteristics that make it internally unstable, and these are opacity and leverage.

From this vantage point, he then develops LPB as a system of equity structured mutual funds, which fulfill all the requisites of today's banking business but remove the associated risk. This system may stand on its own or be the steady-state operational methodology of the Chicago Plan.

His résumé is found at the end of this chapter.

LARRY KOTLKOFF:

It's a great pleasure to be with you all. I'm going to follow up that extremely interesting and insightful talk by Michael [Kumhof, whose talk is presented in the previous chapter in this book] with a discussion of Limited Purpose Banking and how to fix the global financial system with all its instabilities. I am going to look at the issues from a somewhat different angle and try to talk about the fundamental problems. Michael was concerned about banks creating money out of thin air and causing instability from that, and I think that is an important concern and issue, but I'm going to talk about two other issues that I think are more fundamental.

I'm going to get to that in a second, but I want to first of all summarize where we are. I think the big thing to say is that Wall Street, broadly defined, has become a very dangerous place for Main Street. We have had two global financial crises

> Wall Street…has become a very dangerous place for Main Street

in the last five or six years and devastating impacts on hundreds of millions of workers and retirees. One was centered in the United States and one was centered in Europe. I believe it's fair to say, they are still ongoing in both places. The next one might be centered in China.

Or Bad Banks?

Bear Stearns, Country Wide, Lehman Brothers, Northern Rock, Royal Bank of Scotland, HBOS, BNP Paribas, UBS, Anglo-Irish Bank, MBIA, Citigroup, Merrill Lynch, Fannie Mae, Freddie Mac, Washington Mutual, Glitnir, Allied Irish, Bank of Ireland, Dexia, Landsbanki, AIG, Lloyds, Barclays, Bradford and Bingley, ING, ABN AMRO, Fortis, …

Figure 5.1: List of Bad Banks

So, what is really going on? Well, some people think it is bad assets, and here are a couple of examples—sovereign debt, subprime real estate mortgages, definitely bad assets. Other people think it is just bad banks. The bankers are the bad people here, and we've got all these banks. I should have added a couple of Cypriot banks to my list of bad banks, such as the Bank of Cyprus and Laiki. So it's about twenty-nine bad banks we could list right away.

Other people think it is bad regulators, bad financial rules, bad governance, bad politicians, bad bankers again, bad disclosure, bad leverage, bad luck.

(*Laughter.*)

Or

Bad Regulators?

Bad Financial Rules?

Bad Governance?

Bad Politicians?

Bad Bankers?

Bad Disclosure?

Bad Leverage?

Bad Luck?

Figure 5.2: Other Potential Causes

Regardless of the precise cause, what we do know is that asset prices plunged and banks failed. And the question is, do banks always fail when asset prices plunge? Not true.

> Do banks always fail when asset prices plunge?

If you look at the dot-com bubble, the NASDAQ fell 70 percent, the S&P fell 50 percent. There were no major bank failures. So why didn't the banks fail when the dot-com bubble burst? Well, they weren't holding the dot-com stocks, which were the bad assets of the day.

So maybe the answer is to make the banks hold only good assets. That's one view that some people have, but that would kill the market for the bad assets. So maybe the answer is to have only good banks that hold good assets and have bad banks that hold only bad assets. And what are the good banks?

We are told:
Good Banks Are Commercial Banks and Have Retail Customers, Issue Insured Deposits, and Run the Payment System

Bad Banks Are Investment Banks, Hedge Funds, SIVs, Mortgage Companies, etc. and their Customers are Corporations, Rich Foreigners, and Other Bad Banks

Figure 5.3: Good Banks versus Bad Banks

These are supposedly good banks, commercial banks that have good customers, which are retail customers, and they issue insured deposits and they run the payment system. Then you've got the bad banks that are investment banks and the hedge funds and the structured investment vehicles and the mortgage companies, and their customers are bad customers. They are corporations, rich foreigners, and other bad banks.

So, this answer can be refined. This is not my answer, by the way.

This Answer Can Be Refined:

1. "Good" Banks Hold Only "Good" Assets
2. "Good" Banks Behave – No Trading and No Derivatives
3. All Banks Hold More Capital Against Risky Assets
4. Stress Test Banks and Adjust Asset Mix as Needed
5. Let "Bad" Banks Fail, But Arrange Quick Funerals
6. Let All Banks Operate with Up to 33 to 1 Leverage

Figure 5.4: A More Refined Answer

This is the conventional answer as being currently defined. The good banks are supposed to hold only good assets; good banks are supposed to behave.

They don't do any trading in their derivatives. They don't hold any derivatives. All banks hold more capital against risky assets; we stress test banks and adjust the asset mix as needed. We

> It's the wrong answer!

let the bad banks fail, and we arrange quick funerals for the bad banks when they fail. But we still let all the banks basically leverage thirty-three to one. This is the new financial architecture; this is Basel III; this is Paul Volker's view, Dodd Frank's view, the Vickers Commission answer. There is a supposed solution in the eurozone that is coming up with the same answer. Good banks, bad banks. It's the wrong answer.

Here's why this is the wrong answer. This answer has four fatal flaws.

The Answer's Four Fatal Flaws

1. "Good" Assets Do Bad Things

2. "Bad" Banks are Too Big To Fail

3. The Stress Tests are Jokes

4. Macro Problem Is Funerals, Not Funeral Arrangements

Figure 5.5: Four Fatal Flaws

First, good assets do bad things. Think about Greek government bonds, Italian government bonds—excellent, safe, good assets. They did bad things. Bad banks are too big to fail. Remember Lehman Brothers? That was a bad bank. That was allowed to fail. Now, other banks failed, but they weren't allowed to fail in a clear-cut way like Lehman Brothers. They weren't allowed to go bankrupt.

But even short of bankruptcy, you know Bear Sterns failing, it got rescued, it ended up being sold for, in effect, two dollars per share, but it failed. We had twenty-nine banks now that have more or less failed, and whether they failed through bankruptcy or just through some shotgun wedding or some rescue by the FDIC or some similar agency, these are failures, and they are too big to fail in the sense that they psych the economy out. That is the problem with these banks failing, and in addition, they lead to the financial highway system breaking down, the financial exchange breaking down.

The stress tests I think are jokes. Lehman Brothers would have passed perfectly fine only three days before it went under. There was a stress test on Lehman Brothers, and Lehman put out a statement that was approved by the SEC, which is Lehman's regulator. The SEC was inside Lehman Brothers for about seven months. Lehman Brothers did better on that stress test than any of the top banks in the United States would today.

(*Laughter.*)

So, these things are jokes.

The macro problem is the funeral, not the funeral arrangements. Think about what happened after Lehman failed, which was at the end of many other banks failing. We had total panic in the financial system, and whether or not this mattered all that much in fundamental terms to the economy, it psyched out millions of employers, at least in the case of the United States. They recognized that President Bush was saying, this sucker is going to blow and John McCain was cancelling his campaign to "save the economy" and President Elect Obama was whispering about the Great Depression and everybody in the media was saying, "we are going to have a Great Depression." And Google searches for the Great Depression spiked like crazy in September 2008. Therefore, employers asked, do I want to still be employing these people when my customers don't show up? No. I'm going to start firing my employees because I'm sure everybody else is going to fire their employees. And so then we had a great piling on of firing employees. I'm going to fire my workers because I think everybody else is going to fire theirs, and I don't want to wait to do that.

So over the next seventeen months, we had 8.5 million Americans fired. It was like a pile-on. In some months, it was 500,000 people being laid off per month. Had this all happened in one day, and 8.5 million people had been fired on September 16, the day after Lehman failed, we would all have seen that this was a coordination failure. This was a collective panic. Everybody at the micro level took actions to make a terrible macro outcome. This was a condition of **multiple equilibria**, as we economists say, that we could have people being confident about the economy and not firing or people being sure everybody else was firing and fire and make that outcome happen, make it a self-fulfilling prophecy.

So, when the banks go down, they change the broad confidence level. They destroy a very important public good, namely confidence, because we have more than one place this economy can go to, and it depends on people's confidence. The banks are in charge of two public goods—the financial highway system and public confidence. That is why we cannot let them gamble, but that's what they did.

So, here are some examples of good assets that have gone bad—Lehman Brothers' bonds, AIG stock, these are bad assets. They were good assets,

> Banks are in charge of two public goods

perfectly good assets. Now, what are the next good assets to go bad? Maybe Chinese mortgages, maybe US treasuries. I think US treasuries are probably the riskiest asset in the world right now. I wouldn't touch them; thirty-year bonds, Treasury bonds—I wouldn't touch them with a thousand-foot pole.

Will We Let Big "Bad" Banks Fail?

No!

We ran this Experiment With Lehman and It Blew Up in Our Face.
Figure 5.6: Will We Let Big Banks Fail?

Now, will we let the big, bad banks fail? No! We ran this experiment with Lehman Brothers, and it blew up in our faces. So all we're doing in saying that we're going to let these big, bad banks fail is we're inviting a run on them and, thereby, making runs even more likely, creating greater instability. So what about the "Treasury's No-stress Stress Test"? Well, again, sixteen of the nineteen top banks have less or much less capital than Lehman had only three days before it declared bankruptcy.

So in 2008, trust took a holiday. No one trusted Lehman's books, not the Treasury, not the Fed, not the SEC, not the banks—and not anybody else was trusting Lehman's books. So this was, again, a coordination failure. The sentiment was, I believe nobody else is trusting this financial institution and I don't want to be the last one to try and get my money out. That's what caused the run.

When the Panic of 2008 Hit,
Trust Took a Holiday

No One Trusted Lehman's Books –
Not the Treasury, Not the Fed,
Not the SEC, Not the Banks, Not the Public

And No One Trusted That Others
Would Trust Lehman's Books

Figure 5.7: Trust Took a Holiday

It could well be that Dick Fuld, who ran Lehman, had it right—that Lehman was perfectly solvent in some sense. It had great assets. Lehman had a book of businesses that nobody could understand, not even the SEC or the Treasury. It was too opaque.

So, I'm trying to get across the point that it wasn't the funeral arrangements; it was the actual funeral—the fact that these entities failed and we had nationalizations, federal bailouts, one bankruptcy, shotgun weddings. It all psyched the economy out. That's the macroeconomic problem. It caused a massive coordination failure. Overnight, we had millions of households and individuals, consumers, taking steps to produce a very bad recession.

It wasn't the flower arrangements that caused the recession, it was the funerals themselves. So, what's the real problem with the banking system? The real problem with the banking system consists of two things, which are barely mentioned. If you look at the most recent British reform, which is the Vickers Commission [see Larry's written response to this[28]], the word *opacity* is hardly even used; I think it might even be used zero times in that entire 250-page document. The real problems are leverage and opacity.

So here's the point. Markets don't operate well in the dark. If you can't see what you're buying and you're buying a promise that you can't really

> The real problems are leverage and opacity

verify, it's a promise that might be fraudulent. So as soon as there's kind of a whiff of concern about that promise, your tendency is to start to try and get your money out and get it while you still can.

Let's think about the 1982 Tylenol scare as an analogy. This is a good example of opacity. Now, what happened in 1982? How many people remember the Tylenol scare? Okay, most younger people didn't raise their hands because they're not familiar with it. So what happened was that, in Chicago, there were four bottles of Tylenol that were laced with cyanide, which is a poison. Around the world there were thirty million bottles of Tylenol, and overnight they became a truly toxic asset. Nobody would buy them. Their price dropped to zero. This was a run on Tylenol.

And why did people not buy those Tylenol bottles in Frankfurt, even though there were only four bottles in Chicago that had been tainted? The people in Frankfurt, Germany, or Istanbul, Turkey, wouldn't buy the stuff because they didn't trust what was inside. What was the type of sealant on those bottles back then? Basically nothing. You could open those bottles; there were no safety seals.

---

28   Laurence Kotlikoff, *The Economic Consequences of the Vickers Commission*, (Civitas: The Institute for the Study of Civil Society, 2012), 42–48.

And you could stick in some cyanide and close the bottles up, so there was no disclosure of what was inside the bottles. It was all trust.

This was opacity. Nobody knew what was truly in those bottles, whether it was straight Tylenol or Tylenol plus cyanide. So there was a huge run. Johnson & Johnson didn't try and bribe people to buy those bottles or reassure them. It just recalled them, threw them out, and repackaged 30 million bottles with safety seal containers. That's why we can no longer open things.

(*Laughter.*)

There's a story here.

And in disclosing what's in those bottles, we were able to preserve this market for medications and we eliminated the concern about Tylenol fraud. So, fraud, suspicions of fraud, and suspicion of suspicions of fraud can trigger financial runs when you have products which are not being disclosed.

> Fraud, suspicions of fraud, and suspicions of suspicions of fraud create bank runs

So governments, what do they do? They try and prevent these runs by promising to keep the banks' promises. And in so doing, governments make promises they can't keep. So that's kind of where we are today. We have the government having printed lots and lots of money to try and protect these promises. And they're promising that they can actually cover their promises, that all this money creation is not going to lead to a lot of inflation, which I think it will. That's in effect a promise that they can't keep.

Let me just give you an example with respect to the FDIC. What would happen if we had a run on the banks in the United States today? The FDIC has perhaps $18 billion in reserves; I'm not exactly sure what it is. However, it's insured about $6 trillion in deposits. In addition, there's another $3 trillion in money market funds that are effectively insured by our government because the last time there was a run, the government came right in and insured them. Then there's $3 trillion in cash-surrender value policies of life insurance companies that most people don't realize, but they're just like checking account deposits because people can just take their policy into a life insurance company and say, "Give me the cash right now." Three trillion dollars! So that's $12 trillion the Federal Reserve would have to print if people really expected inflation and caused a run. And then, people would expect there to really be inflation. And if you expect prices to go up, you're going to want to run even more, right? Even if you expect that the FDIC is going to make good on your money that's in your checking account, you're going to want to get it out before prices go up.

In 2002, there was a run on the banks in Argentina after they went off the dollar peg. It wasn't that people didn't trust the banks would pay their pesos; they expected inflation, so they ran. So this

> Governments make promises they can't keep

guarantee of your deposits, well, it's a guarantee of pieces of paper. It's not a guarantee of canned soups. It's not like the FDIC or the Federal Reserve has cans of Campbell soup.

All it has are these pieces of paper; I know this is probably an illegal act (*ripping a one-dollar bill into small bits*), but this is just paper. And when you rip it up, you will see that it's just paper. It's worth trying to do that just to get the feel of it.

(*Laughter.*)

Just remind yourself that it's only paper.

We could have a run tomorrow on our banking system, and FDIC insurance would do nothing. And that run could happen because Cyprus had a run. And people in Greece, from one day to the next, start panicking, have a very public run. It could spread all through southern Europe into France and Belgium. God knows their banks are underwater, too. The Deutsche Bank is leveraged fifty-five to one, I understand. It could spread there.

You could have Rush Limbaugh saying, "Get your money out of the banks," and people in Alabama start running to their banks, and it starts spreading through the country. Bingo. We're off to the races. This is what we call multiple or flipping equilibria—flipping from one state in the economy to another, all of which would be solutions to the same underlying set of equations. We want to prevent this from happening.

Anyway, so here's my bottom line. Our "trust-me" banking system is inherently unstable; managing systemic risk can produce systemic collapse. We have the president of the United States saying, "This sucker is going to run." You have Treasury Secretary Paulson literally begging Nancy Pelosi to come up with $720 billion or so to bail out the financial system.

This causes panic and undermines the public's confidence. And guess what? We can have a major recession and we can likely even have a depression. When you have an urgent need to eliminate

> We need to move from "trust me" to "show me" banking

promises that can't be kept, we need to move from "trust me" to "show me" banking.

Limited Purpose Banking does this and it ends up with a solution that, in some ways, is similar to Michael's but, in some ways, is different. But it moves from "trust me" to "show me" banking. And it limits banks to their true purpose, which is not printing money out of thin air but financial intermediation.

Limited Purpose Banking

➤ Moves from "Trust Me" to "Show Me" Banking

➤ Limits Banks to their True Purpose – Intermediation

➤ Full Transparency and Disclosure and Zero Leverage

➤ Households and Firms Borrow, But Not Banks

➤ Non-Leveraged Banks Can't Fail =>Financial Stability

Figure 5.8. Limited Purpose Banking

Think about gas stations. A gas station is intermediating between a refinery and a driver, but they're critical for the highway system. If all our gas stations were going to go out and gamble with their businesses what would happen? For example, they could all take in money from their customers and say, "Look, here's a guarantee. Give us some money now, and we'll guarantee to pump gas for you at five dollars a gallon. Pay us now, and you can pump as much gas as you want at five dollars a gallon." And suppose the price of gas goes up to twenty dollars a gallon. If they all did this, every single gas station in the country would go broke the same day. They'd all walk away from their gas stations with the keys to their pumps. The highway system would break down. We wouldn't be able to use this public thing called the highway system.

Now, what do you think Congress would do the day after that happened? They would say to the gas station owners, "You can go gamble on your private account, but you cannot gamble with your business. No gas station can actually do anything but buy gasoline and sell it. You cannot engage in gambling with this business because you're running a public good." That's what the banks are doing, too. They're running the financial exchange system. If you want to see proof of that, go to Cyprus today and you'll see businesses that cannot pay their suppliers, cannot pay their workers, because they can't get more than three thousand pounds out per week from their banks and pay their creditors.

So what we need to do is get the banks out of the gambling business. And we need to get them into the disclosure business. And we need to force them to just run the highway system. This is a public good.

> We cannot let banks gamble with public goods

They're maintaining a public good; they're running a public good. We cannot let them gamble with public goods; it's that simple.

But fortunately, I'm not a banking economist or a finance economist. I'm just an economist who works in other areas, like public finance and some macroeconomics. So, when I look at this, I see the core problems because I'm not trapped in the literature. I haven't contributed to that literature, so I don't think what I think because it's what other people think. I think it's a combination of two key things, one being leverage—a lot of people do think leverage is an issue—and opacity.

What we need is full disclosure and zero leverage because the intermediaries, the banks, should not be gambling, and that's leverage. And it's fine for households and firms who are not financial firms to borrow, but the banks themselves should not be engaged in it.

Prominent Economists and Policymakers Endorsing
Serious Consideration of Limited Purpose Banking

- Mervyn King, Governor of the Bank of England
- Seven Nobel Laureates in Economics (Ackerlof, Lucas, Prescott, Phelps, Fogel, Merton, Sharpe)
- Former U.S. Secretary of Treasury (George Shultz)
- Former U.S. Secretary of Labor (Robert Reich)
- Former U.S. Senator (Bill Bradley)
- Two Past Chairs, Council of Economic Advisers (Michael Boskin and Murray Weidenbaum)
- Two Former Chief Economists of the IMF (Harvard's Ken Rogoff and MIT's Simon Johnson)
- Former Chief Economist of the SEC (Susan Woodward)
- Former Deputy Comptroller of the Currency (Robert Bench)
- Former Vice Chairman of Joint Chiefs of Staff (Admiral Williams Owens)
- Jeff Sachs (Renown Macro Economist and Head of Columbia's Earth Institute)
- Jagadish Bhagwati (Renown International Economist)
- Martin Wolf (Senior Economics Columnist for the Financial Times)
- Steve Ross (MIT's Premier Financial Economist and Father of Arbitrage Pricing Theory)
- Niall Ferguson (Harvard's Distinguished Economic Historian)
- Kevin Hassett (Distinguished Economist at AEI and McCain's Former Chief Economic Adviser)
- Paul Romer (Stanford's Distinguished Growth Theorist)
- Domingo Cavalo (Former Economic Minister of Argentina)
- Wiliam Niskanen (Chairman Emeritus, The Cato Institute)
- Preston McAfee (Chief Economist, Yahoo)
- Other Very Prominent U.S. Economists

Figure 5.9. Prominent Endorsers of Limited Purpose Banking

So here's this proposal I'm going to give it to you. And I want to show you that we've got a lot of support for this. Here are pretty interesting names. Mervyn King—these people haven't all formally endorsed Limited Purpose Banking, publicly endorsed it, but most of them have—Mervyn King is really the one exception who hasn't publicly endorsed it, but he's publicly talked about this proposal, including to Parliament. And he said on several occasions that it deserves serious consideration. There are seven Nobel laureates who have either publicly or informally endorsed this while talking to me, including George Shultz, former Secretary of Treasury; Robert Reich, former Secretary of Labor; and Bill Bradley, chairman of the Council of Economic Advisors, a very prominent economist. You're going to hear from Jeff Sachs. He wrote the preface to my book, *Jimmy Stewart is Dead*, which discusses the banking system and how to fix it.

And this is not an ego trip for me. I mean, it's partly an ego trip.

But it's to try and point out that there are a lot of people who have a lot of experience and knowledge, much more than I, about financial systems who think this is a good idea. And it's not actually just my idea. Ideas, good ideas, aren't isolated with one person. Other people come up with them. I think the Bank of England was working on this idea before I started talking about it publicly. Mutual fund banking, which is what Limited Purpose Banking is, is 100 percent equity-financed mutual fund banking. That idea has been around for a while among economists. Jim Tobin talked about it; Milton Friedman had some discussion about it, as did Charles Goodhart. Nobody has taken it to the extreme that I have, but it has been in the air.

Limited Purpose Banking

- Mutual Fund Banking
- Federal Financial Authority
- Auction Market

Figure 5.10: LPB #2

This proposal is very simple. It's mutual fund banking with no leverage with a federal financial authority to do the disclosure and an auction market for the securities that have been disclosed to be bought and sold by the mutual funds.

It draws a line based on limited liability. It's not a good-bank-versus-bad-bank line. It's not a commercial bank; it's not the Glass-Steagall commercial-bank-versus-investment-bank line. These lines, which regulators have drawn to create safety, well, they're just crazy; they're not economic lines. So let's draw a line that's economic. If you want to be a limited liability financial company, no matter whether you call yourself an insurance company, a credit union, a hedge fund, a private equity company, a commercial bank, or an investment bank, then you're just going to have to be transformed into a mutual fund company to do your business. All of your business can be done as a 100 percent equity-financed mutual fund.

If you want to have leverage, you have to have unlimited liability. You have to put your own car, house, and all your money on the line. If you want to gamble with the financial system, be our guest, risk everything. Richard Fuld would have been penniless under this scheme had he ran his bank the way he did.

Limited Purpose Banking

All Financial Companies Operating with Limited
Liability Must Operate Solely as Mutual Fund
Holding Companies Issuing 100% Equity-Financed
Open and Closed End Mutual Funds

Figure 5.11: LPB #3

So we're going to have regulation based on function, not form. All financial companies that are working with limited liability have to operate as mutual fund holding companies, issuing a 100 percent equity-financed, open and closed-end mutual funds. Now, there's going to be one special type of mutual fund that's going to be used for the payment system, and this gets back to Michael's proposal. It's a cash mutual fund.

A cash mutual fund will hold only cash. I buy shares of cash mutual funds, and I put my money in cash mutual fund with, let's say, Fidelity Investments. Fidelity Investments holds the cash in the vault. Think about its dollars being held in the vault. Now, I can write a check against that, I can use a debit card to access that money. I can get cash out of an ATM machine, based on my cash mutual fund. That's going to be used for the payment system. That's very much like Michael's deposits being backed by reserves. In my case, the cash is the reserves, and the deposits are the shares of the cash mutual funds.

Now we have a payment system you can never have a run on because the money's always there. You always know that your money is there. All shares are cash. I've got an equity position in there. Of course, then I'm also going to personally be holding shares of other mutual funds like equity mutual funds, mortgage mutual funds, Chilean stock mutual funds, or real estate mutual funds. Some will be closed and some open-ended.

We have a very big mutual fund industry in our country. We have more individual mutual funds, separate mutual funds, than we have banks. We have about 10,000 mutual funds and about 9,500 banks. Most Americans do most of their banking via mutual funds because most of us have most of our assets in 401(k) plans, which are equity-financed mutual funds. All the equity-financed mutual funds had no trouble weathering the crisis. The only part of the mutual fund industry that had trouble was the leveraged mutual funds, and they were the money market funds because they had made a promise that couldn't be kept. They made this fraudulent, back-to-the-buck promise that couldn't be kept. Those were the ones that got into trouble.

Under my proposal, money market funds would exist, but they would not be leveraged. They would be floating, just like all the other mutual funds. And from one day to the next, they would break or make the buck. They would not ever be allowed to "back the buck." So it would be marked to market every day.

Just to be clear, under this proposal, the money multiplier equals one, which is something the Chicago Plan wanted to have and

Milton Friedman was a big advocate of. So where's your money going to be? It's either going to be held in the vaults of the cash mutual funds or it's going to be in your pocket. And so, that's going to be the money supply; that's going to be M1. The government can make M1 as big as it wants; it can print money and buy lunch for the president with it. That will put more money in circulation, and M1 will be bigger. So this is not reduction in the size of M1. It can be as big as the government wants it to be.

What else? How do insurance companies fit in? Well, let's think about running derivatives. Suppose you're AIG and you want to run a derivatives market. You want to, for example, sell **CDS**s [Credit Default Swaps]. You want to ensure that Cypriot bonds will not fail, will not default. Here's how we can set up that market through AIG's Cypriot bond and mutual fund. And here's how we do it.

I'm just going to give you an analogy of a horse race. Suppose I run a horse race. We've got horse "A" and horse "B." And I'm at the track. You guys come to the closest track, Delaware Park. A third of you bet on horse A, and the rest of you bet on horse B, and you give me your money. I'm behind the window.

I take in your money. I keep your money right here, safe—all of it. This is called a pari-mutuel bet. Pari-mutuel betting has been in place since 1857. Think of the word *mutual*. So what happens? Whoever wins the race gets the pot I've got after I take my fee. I'm running a mutual fund. It's a closed-end mutual fund. That money comes in; I close the window; the race is run. Whoever wins, those who bet on horse A or those who bet on horse B, I pay out the whole pot, less my fee, to the people who won in proportion to their bets.

Let's make horse A that Cyprus defaults at the end of the year and horse B that Cyprus bonds do not default. Now, we've got a CDS market, but it's a fully collateralized bet. It's not like AIG, who promises to pay off and can't actually come up with the money because they've taken in some premiums and then gambled with them. Instead, all of the money is right there.

This is an equity-based mutual fund that can never leave the liability to the taxpayer. This is a safe way to run derivatives in general. Think about the bet being that IBM shares go above two hundred dollars over the course of the year. That's an option market right there. It's a perfectly safe way to have derivatives.

So we can have derivatives; we can have modern finance without leveraging the taxpayer, without gambling with the economy. That's how you can allocate aggregate risk—how you can have markets for aggregate risk, financial markets for aggregate risk, and an equity-based mutual fund system. We've never had a horse race where the taxpayer had to come bail out the loser, right? Never happened.

What about idiosyncrasies like life insurance? Well, right now, we have a life insurance industry that is selling two products—life insurance and annuities. They have about $19 trillion in commitments out there, and they could go broke the next day. The life insurance reserve funds that are run by the states have no money. They're like the FDIC; they're lying. They have an empty shell. There's virtually no disclosure.

> We can have modern finance without leveraging the taxpayer

What happens if we had a swine flu breakout? I guess it has broken out recently in China, right? Swine flu kills young people. And then we have a cure for cancer developed that would keep old people alive. So, what if that happens simultaneously, maybe in a couple months? The insurance company is going to lose on both sides of their hedging strategy. They're going to have their annuitants live much longer than expected, and they're going to have their life insurance customers die off in droves.

In the 1920s, the swine flu produced a major increase in the worldwide mortality rate. About 2.5 percent of the world's population died from this. It killed more people than World War I globally. So now you've got insurance companies losing money on both sides of their hedge, and they go under. Now there's a run on the insurance companies, which kicks off a run on everything else. This will be a $3 trillion run because these cash-surrender value policies would start being cashed in right away.

So what about running life insurance a different way? Let's say you're all male and about fifty-five years old. You're in good health, and you want to buy insurance. So you put your money into my mutual fund, and the bet is whoever dies within three months gets the pot, less the fee, in proportion to what they put in. All the money is there.

If more of you guys die because swine flu breaks out, less is paid out per person who dies. Less is paid out per decedent. This is a way of running a safe, idiosyncratic insurance market—to run life insurance in a way that's not going to threaten the economy. You can do this with health insurance; you can do this with casualty insurance; you can do this with longevity insurance.

The original such insurance market was the **tontine** which was established in 1637. How many people have ever heard of the word *tontine*? How many people in this room have heard it? We've got two, three, four. Okay, how many people know the first, physical location of the New York Stock Exchange? What was the name of that?

It wasn't the Buttonwood Tree because that was not a proper physical location, as it had no roof over it. It was just a tree. People met there, and then they decided it was raining and they wanted to go inside. So they chose a place to go inside and meet. What was the name of that place? It was called the Tontine Coffee House. Everybody in that century, in the century before and the century before that knew what a tontine was. It was an everyday term. Countries like France and England financed themselves by issuing tontines, by setting up tontine markets.

We could use ancient finance to fix up our modern financial system. Let me just say a couple of final things. We don't need to have Angelo Mozilo, who ran Countrywide Financial into the ground and, in the sale, ran Bank of America into the ground, to verify whether George here (*pointing to a member of the audience*) actually has a job, whether he actually has a credit rating that he says he has or whether his house that he's trying to buy is worth what he says it's worth or some crazy figure.

We can have the federal government actually verify that he's got a job and what he's earning. So we can use the federal government to verify things—just like we have an FDA that verifies that our medications are actually not lethal. This is why the FDA came along, to make sure that we weren't selling snake oil. And that's what people were selling back then. Useless or even lethal drugs were destroying the drug industry. So, the FDA was used to do the verification. We need an FDA for the financial sector, and I am suggesting the FFA, the Federal Financial Authority. They do the verification.

The last little bit of this proposal is that mutual funds will buy and sell their securities at auction. So if I'm a small company for example—and I do have a small company—and I wanted to float my paper, it would be verified by the Federal Financial Authority.

The FFA would come and verify my company and my earnings history and put everything they can reasonably say about my company up on the web in real time.

The Federal Financial Authority (FFA)

•Verifies All Securities Purchased by Mutual Funds

•Private Verification Companies, Working Exclusively for the FFA, Verify Income, Employment, Tax Returns, Credit History, Collateral Appraisals, Etc.

•No More "Liar Loans," "No-Doc Loans," "Ninja Loans"

•Real-Time, Ongoing, Web-Based, Micro-Level Disclosure

•Mutual Fund Investors Know What they Are Buying

Figure 5.12: The Federal Financial Authority

Then I go with my paper—irrespective of whether I want to borrow money or sell shares—up to the auction of the mutual funds that are investing in small company paper. This would give us an efficient means for small companies and large companies, as well as households, to get their papers onto the market, and they'd get the price for the paper and the lowest interest rate.

Transition To Limited Purpose Banking Is Simple

• Financial Corps. Re-Chartered as Mutual Fund Holding Co.s

• Convert Investment Banking Operations into Consulting Service

• Convert Trading to a Matching Business with No Open Positions

• Convert Checking Accounts to Cash Mutual Funds

• Convert Other Short-Term Bank Liabilities to Money Mkt Funds

• Convert Long-Term Bank Liabilities to Closed End Funds

• Insurance Companies Issue Only Tontines and Pari-Mutuels

• Establish the Federal Financial Authority

Figure 5.13: Transition to LPB

The very last thing to say is that we have all these problems—we have fraud, insider rating, director sweetheart deals, corporate governance problems, political bribes, **regulatory capture**, moral hazard, nondisclosure, off balance sheet bookkeeping, government bailouts, and failure to mark to market. Every single one of these things goes away with Limited Purpose Banking, every single one. We will then have a safe financial system; a banking system that can never fail; and, therefore, a much more stable economy and a much more efficient economy. This can be done pretty much overnight, and it should be done immediately in Europe for sure and certainty in the United States too. Thank you.

A System Built For Hucksters Disappears

- Fraud
- Insider Rating
- Director Sweetheart Deals
- Corporate Governance Problems
- Political Bribes
- Regulatory Capture
- Moral Hazard
- Non-Disclosure
- Off-Balance-Sheet Bookkeeping
- Government Bailouts
- Failure to Mark to Market

Figure 5.14: The Huckster System Disappears

LAURENCE J. KOTLIKOFF, PhD

William Fairfield Warren Professor and Professor of Economics at Boston University

Laurence J. Kotlikoff is a William Fairfield Warren professor at Boston University, a professor of economics at Boston University, a fellow of the American Academy of Arts and Sciences, a fellow of the Econometric Society, a research associate of the National Bureau of Economic Research, and president of Economic Security Planning, Inc., a company specializing in financial planning software. An active columnist, Professor Kotlikoff's columns and blogs appear in *The Financial Times*, *Bloomberg*, *Forbes*, *Vox*, *The Economist*, Yahoo.com, and *The Huffington Post*. Professor Kotlikoff received his BA in economics from the University of Pennsylvania in 1973 and his PhD in economics from Harvard University in 1977.

From 1977 through 1983, he served on the faculties of economics of the University of California, Los Angeles, and Yale University. In 1981 and 1982, Professor Kotlikoff was a senior economist with the President's Council of Economic Advisers.

Professor Kotlikoff is author or coauthor of sixteen books and hundreds of professional journal articles. His most recent books are *The Clash of Generations* (co-authored with Scott Burns, MIT Press), *The Economic Consequences of the Vickers Commission* (Civitas), *Jimmy Stewart Is Dead* (John Wiley & Sons), *Spend 'Till the End*, (coauthored with Scott Burns, Simon & Schuster), *The Healthcare Fix* (MIT Press), *The Coming Generational Storm* (coauthored with Scott Burns, MIT Press), and *Generational Policy* (MIT Press).

Professor Kotlikoff's writings and research address financial reform, personal finance, taxes, Social Security, health care, deficits, generational accounting, pensions, saving, and insurance.

Professor Kotlikoff has served as a consultant to the International Monetary Fund, the World Bank, the Harvard Institute for International Development, the Organization for Economic Cooperation and Development, the Swedish Ministry of Finance, the Norwegian Ministry of Finance, the Bank of Italy, the Bank of Japan, the Bank of England, the government of Russia, the government of Ukraine, the government of Bolivia, the government of Bulgaria, the Treasury of New Zealand, the Office of Management and Budget, the US Department of Education, the US Department of Labor, the Joint Committee on Taxation, the Commonwealth of Massachusetts, the American Council of Life Insurance, Merrill Lynch, Fidelity Investments, AT&T, AON Corp., and other major US corporations.

He has provided expert testimony on numerous occasions to committees of Congress, including the Senate Finance Committee, the House Ways and Means Committee, and the Joint Economic Committee.

CHAPTER 6

Implications for Global Development

DR. JEFFREY SACHS, TWICE MENTIONED by *Time* magazine as one of the hundred most influential people alive, describes the international reverberations of the ethical and regulatory failures of our finance system. He castigates the collusion found between our political and banking establishments. Both the fractional reserve banking system and the shadow banking system, in their very essence, foster ethical deviations by both individuals and institutions due to their complexity and opacity.

This chapter may appear to have a different theme from the rest, but seeing it as part of the whole is important. Here Dr. Sachs describes our system as out of control. The analogy that comes to mind is of a divided highway. We do not need policemen manning the exit ramps to stop drivers from entering the freeway in the wrong direction, as the system is self-policing. If drivers enter a divided freeway in the wrong direction they will most likely get killed, and so they do not do it unless drunk or exceedingly confused. Our banking system is not internally self-correcting in that manner, which is why we do need the policemen—that is, the system regulators—patrolling at every off and on ramp. As is evident by Dr. Sachs's presentation, some on and off ramps are being missed.

His résumé is found at the end of this chapter.

JEFFREY SACHS:

I've been asked to talk a little bit about the international implications, especially the development implications of the financial crisis and of the banking sector. And maybe it's useful to just share with you a sense that I received a few days ago when meeting with about a hundred UN ambassadors who are discussing the global economy and global policy framework for the period from 2015 to 2030, which is very much the United Nations' agenda. What was palpable in the room was a very, very deep sense of anger and grievance at the American financial system.

I think this is important to state because we have our debates as if we're sometimes operating in a cocoon, and the rest of world, especially the developing world, feels that they have been the victims of the United States and its mismanagement over the last few years. I think it's a geopolitical reality that is very real and very justified.

> Int'l ambassadors: why should we take advice from those who have so badly mismanaged?

In other words, the sense of the 2008 crisis is, "You did this to us." And the failures of regulation in the United States have contributed markedly to instability and economic stresses in other places.

As several of the ambassadors reflected, the United States and the International Monetary Fund more or less treat the policy discussions as if nothing really has happened, and what several ambassadors said is, "Why is it we're taking advice from the people who have mismanaged the financial system so badly?" This is not an insignificant context; it's hard for the key currency and the center of the world financial system maybe to hear this very well and to take it as seriously as it should be taken. But the backdrop from the world's point of view is that the United States has failed badly in financial management and the implications of that are felt around the world.

My feeling about this is similar, and I think it is worth speaking outside of the monetary and macroeconomic framework for just a moment. And that is to reflect on the Fed's role as regulator and on the real lessons of the financial crisis since 2008. The angle that I would emphasize—again, I think it's not typical for us as economists—is the massive illegality that has been exposed in the system.

I am systematically tracking the news every day of new settlements of the financial markets with the SEC and other legal proceedings. We have really a mountain of criminal and fraudulent behavior that is very much part of the 2008 scene. And we don't usually speak in these terms; we usually speak in terms of bubbles and mistakes, misjudgments and so forth.

But the amount of what I would regard as utter criminality and financial fraud is absolutely enormous. And it's almost daily, whether it is the insider trading scandals, the **Libor** scandal, or **ABACUS** and similar settlements on selling toxic assets by the investment banks. Because we're the inside of this, I think we are not actually feeling the full weight of not only regulatory failure and moral failure but the massive legal failure that is implicated in this as well.

Today just as an example, I clipped three stories from the news. One was that yesterday a judge approved the settlement with SAC Capital, a $602 million fine for civil insider trading. That's a modest fine, the judge expressed his concern that SAC Capital did not have to admit or deny any of the claims that were made in this. So this is a settlement without any resolution of the substantive topic.

When asked whether a $602 million fine is likely to have much effect, well, the same day we had the story that the owner and CEO of SAC Capital personally took home $1.4 billion last year in compensation. So the company is paying a $602 million fine and at the same time, Steven A. Cohen takes home $1.4 billion in personal compensation for his management of the company. If we go back just a few days, his top trader was arrested and led off in handcuffs from his apartment on Park Avenue.

> Massive illegality
> has been exposed
> in the system

This is what is called the American financial system at the moment. It's really mind-boggling to me, and it is an unregulated, essentially lawless environment that is not getting any more lawful.

I checked Steven A. Cohen's political engagement this past year, and he gave $217,000 in campaign contributions. And this is a pittance from the point of view of his wealth, obviously, as a share of a $1.4 billion paycheck. But $217,000 with our cheapskate politicians actually goes a long way to making sure that Mr. Cohen will be very well treated by his senators and by others who are giving ample protection to all of this.

This is where I would start actually. I think the macroeconomics is important, but I think that the lawlessness and the sense of impunity of the system is absolutely massive. Wherever we look, we see the same thing continuing till today; and that is massive bonuses at the top of the financial markets, massive civil fines being paid for really incredible behavior, and massive campaign contributions going from this financial leadership to the political class.

Yesterday's front-page story in *The New York Times* gave eight salary figures—David Tepper, $2.2 billion paycheck; Ray Dalio, $1.7 billion;

Steven Cohen, $1.4 billion. By the way, half of these companies didn't even beat the market last year. It doesn't matter. They have a fee structure that is independent of any real performance, and when they fail, of course they don't have to give back anything, including last year's billion-dollar compensation holder John Paulson, whose gold price bet is announced today to have lost $1.5 billion for his shareholders. But I can guarantee you he's not putting $1 billion back into his company. It's only upside, no downside.

Look at the political linkages of all of this. Daniel Loeb, who gets only $380 million of compensation, gave $551,000 in campaign contributions last year. Ken Griffin, who took $900 million for Citadel, gave $2.7 million in campaign contributions; David Tepper of Appaloosa gave $601,000 in campaign contributions; and so forth. Many of these companies are involved in these civil lawsuits—payments for fraudulent behavior that is neither admitted nor denied.

The final thing I would add to all this shocking behavior is that we have perfected not only this system but we have perfected the system in which these companies are domiciled in the Cayman Islands or with partners in the Caymans. This takes away any accountability and not only masks them from tax liabilities on these earnings but also masks them from many legal liabilities. The latest, of course, is they created reinsurance companies in Bermuda and in the Cayman Islands that allow them to invest in their own firms through a tax-sheltered mechanism that is only a shell from the point of view of insurance.

So my question to you, as part of the Fed, is where is the Fed? Because this is about basic regulatory practice. It seems to me in truth that we have a system that is out of control right now. It is politically out of control, out of control in terms of regulation, out of legal bounds, and out of responsibility. And we've invented a system where you get to take home billions of dollars in personal compensation. Your shareholders pay hundreds of millions of dollars in fines, you shelter your money in the Cayman Islands in agreement with the IRS, and nobody seems to control it at all.

I sit with the diplomats in New York, and I can only tell you that the level of unhappiness has risen to very stark degrees. I can only agree with them that I don't see any real progress being made in getting this right. So this is my brief

> We have a system which is politically, legally, and regulatorily out of control

message: I think we're beyond the macroeconomics right now. We're beyond the prudential issues. We're to a very gut level of legal accountability, tax regulation, transparency, and a basic sense of fairness. And my view is that we don't have it right now. Wall Street is pretty lawless, and unfortunately the regulatory system that we have is nearly broken down. That's my take from this end.

WILLIAM DUNKELBERG. If you have a few minutes, we would like to open our floors for questions to you. So, questions for Professor Sachs?

JEFF. I like to hear views about why I got this wrong actually.

QUESTIONER. Thank you very much, especially for what appears to be moral outrage. Some of us are more on the limited government Tea Party side and see this as a failure of government and just to bring it down to a very gut level, as you said. We have a trial at Philadelphia; it's an abortion clinic trial. But the scandal is that, for seventeen years, this clinic was not investigated or regulated.

Law requires that a facility, much the same as what you're talking about, is supposed to be regulated; you have SEC, FDIC, etc., etc.

There is a failure of government from your level, from what you're talking about, all the way down to a medical facility, and there were alerts that the people could have stepped into it.

And I'm wondering whether you see a failure of government, because now you're telling me that the international communities are looking at our country and naming it a failure of government in a very negative way. And this is—I'm an American—this is very upsetting.

JEFF. I think this is a profound failure of government without question. I think it is seen in that way from the Tea Party to, if I could say, the left, where I probably would be classified. I think we would agree that the symptoms are government failure, massive legalized corruption of large money interests that have taken over the regulatory process, regulatory capture. Probably the diagnosis would be pretty similar from many different points of the political spectrum.

> This is a failure of government

Let me describe two questions on the response to this. One response is that we ought to make government work. The other response is that we can't make government work, so we ought to understand that and basically close down another part of government. These are both logically consistent positions in my view. My own position, though, is the first. We need government and should and can make it work.

One thing to add to the evidence base, when the financial crisis hit on September 14, 2008, *The Wall Street Journal*, which is normally a voice of libertarian free markets, ran an editorial a few days later essentially saying, "Are you crazy? Don't you understand market failure? Of course we have to bail out the banks; the whole world economy will fail if we don't bail them out!" and so forth.

You could call that a loss of nerve, you could call it hypocrisy, or you could call it a diagnosis—whichever one you want. But the point is, very soon after the financial crisis hit, there was a call, even from the free-market right, for bailouts. Another example of that is Paul Ryan, who purports to be a voice of libertarian thinking but who voted for **TARP** at the same time and said, in effect, "Of course we have to bail out these institutions; otherwise, the markets will collapse."

So that of course only deepens the puzzle; it doesn't solve the basic conundrum of whether this is irremediably broken or whether this is hypocrisy that needs to be solved. The hypocritical part I find is that the moment the bailout actually happened, *The Wall Street Journal* immediately reverted to form in its language and its claims. It went back to its free-market stances as if nothing had happened.

I think that there are at least two parts of a good answer to this. One is to create a situation, maybe along the lines of Larry Kotlikoff's Limited Purpose Banking [see Chapter 5: "Limited Purpose Banking"], maybe along the lines of downsizing banks so that they are not too big to fail, so that you really could let these institutions go under to an important extent and get away from this compulsion of not only bailouts but also the hypocrisy that comes along with it. I think that is certainly part of the answer.

I do think that there is a truth, though, to the fact that the fractional reserve banking system—if we're going to keep it, and we probably are—is, as Milton Friedman rightly said, "inherently a fragile institution that is subject to self-fulfilling collapse." As he wrote, one stone can start the avalanche and it's the job of the Fed to prevent that from happening. This means that

> The fractional reserve banking system is subject to self-fulfilling collapse

bailouts, in some sense, some lender of last resort fulfillment, are going to be inevitable, and in that context, prudential regulation is also going to be inevitable.

I don't think we're going to really get around the need for some regulatory performance, and we need to analyze why it is that the current regulatory regime has been such a complete failure. Part of it is technical no doubt, that markets can deregulate around regulation, but part of it is really political corruption that could be addressed in a more straightforward way.

I'll personally say a word of moral outrage; I don't believe that there is any theory in the world that justifies the incomes that these people are taking. This is, in my view, a prima facie market and political failure. I know a lot of these people; there's no way in the world that their marginal productivity is in orders of magnitude close to their income levels.

And I find it completely disgusting that they are allowed to make large political contributions. You know we have the Hatch Act. We have other limits on political contributions, and I think the Fed should be a lot more serious in pointing out these contradictions and trying to create space for itself to be a decent regulator again.

WILLIAM. All right, we have the next question from one of our speakers.

LARRY. Hey Jeff, it's Larry [Kotlikoff]. To me, I think the banking system is getting a big pass by from the judicial system and the politicians because they have this control over this public good, which is the financial exchange system and also public confidence, business confidence. If these big companies are seen to be engaging in fraud, then suspicion will land on all the other companies like them because nobody can tell what they are actually up to because there is no disclosure. So to me, this thing only ends when we get these entities out of the leverage and opacity game and into a radically new and safe system, where they can't fail and they can't leverage and they have to disclose what they're actually buying on behalf of the client.

JEFF. I think your point, Larry, is a very powerful one. And at a not literal level of Limited Purpose Banking but of a more general level, Glass-Steagall successfully did that for quite a long time. Its removal was a very cynical play by Rubin, Summers, Clinton, Graham, and others, who all had very strong interests, personal interests, in the outcomes of that deregulation. They exploited the gaps that they created and then, to the chagrin of some of us at least, were invited right back into the White House in early 2009 after they had made this calamitous mess, to be the ones supposedly to fix it. I know that Summers for example continued to really institute moral hazard policies right and left by fighting against any limits on compensation of these people who had entered into the breach.

So this is a case where institutional reform of separating fractional-reserve banking and basically the provision of liquidity from gambling should be done. But I would add this

> Those who exploited the gaps were asked to come back in to fix them

other point, which is that a lot of what has actually happened and what has been revealed is, in my view, prima facie illegal behavior. It's financial fraud on a very large extent. There's also a tremendous amount of insider trading, and you can even see how it works when you're living in New York. It's not so mysterious, but we don't act.

I take John Paulson for example. Paulson worked together with Goldman Sachs to massively defraud many European banks, which bought the toxic mortgages that Paulson had put together. When this ABACUS deal was taken up by the SEC, Goldman ended up paying a small fine. The chair of Goldman, of course, continued in his position and continued at White House State dinners. And Paulson wasn't even mentioned once in any of the proceedings. He took home a $1 billion paycheck, even as Goldman was paying a roughly $700 million fine—if I remember correctly—for the abuse that Paulson was part of.

I can't believe, no matter what the financial regulations, that we can't do better than that. That's really pathetic.

QUESTIONER. As a former congressional staff attorney and retired tax lawyer, looking at the possibilities of small steps that might be taken, how affirmative would you think reenactment of Glass-Steagall would be?

JEFF. I think that it is quite important to recreate a mechanism where liquidity is separated from large-scale financial gambling. It's really, in my opinion as a macroeconomist, the collapse of liquidity that is the real macro-danger. The rest is the collapse of confidence, lawlessness, decency, and so on.

But what made Lehman so damaging, of course, was how it infected the money markets, the interbank loans, and the complete drying up of commercial paper. This was the devastating effect. It was basically March 1933 replayed. So liquidity is the real value here from a macroeconomic point of view. Loss of wealth is not my concern. I don't even particularly care whether bankers make big money, except I think a lot of them are crooks and that it's based on a lot of nefarious behavior.

> The collapse of banking liquidity is the real macro danger

But the macroeconomic significance is kind of a **Diamond-Dybvig** banking crisis, which we know to be part of a fractional-reserve banking system. It seems to be, analytically, that we have basically two levels of decision-making. One is separating liquidity in the banking sector from other kinds of speculative financial activity. This I would do for sure. I would never have put Goldman Sachs back under the Fed's protection as a banking unit, so that it could receive direct loans from the Fed. That's ridiculous and sad, actually.

But the second point then is Larry's point. This is whether fractional-reserve banking itself has value enough to keep it in its current form. I'm not convinced one way or another. I grew up in a fractional-reserve banking system. I do believe that it provides liquidity in normal times if regulation is good. I tend to believe that there is value in reserve banking. But it's also highly volatile, as theorists have recognized for at least 150 years and as Milton Friedman agreed. I think we have the choice. Could we really have liquidity without fractional-reserve banking?

If we could, we might be able to address another degree of this problem. The final point, of course, is separating the politicians from the crooks. But maybe that's so close together that they can't actually be separated. Maybe it's just the same community.

MICHAEL Kumhof: I have a different question, but I just wanted to say it is possible to separate liquidity provision from credit provision. And that's what the Chicago Plan is all about, and I think that should definitely be tried.

My question was on your international experience; you're starting off by saying you're talking to a lot of international decision-makers. What is the sense there, about the readiness to try different monetary and financial approaches to what we have today? Do they feel that they could start to do that on their own in their own countries? Or do they feel that they depend on the center countries like the United States and the Europeans to do something first?

JEFF. I think in general, for most small or developing countries—I'll put aside the very largest ones—there is a sense of almost complete dependency on the international system, for their payments, their lines of credit, interbank markets, and the need for swap facilities with the Fed or the ECD. The pervasiveness of tax havens, the extent of flight capital from their countries, the legal structures where, basically, very clever US lawyers help to free all of these countries from their tax revenues.

They feel very much dependent on a system that they feel is dysfunctional. However, they've also been well-schooled in that, for the last twenty-five years, their goal was to be part of the international system. They just woke up to a system that they find very destabilizing, and they don't see any clarity of the way forward; but most of the advice that they get is to be part of the system and be quiet, basically. This is how the system is. You join it. You stay in good terms with the Fed, with the IMF, with others. And there is very little sense of autonomous potential among these countries. Really, I can only emphasize that the palpable anger and vulnerability that's felt right now is very high.

> Smaller countries are dependent on a system which they feel is dysfunctional and destabilizing

DENNIS. My name is Dennis Peacocke, and I represent the faith-based side of macroeconomics. And I just want to congratulate you that you pulled us back to the reality that, in spite of all the complexities and theories and mechanics that we deal with in economics, economics is really about values and the values and ethics of people. Thank you very much.

JEFF. Well, thank you very much for saying it and practicing it.

I'm just going to end here because I'm being pulled out. I have to go to the UN, in fact, right now. I believe that we have a crisis of values that is extremely deep because the regulations and the legal structures need reform. But I meet a lot of these people on Wall Street on a regular basis right now.

I'm going to put it very bluntly. I regard the moral environment as pathological. I'm talking about the human interactions that I have. I have not seen anything like this, not felt it so palpably. These people are out to make billions of dollars, and nothing should stop them from that. They have no responsibility to pay taxes. They have no responsibility to their clients. They have no responsibility to people, counterparties, in transactions. They are tough, greedy, and aggressive and feel absolutely out of control in a quite literal sense. And they have gamed the system to a remarkable extent, and they have a docile president, a docile White House, and a docile regulatory system that absolutely can't find its voice. It's terrified of these companies.

If you look at the campaign contributions, which I happened to do yesterday for another purpose, the financial markets are the number one

> The moral environment is pathological

campaign contributors in the US system now. We have corrupt politics to the core, I'm afraid to say. Both parties are up to their necks in this. This has nothing to do with Democrats or Republicans. It really doesn't have anything to do with right wing or left wing. The corruption, as far as I can see, is everywhere.

What it has led to is this sense of impunity that is really stunning. You feel it on the individual level right now, and it's very unhealthy.

I have waited for five years now to see one figure on Wall Street speak in a moral language. I've not seen it once. That is shocking to me. If they won't, I've waited for a judge, for our president, for somebody, and it hasn't happened. And it's not going to happen anytime soon, it seems.

JEFFREY SACHS

Director of the Earth Institute at Columbia University

Jeffrey D. Sachs is a world-renowned professor of economics, leader in sustainable development, senior UN advisor, bestselling author, and syndicated columnist, whose monthly newspaper columns appear in more than eighty countries.

Professor Sachs serves as the director of the Earth Institute, Quetelet professor of sustainable development, and professor of health policy and management at Columbia University. He is special advisor to United Nations Secretary-General Ban Ki-moon on the Millennium Development Goals, having held the same position under former UN Secretary-General Kofi Annan. He is cofounder and chief strategist of Millennium Promise Alliance and is director of the Millennium Villages Project. Professor Sachs is also director of the UN Sustainable Development Solutions Network. He has authored three *New York Times* bestsellers in the past seven years—*The End of Poverty* (Penguin Books), *Common Wealth: Economics for a Crowded Planet* (Penguin Books), and *The Price of Civilization* (Random House Trade Paperbacks).

CHAPTER 7

Panel Discussion with Larry Kotlikoff and Michael Kumhof

SEAN. GENTLEMAN, THANK YOU FOR your talks. Sean Hallihan here. I was a Wall Street guy eons ago and then a technology guy. The thing I would like to ask is, what are the possibilities, the real possibilities, and what's the manifestation of no possibilities? What are the possibilities that we could actually move away from the fractional-reserve banking system that we have, to one which I think requires greater capital adequacy, to move all the way to the things that you're suggesting?

Since I've been away from this conversation for decades, it seems to me like a very far way to travel. Can you tell us what's going on in the Senate, in the House, and academia and where the best possibilities for reform are?

LARRY. I'll start. So you saw some of the people who endorsed Limited Purpose Banking. That's encouraging. I've been asked to speak about it all over the world, at different central banks from New Zealand to Sweden. So the word is getting out. The people in the Fed have asked me to speak, so I've spoken at different Federal Reserve banks. And there are people within the Federal Reserve at pretty high levels who are very interested in the proposal.

But we don't have any legislation pushing through Limited Purpose Banking at this point. There's a lot of vested interest, obviously, in the status quo. Let me just say, I think if we had a small country that did this, it would be a model that would spread to other countries.

> What is the probability of actually moving from the fractional reserve system?

But let me say how you can do the transition pretty quickly. Right now we have a huge amount of excess reserves. From day one, the banks could take the deposits and convert them into cash mutual funds so that a depositor would have to sign an agreement to have his deposit turned into shares of a cash mutual fund. The reserves then could be put in as cash to back these cash mutual funds, so that the bank now sets up a cash mutual fund and takes its reserves. And now, there's a dollar of cash for every dollar of shares outstanding.

Then the short-term liabilities of the banks could be turned into money market funds that the banks would then set up, money market mutual funds that are floating, so they're not valued to the buck. And then, the longer-term credits of the banks could be transformed into shares into closed-end mutual funds that are holding the liquid bank securities.

Now, all of this can be done by having the Fed help grease the wheels. It could buy up all the banks' assets and pay off all the creditors, have the creditors turn around and buy the assets through the mutual funds and the creditors invest in mutual funds. The mutual funds then buy the assets from the Fed that it just bought up.

So I think all of this can be done pretty quickly and safely. And it just takes somebody to try it. Now, in terms of the politicians, the summer after Dodd-Frank was enacted, Barney Frank had me over to his office in Boston. I had met Barney Frank once before, and it wasn't a pleasant meeting. He's a tough character. He's not an easy guy to interact with. I stood there for fifteen minutes in his office. He was sitting at the desk not looking up. I said, "Hello, Mr. Frank." Nothing.

After fifteen minutes, he looks up, and he starts yelling at me. That's the typical Barney Frank encounter. It's not especially me.

This time, I walk in and I say, "Do you know anything about Limited Purpose Banking?"

He says, "I know everything about it; it's exactly the way to go, and we're going to do it as soon as I get back to Washington."

And of course, he gets back to Washington. But his party is not in the majority anymore, and so he's out of office in terms of being Chairman of the House Banking Committee.

So he's certainly gone. After having just legislated Dodd-Frank, he told me point blank that Dodd-Frank was an interim solution, that the real solution was Limited Purpose Banking. This is Barney Frank. I don't know whether he'll remember that conversation, but that's what he told me. I don't know what the political links are, but I know that, if we can have people talking about this, it could happen. It at least has a chance of happening.

MICHAEL. So, I have also presented this work at leading central banks, at the Bank of England twice, at the ECB, at the Fed only two weeks ago. There's general interest, but those presentations are typically in more of a research setting and not, in my case at least, with the top people in the institution. But I think the word is spreading.

There are various efforts underway around the world to draw attention to this. For example, in the UK, there's the Positive Money campaign, which has a very similar agenda. In the US, there's the American Monetary Institute; in Germany, there's Monetative; in Switzerland, there is an initiative around Professor Binswanger, called Monetaere Modernisierung. As well in New Zealand and Iceland there are embryonic political movements that are trying to push something along these lines. Some of that is happening in Germany as well. So these ideas are out there.

But I think what it would take is some really shocking event to move such a drastic step—an event whereby we would have our backs against the wall and we needed to do something, and it might as well be the right thing. Even if we in this conference don't deem it to be a drastic step, to many, this is a drastic step. I think that's what it would take to get there

For example, I presented a proposal right at the end that was like a mini Chicago Plan, basically addressing the problems of the banking system in very acute distress where you need to do something. Once you realize that bailing-in not bond debtors, but ordinary depositors, destroys the money supply and makes the remaining money supply precarious, you're probably going to think twice or thrice about that. And then, once you realize that the option that I presented is painless, clean, and has been done before, more or less fifty years ago. Then maybe something like that would be considered.

> Bail-in destroys the money supply

It would go very painlessly, I think, as it did historically. This would be a perfect example of "where should we go in the long run?"

because this would be a mini version of the Chicago Plan, where you then just tell the banks you have these reserves and you're essentially bailing them out by doing this, by buying those bad assets from them. But these need to be kept as reserves for the checking accounts. Once that is done, people can see that this is a solution that does, in principle, work.

But it has one drawback, and the voters are going to see that. The drawback is that what is being bailed out here is essentially just the bad loans of the banking system. So you're basically then just saying, "We're helping out those who have taken on more debt than they should have and nobody else gets a crumb." That perspective, though, is not quite right because it will prevent the economy from tanking by doing this, so everybody else at least gets an economy that doesn't tank.

But if you were instead to say, "Look, everybody gets the same"— it's the citizens' dividend that I described in my presentation— "everybody gets the same amount and gets out of debt by the same amount," then this would also help to cover these nonperforming loans. It would also put the banking system right, but there wouldn't be any perceived injustice in this. This could be done in a way where everybody perceives they are being justly treated.

So what I am trying to say is, "Look, you can do this partial solution here, but it isn't just, so why not go all the way?" Maybe I'm hoping for more than what can be achieved, but that's how I look at it now. Thank you.

MARSHALL. Hi, my name is Marshall Pagan. My question is, aren't the varieties of QE that we've experienced a form of Chicago Plan lite? In the sense that, if I understand correctly, if you had a Chicago Plan, you would need to have reserves at a level between $12 and

$15 trillion, perhaps more? And the Fed's balance sheet has gone from $800 billion to $3.2 trillion with the consequence that you have substantially greater excess reserves. But effectively, it seems to me what the Fed has been doing is sort of moving, in a somewhat ad hoc way, in the direction toward what would be required if you were, in fact, in a Chicago Plan environment.

I guess that's the first question. The observation, it seems to me, is if we're transitionally moving to a Chicago Plan, one of the first issues you're going to face is whether or not there's adequate collateral to back the Fed's increased balance sheet. And the implication of that would be either you'd have to have, substantially, all of the federal debt being held by the Federal Reserve or the Fed holding a greater variety of assets than just federal treasury paper. And I guess the question in that context is, isn't that what the Fed's been doing?

MICHAEL. I guess (*looking toward Larry at the front*) that was more about the Chicago Plan than Limited Purpose Banking.

What the Fed has done is created a lot of reserves. This is certainly true. But there's a sense that these will eventually be withdrawn once the economy has normalized or at least, to a significant extent, withdrawn. And there is no sense that this is more than a temporary emergency measure where "temporary" could be many years, but nevertheless, an emergency measure.

And what this doesn't really do is to prevent the banking system from continuing to run as a fractional reserve banking system the way it has always been run. So at the margin, the banks are still fully in control of the broad money supply and how it is created because these reserves are not really constraining them in any way. What they're doing is providing a temporary cushion against lack of liquidity and potential insolvency of the institutions involved.

And so this is not really the Chicago Plan. It could be turned into that by saying to the bank, "Look, these are reserves that you have now. We're now requiring that these are not going to be withdrawn and you have to hold at least reserves against all checking accounts."

Your second question presents a very common misunderstanding. You basically said, "Under the Chicago Plan, the Fed would have to have adequate collateral to back its balance sheet, that is, it's issuance of money." This is

> QE increases reserves but does not move toward a Chicago Plan lite

a notion that goes back to the gold standard, whereby money has to be backed by something else, which, actually in my view—and excuse the language, it's not personal because this is a very common understanding—but I think this is nonsense. The gold standard was a barbarous relic, and this aspect of it was a barbarous relic. That is, this notion that money has to be backed by something else—under the gold standard, by gold, and then later on by some form of debt.

Money does not have to be backed by anything. Money is a token that is used in exchange and that can be issued simply as that token. The government, or whoever it is that issues that token, can take the seigniorage revenue that comes along with that. There does not need to be a backing in any sense.

So basically what happens in my version of the Chicago Plan is that, when the money is issued, seigniorage is treated as a one-off revenue and, as I call it, equity in the commonwealth of the nation. So, I hope that addresses that second question. If not, let me know.

QUESTIONER. I have three questions/observations. One is addressed to Michael Kumhof primarily. If you could just comment on the impact of the substantial wealth effect of the debt repayment through commonwealth equity on inflation? Even if the total sum of money is unchanged, presumably if you write off basically 100 percent of GDP's private debt, mortgages, and consumer credit, that would have some impact on pertinent income, consumer spending, and so on.

The second is, when you repay/replace mortgage and consumer credit in this transaction, how do you intend to compensate the banks for the loss of excess spread that they would expect when these assets are replaced or reserved? Presumably, you buy these back at market value rather than book value, would you not? So another way of asking the same question is whether you intend to basically redeem these bank assets at market value rather than book value?

And the third question is slightly more technical. You mentioned that, when you moved treasury credit supply to investment trusts and the lending institutions in the economy, you would do this by managing the cost of treasury credit. Any particular reason why you wouldn't just manage it in the same way as you manage money? You can just fix a growth rate and let interest rates set themselves.

MICHAEL. All excellent questions.

First, the wealth effect on inflation. That is a very common misunderstanding. The first time I actually discussed that question was with [Lord] Adair Turner a few days after the paper came out. And so, the answer is the following. Start off with the economy before the Chicago Plan and you have—in the model, and I hate to talk about it in terms of my model—basically some rich and financially unconstrained households holding deposits in the banking system. The borrowers of that banking system are financially constrained households that need to, for example, have mortgages, etc. I am simplifying it here, but the essence is captured in what I'm saying.

So, at that point, basically, there's a flow of interest. The wealth effect is the present discounted value of the interest payments and how these change, right? We have a flow of interest from a constrained household to an unconstrained household. Now, you implement the Chicago Plan.

Basically what happens is that the government steps between the constrained and the unconstrained household. It says to the unconstrained households, the holders of the big deposits, "Look, you still have your deposits in the bank, but now they are backed." I'm using the word *backed* not in the sense of collateral, but the deposits now represent reserves of public money. For the unconstrained households, the rich guys if you wish, they still get the same interest. So for them, there is obviously no wealth effect. They get the same interest from the government. Obviously, there is no debt forgiven here because they start off without debt.

The constrained households are now paying interest, not to the rich guys anymore but to the government instead because the government now provides Treasury credit. That is how credit is now funded to the constrained households. The balance sheet that I showed right at the beginning, right after the transition to the Chicago Plan, was essentially only the government lending into the credit system. I'm abstracting from a lot of things that come later in the transition period in order to tell you just the essence of the story because, in the end, the government ends up not funding the credit.

Let's just talk about that case. The government now is lending to these constrained agents. It's a step in between. Now the government says, "I am forgiving you a lot of this debt." You could call it that or you can tell my story of the citizens' dividend. This government in this simulation has a structural deficit, which is what many governments have these days, which means in the long run I'm targeting a certain deficit to GDP ratio.

If the government now says, "I give up a lot of these interest payments from these guys by forgiving them the debt," then the government has to make it up somewhere else by raising taxes or something else. Ceteris paribus (everything else being equal) that's what would have to happen. If those taxes were to fall on those constrained agents whose interest charges have just been forgiven, then they come out plus or minus zero. They have really not gained anything. This is really just an accounting issue. The government has forgiven something to people, but it has a balanced budget that it likes to maintain. So if it forgives something, it has to get it back somewhere else. Because these people whose debts have just been forgiven represent the majority of people in this economy, the government is going to get the needed income back mostly from them.

So there is no wealth effect from this. This actually comes through very clearly in the simulations. Of course, there are all sorts of other things going on because this also stimulates the real economy so there's an increase in the demand for money, there's a drop in interest rates. All of that I've abstracted to just tell the essential story; there is no positive wealth effect from this debt forgiveness.

The next question was how do we compensate the banks. Essentially, yes, the assets would be bought back at market value. That's what the model simulation assumes. The shareholders now have far too much capital in the banks because the capital that was in the banks before the Chicago Plan is no longer needed because the capital adequacy regulations don't call for it. If I have half as much of a balance sheet as before, then I can just pay a one-off dividend to my shareholders, again at market value, and let that capital be deployed somewhere else—not in the financial system but somewhere in the real economy. Nobody needs to lose any money over this.

As far as Treasury credit is concerned with respect to one of the slides used, you asked if I only have a price mechanism. How about a quantity mechanism? I have some other slides here, but I think I can tell you the story verbally. There are a number of things you can do with credit. Let me put this into perspective first. There is money in credit now. For money, I want the government to be very firmly in charge and I'm on completely the same page as the Chicago School economists of the 1930s, the laissez faire economists of the 1930s. They were all about laissez faire in industry but not in finance. That "laissez faire everything" only started much, much later. I'm talking about controlling money.

As far as credit is concerned, you can think about a whole spectrum of policies. The policy that I modeled in the paper as the baseline is where there are investment trusts, funded by private equity, private debt, and a little slice of Treasury credit. And that Treasury credit can act as the lender of last resort; if the government wants to stimulate lending by these investment funds, it can inject additional money—lend money into circulation so to speak—and it can set an interest rate for that. That's how I conceptualize it.

Now the government also sets an interest rate; that's the **federal funds rate**. That's on a different asset class; that's actually on a liability of the government. This would be an interest rate on an asset of the government, a rate at which government lends to the private sector.

If you wish, that could be the end of the story. But I don't think that's a good idea. I think it does make sense to give some influence to regulators and also the government over the aggregate quantity of credit. Not so much over the allocation, although even there an argument could be made; maybe you could try to encourage certain types of credit, like investment in machinery, and discourage other types of credit, like asset speculation or things like this. There's a scholar at the University of Southampton in the UK, Richard Werner, who has done extensive research on this policy called Quantitative Lending Guidance or Window Guidance.

Some people, when they read my paper, say, "This is communism." That's complete nonsense because that sort of system was practiced all over the Western world and East Asia in the decades immediately following World War II—exactly what you were alluding to with your third question, being a more direct control over the quantity of credit. It was actually something that was originally pioneered by Germany prior to World War I. It was then adopted by various East Asian countries, and it was practiced all over Western Europe as well after World War II. Werner's evidence shows that, most of the time, this was a very successful policy. This is something I would like to work on in the future.

Actually, if you look at the new Basel III regulations that are now being put out, there is a regulation in there that says countercyclical capital buffers can be used whereby that buffer would be raised in response to an increase in the credit to GDP ratio.

LARRY. I think you're getting into the weeds a little too much in this stuff. Let me try to answer your question slightly differently. Suppose we want to go to Limited Purpose Banking, and I'm the Federal Reserve and you guys are all the banks. I just print a whole lot of money and buy up all your assets. You take the money that I give you, cash, and you pay off your creditors, the depositors, and all the other creditors of your banks, and you yourself shut down. I've got all your assets, and your creditors have all the cash I just printed.

Now day two, you open yourselves up as equity-financed mutual funds and you sell shares to your mutual funds. Some of you are selling mortgage mutual funds, and some are selling real estate mutual funds, and some are selling cash mutual funds. You take the money back in from the public that you just gave them in exchange for shares, and then I, the government, sell these assets back to the mutual funds. You're now mutual funds. I've pushed the money in, and I've taken it out. There is no wealth effect.

> There is no wealth effect in the system conversion

Now we're in a situation where, if you look at the mutual funds, there are all different types; some are cash mutual funds, some are equity mutual funds, and some are bond mutual funds and money market mutual funds. They're all floating; none are backed to the buck, except the cash mutual funds because it's just cash. If you aggregate all these mutual funds, they've got liabilities, which is equity, and they've got assets, which are all their holdings. That's Limited Purpose Banking.

Now if you go there and say, "How do you go from Limited Purpose Banking to Michael's Chicago Plan?" It's taking these noncash mutual funds and allowing them to leverage. You've got to ask yourself the question, "Would you want to do that?" My answer would be, no, because the big problem with our financial collapse was not in the deposits and a run on the deposits in the commercial banks. It was a run on the investment banks. It's because they were leveraged, and it was the specter of their failing; it wasn't whether or not they hurt the individual household and whether he could get his money out. It was the specter of those big institutions failing and bringing down the financial system and just scaring the public in terms of the level of confidence in the economy.

Lehman was not going to be cured by the Chicago Plan. Get that out of your minds. That's not an answer. The Chicago Plan is not going to fix what happened with Lehman and Bear Stearns because they would all be, in effect, leveraged mutual funds under Michael's proposal.

> The financial highway must not be leveraged

What I'm proposing is that these leveraged mutual funds not be leveraged. They have to be 100 percent equity financed. So if Lehman has sold mutual funds and invested in bad mortgages, then the people who hold these non-leveraged mutual funds, hold the mortgages through those non-leveraged mutual funds, would get hurt. And life would go on. That's what I think you need to be thinking about.

When you're thinking, do you want leverage in the financial system? Do you want people gambling with the financial highway, with what is a public good? That's the key question. Do you want them operating with opacity? Do you want them able to borrow money and invest in things nobody can see and have no government oversight and disclosure of what they're investing in? That's the key question you should be asking—not details about whether there's a wealth effect or exactly how this mechanism's going to work because that's going to miss the main point.

MICHAEL. But I think the question about the wealth effect was very relevant. As a macroeconomist, I have to ask, if I do a reform like the one I'm proposing, is that going to be inflationary? That's always the knee-jerk reaction of monetary economists out there, and it's just plain wrong.

LARRY. You can see that by the money going out and coming back in.

MICHAEL. I think Larry and I differ on an aspect of what theses mutual funds should look like. His exclusive type of mutual fund is the equity funded one, where I'm not necessarily convinced of that; you can still have risky fixed income instruments out there in mutual funds. They can be leveraged. But what is absolutely critical is that, when they screw up with their lending decisions it has no effect, zero effect, on the safety of the means of payment. The means of payment will be completely separate from what those guys do.

And by the way, if you have a monetary system where there is no private source of funds anywhere in the economy, as there is today, where private agents can just freely print money, then Lehman, or any other type of institution, will have a much harder time leveraging up the way they did. It doesn't work so easily because you have a given money supply that is provided through the government; you can, perhaps, affect the velocity of that, but there's policy toward that too.

But otherwise, this is the money supply, and people hold this money supply for transactions. And if a Lehman wants to leverage up, nobody can create money out of thin air to allow Lehman to leverage up. This is a very different world. It's one thing to talk about how do we resolve Lehman, given we are where we are, but the Chicago Plan is how do we never get a Lehman in the first place.

BILL POOLE. I have a question on this banking discussion, but I also have a comment on Jeffrey Sachs. The banking system grew up as a market phenomenon over, what, three hundred, four hundred, five hundred years? Something like that. The banking system really, in the scheme of things historically, is only relatively recently subject to a great deal of government regulation. The basic characteristics of the banking system have been a market phenomenon.

The question I have is, when we have a redesign, whichever one we were to choose, what happens if the market system produces, call them "near banks" or whatever organization you want to call

> How do we control the shadow banking system?

it, because there is a demand and a supply for firms with those characteristics? I think it's an important question because the system that you're advocating will not be a stable system over time if there are market forces that create different kinds of firms.

Now let me make a brief comment about Jeffrey Sachs. I reacted very badly to his presentation. Maybe you heard it differently. I heard no economic analysis. I heard no facts. I heard lots of highly charged words that seemed to me not to be appropriate in, I'll say, an intellectual discussion like this.

I'll tell you a little story. About twenty years ago, my youngest son married a Romanian woman he met studying in Switzerland. I got to know her father a little bit. Most of his life was under communism, including the brutal Ceaușescu for the last twenty years or whatever period he was in power for. Levu was his name. Levu's attitude was, even after the fall of communism, that anybody who has accumulated any wealth is a crook—has to be a crook. That's the way it was under communism. The only way you accumulated wealth under communism was to be a crook. And you got it through the state, not by following the grand rules of Marxism.

I believe that some of what we heard from Jeffrey Sachs was exactly like that; these hedge fund managers have to be crooks. They couldn't possibly be providing economic services that are worth anything like that. Now we know that quite a few hedge funds have, in fact, been closed down. Some hedge funds have not done very well, and the investors have walked away and they've been shut down. I think that, without an economic analysis of what these funds do, it is simply improper, quite frankly improper, to assume that the wealth that they accumulated was a matter essentially of criminal activity or theft.

LARRY. Let me just respond quickly to both points. What I'm proposing is that for any nonfinancial corporation—like a General Motors that tried to get into the banking business with GMAC—that subsidiary would have to be operated as a100 percent equity-financed mutual fund. Clearly, there are going to be some issues of judgment, and that's where regulation would come in. But in general, there's a whole lot less regulation under what I'm proposing because you don't really have to; you've got maybe 130 different regulatory bodies in the United States to make sure that this leverage, this gambling on the part of the banks, doesn't kill the economy. The banks have invested in risky ways, and so you have to see exactly what the banks are investing in to make sure that they don't go under and, therefore, kill off the economy and destroy the public good.

I'm saying let's have disclosure by a single government agency, not 130, of what the mutual funds are investing in and if the investments go poorly the shareholders lose value and things go on. None of the equity-financed mutual funds—and by the way I don't do any consulting for any

> Not a single equity financed mutual fund got into trouble during the crash

of these mutual funds just so you know—none of these equity-financed mutual funds got into any big trouble in 2008. Not a single one of them. We had a financial earthquake, but they were built out of stone. All the companies built out of straw, that is the highly leveraged banks, collapsed—not all of them but most of the big ones.

So what do we do? We rebuild in straw. That's what's going on here, and we can't even see the fact that the non-leveraged mutual fund companies did not collapse. I think that that is an issue, albeit a minor one. The big thing is that there are about ten thousand mutual funds and none of them collapsed, and we're not even looking at that.

The other thing about Jeff's [Sachs; see Chapter 6: "Implications for Global Development"] comments is that I agree with Jeff. If I'd had the opportunity, I would have said the same thing if I were talking on that topic. To tell you the truth, we have documented by the SEC something like seven hundred cases every year where none of these guys go to jail. It's in the paper day after day. Day after day, this is criminality of a sort that's not really being dealt with in any strong manner. It's being dealt with by a company signing a paper, admitting to nothing, and then going about its business and paying its fine. This is slapping of the hands.

We have a revolving door between Wall Street and Pennsylvania Avenue. It's obvious. You have Larry Summers earning $5 million for mismanaging money, and then he goes to work in Washington and now he's back probably working on Wall Street on the side. Robert Rubin leaves Wall Street. It's endless. We have a corrupt political system in my mind.

I think Jeff's trying to lay that out and talk about the need for the

Federal Reserve—we're at the Federal Reserve now during this conference and there are Federal Reserve people here—the need for the Federal Reserve and other regulatory bodies to actually do their job. Excuse me, but it just does not seem to be done. Also, we need change in the structure of the financial system so that we don't have the ability for so much corruption, so much leverage. I think that is the way to go.

MICHAEL: I completely agree with you. I would have put it even more strongly than Jeff Sachs. And by the way, there is empirical evidence. There is a paper by Philippon and Reshef[29] who have looked at trying to explain the remuneration of financial sector managers by trying to explain them through increased marginal production. That has been used in the empirical literature and found that a lot of their remuneration can only be explained as a "rent"—in other words, as an unearned income that cannot be explained by their productivity at doing anything.

> We need change in the structure of the system to decrease corruption

You started off by saying that banks are a market phenomenon. Excuse me, but I do not really agree with that. If you read monetary history, you will see that banks were very often very closely intertwined with governments and there were very strong banking charters that needed to be granted first. Think about this—who would not want a banking charter? You are getting the privilege of having a money printing machine in your back yard. You would not want that?

Then it is said, "The markets are going to take care of the fact that

---

29   Philippon, Thomas and Ariell Reshef, *Wages and Human Capital in the U.S. Financial Industry: 1909 – 2006*, New York University and University of Virginia, 2008. Complete copy at http://pages.stern.nyu.edu/~tphilipp/papers/pr_rev15.pdf

these guys will responsibly use their money printing machine." Do you buy that? This is an unreasonable assumption, and the Chicago economists of the 1930s were seeing it exactly the way I'm putting it here.

Now you asked one very important question, which is, when we redesign this, would we have "near banks" arising that would produce essentially—you didn't use the same term—but would they produce substitute monies and would that, therefore, interfere with the control over the quantity of money and therefore of inflation? It's an important monetary question. It is answered in the paper [Benes and Kumhof, *The Chicago Plan Revisited;* the paper backing Dr. Kumhof's presentation].

What you could do is the following: First, only government-issued money would be accepted for any dealings with the government including the payment of taxes. Historically, this has been enough to ensure that government-issued money had a complete monopoly. That may be enough. Second, there cannot be any FDIC-type coverage of nonmonetary liabilities anywhere in the financial system, either explicit or implicit. And you don't need it when your money supply is produced directly by the government in a debt-free fashion. The reason why we have to have the FDIC right now is because this made sure that bank liabilities really are perceived as safe and, therefore, real money. When you produce them safely in the first place, you no longer need to ensure that the liabilities of the remaining institutions are safe, and therefore, their debt liabilities can be risky.

> When you produce safe money you don't need to ensure its safety

The third point is you could rewrite the tax laws to encourage equity instead of debt, where right now we have exactly the opposite.

Equity is very unlikely to be treated as a money-like instrument. Fourth, you could have regulations on maturity mismatches. And fifth—if you really needed to, but I don't think you would need to—you could have an outright prohibition against using nonpublic money for any kind of transaction. I don't think you need to go there.

Let me tell you a little example. I met somebody who right now works at the French Treasury. He tells me the following story, for which I still have to check into the details. In the United States and one or two small European countries, money market mutual funds basically are regulated in such a way that the redemption value is sort of safe and money-like. You basically treat this as money— whereas in France, for example, this was not the case and these funds have a fluctuating asset value.

As a consequence, these things never took off in France because they're not perceived as money. They are perceived as something risky. This is not even the major regulation that was in any way intended to make this money or not money. It just happens to be that way, and you get a major response from that. In addition, if you impose all these other measures that I just suggested, I think you would ensure that near monies would not be a prohibitive problem. You would always fight on that front. Henry Simons in his writing was very clear that this was an issue, but I think you wouldn't have a major problem.

CAROL COREN. I have two questions, one of which has to do with the relevance of the credit union system to your models and the experience, worldwide, of the growth and performance of credit unions—which have a moral compass that, in some measures, is affected by the democratic direction of their members who in theory elect the managers of the union (and on an annual basis) and have opportunities to review a transparent report of the performance and holdings of the credit unions—and where this fits in your respective models and views of the banking system.

The other is an observation as to the issues of sustainability that we are witnessing in respect to our food system and the affect that the drive for economies in efficiencies of scale have had on it that have similarly now been witnessed in our banking system, where we have increasingly moved the banking system from local roots and a commitment to community and an understanding of the role that money plays in a community and the relevance of the depositors' commitment to the bank activities and need for money on a secular basis. I would welcome your thoughts on those two observations.

LARRY: I wrote a book called *Jimmy Stewart is Dead*. You know the movie, *It's a Wonderful Life*. Here you have the most moral local banker; this is the Christmas movie that we all watch, *It's a Wonderful Life*. George Bailey is being played by Jimmy Stewart. It's Christmas Eve, and there's a run on his bank because there's been a rumor that he's lost some money in his bank. Everybody knows George; everybody trusts George. But there's this rumor out there because nobody is able to see what George has done with their money.

That's your local credit union; they're honest, good bankers. Maybe George has just invested in something really, really safe like Treasury bills or bonds—thirty-year Treasury bonds—and inflation has just taken off and those Treasury bonds have lost 30 percent of their value and he was leveraged at twenty-five to one or thirty-three to one as Basel II allows. So this very honest, safe, good banker, reliable banker has a problem because he's made a promise he can't keep.

> Both banks and credit unions are unsafe at any speed

In effect, he's made a fraudulent promise to pay off in all states of nature when, in fact, he can't do it.

That's the story with credit unions. They've also promised, like any other bank, even though they might be "better people" or somehow more transparent, they're engaged in something that's unsafe at any speed. This is a banking system set up to fail. It would not be an issue if this was not a public good that these entities were in charge of.

That's the key thing. That's why this is different than another company, say like General Electric failing. Banks set themselves up so that they're not disclosing what they're doing with your money. They tell the depositors, "You can get your money anytime. If you start to see a problem, you can come and get it." They say this because they're trying to pay off the people that have a good insight as to whether or not they're actually in trouble. This is a bribe to get people to give them their money because they're not able to show people what they're doing with their money. So they've set themselves up in a way that they will fail at some point. Credit unions will also fail at some point because they're also not safe.

So we need to have a system that can't fail. It's a public good; it's a public highway system. It cannot be allowed to be brought down. But it has been brought down. Bill is talking about the history of banking, the six hundred or so years of private banking, and how can we change it. We've had six hundred or so years of fraudulent medicine being provided before the government decided to put together the FDA, and now we have a drug industry that actually works. So if we didn't have the FDA, we'd have no drug industry. People would be marketing pills with arsenic and uranium, which is what they did in 1909 or 1905, whenever the FDA came into place.

So we need to have something that works. We need to understand that we don't have Jimmy Stewarts—and even if we did have Jimmy Stewarts running the banking system, what they're doing is playing with fire, with our jobs, and with our retirements. And we've just seen them destroying it. So on that score, that's my answer.

On the size and concentration of big banks, things have gotten more concentrated. Dodd-Frank has made for more concentration; it's going to drive small banks out of business because they

> Dodd-Frank will increase the too-big-to-fail problem

can't comply with all these regulations and they drive out the credit unions as well. And we've made too-big-to-fail a bigger problem. So it should all be fixed with Limited Purpose Banking.

Now Limited Purpose Banking does not eliminate big banks. You can have a very big mutual fund, like Fidelity, that has a lot of small banks within it, which are equity-financed mutual funds. So there's no need to have big or small mutual fund holding companies; they can be big as long they're marketing small banks that are equity financed.

QUESTIONER. (*Inaudible*)

LARRY. Well, fidelity investments—I'm not talking about LLC, I'm talking about TIAA-CREF or T. Rowe Price—any of these mutual fund holding companies have each of their mutual funds as a separate little subsidiary. And they—I'm talking about the ones that are equity financed—they sell shares, they take in money, and they invest in things. And they can't fail.

And, bingo, it's very simple. When you have all the financial entities that are incorporated operating that way, you never have a bank failure again. You never have a correlation between bank failures and economic crises like you see throughout the history of economic business cycles. Just go back in time; you see all these private banks going under and the economy goes down at the same time. It is no surprise.

MICHAEL. I don't really have much to add to that, as I completely agree. In the nineteenth century, the United States had lots of small, local banks, and it was a complete mess. You might have had the odd good bank manager, the equivalent of a credit union perhaps, but the system has within it the seeds of great trouble. You need either the Chicago Plan or Limited Purpose Banking, something along those lines, where you take that seed out.

CHAPTER 8

Money and Debt: Radical Solutions to the Challenge of De-leveraging

LORD ADAIR TURNER HAD JUST resigned as chairman of the British Financial Services Authority[30] when he gave this speech. He homes in on debt, its primary attributes, and how these lead to problems. He uses that as a jumping off point to critique both the Chicago Plan and Limited Purpose Banking, which had been the point of inviting him to speak at the conference.

Speeches and papers of his—given and/or published subsequent to this one—in which he addresses a number of the shortcomings he finds here, may be found online.

His résumé is found at the end of this chapter.

---

30   The British Financial Services Authority is roughly equivalent to the US Securities and Exchange Commission.

ULI KORTSCH. Lord Adair Turner has just resigned as the chairman of the British Financial Services Authority. He has recently joined the Institute For New Economic Thinking, or INET, as a senior fellow. If you are not familiar with that, it is an institute which is, to a large extent, funded by George Soros. It is a research institute and a think tank that is looking at the kinds of issues we're talking about here and, of course, much broader issues.

If I may say so, Lord Turner has been one of the public officials who, while actually in that position, was willing to make public statements of a fairly radical nature. As a matter of fact, there's a one-page description of his most recent speech, or one of the most recent speeches, in the latest issue of *The Economist*. Lord Turner, thank you very much.

LORD TURNER. First of all, can I say that I'm terribly sorry that I couldn't be with you in person this afternoon. I'm actually speaking from Washington, DC, where there is a conference [by the IMF] on macroeconomics and **macroprudential** policy, which is covering some of the issues. And I had to speak here at lunchtime, so I've got to come in by video conference. It's particularly sad that I haven't been with you because I've greatly enjoyed and admired reading the works of both Michael Kumhof, along with Jaromir Benes, and, indeed, Larry Kotlikoff. I think that they've done a great service in making sure that we think about radical ideas of reform—radical ideas which go beyond the incremental improvements in the stability of the system with which, as a public policy official, I have necessarily been involved over the last five years.

> We need radical ideas which go beyond incremental improvements

Now that doesn't necessarily mean that I agree fully with either Larry or Michael, with their precise propositions. But I think there are some underlying principles which they are setting out—and which, as Michael's paper in particular describes, were set out very clearly by mid-twentieth century economists like Irving Fisher, like Henry Simons, like Milton Friedman—and that those principles are very important for us to understand and to use as to guide, as best possible, a policy action. I'm now out of the official public policy role, and that hopefully enables me to be a bit more radical. I'm trying to be relatively radical and straightforward, even while I've been in that role, but when you get to the end, as I have, of four and a half years as a regulator, one of the things that you do is reflect on what we did, reflect on what fundamentally went wrong, and go back to basics to think about whether we need to have a more fundamental reform to make a more stable system.

What I'd like to do is to make five points. One, I'd like to set out what I think are some important issues which were ignored before the crisis, the latest financial crisis, and some principles which I think are important. And I'd like to focus on the problems that debt and banks can create in the upswing. Second, I'll say some words about why that creates particular problems in the downswing as well and the links between some aspects of monetary policy and macroprudential policy.

Third, I'm going to talk about the way that that suggests a possible need for radicalism along two dimensions in macroeconomic policy and in macroprudential policy. Fourth, I'm going to step back and say that the fundamental issue is, do we believe that **maturity transformation** is a good thing or not? And fifth, I'm going to suggest a possible way forward, which is not quite as radical as what Michael and Larry are suggesting. But still I think you'll find this to be a way outside the bounds of what we debated within the policy space over the last four years.

So let me begin by saying I think there are some very important insights into the nature of financial stability and macroeconomics which were almost entirely ignored before the crisis. Olivier Blanchard, the chief economist of the IMF said last year that one of the faults economists had before the crisis was that we thought we could ignore the details of the financial system, and that is largely true. The new Keynesian macroeconomic models largely just didn't have a financial system in it. This is a fairly extraordinary fact, but it's true.

What is also true is that, before the crisis over several decades, we fell into a tendency to believe that financial markets are just markets like any other and that the propositions, which are in favor of free markets and are

> Before the crisis we thought we could ignore the details of the financial system

pretty good in other sections of the economy, apply also in finance. Basically, if we want a good supply of restaurants and a variety of ambiances and price points with good service, there isn't really a better system than having a free market in which entrepreneurs create a concept; some win, some lose, some go bankrupt, some flourish. The free market works.

I think one of the most fundamental things for us to understand is that finance is different. Finance is different because it is linking the present and the future together under conditions of inherent, irreducible uncertainty and because it deals with money, which is a very complex and difficult and distinctive element of our economies. And the fact that we thought the market for money or the market for financial instruments is just like the markets for finance was a major mistake.

Finance is different. It can create instabilities; it can create rent extraction opportunities. Within finance, debt contracts are even more different. And I think there are five reasons why debt contracts, as people like Henry Simons and Irving Fisher described, create risk and why the bigger the amount of debt contracts within our economy, that is the higher the level of debt to GDP, the more fragile is likely to be our macroeconomy.

First, debt contracts are different because of what Andrei Shleifer has called "local thinking," which is a form of sort of partial blindness, a failure to see the world as it really is. If you hold an equity investment, it is obvious to you that you are holding a risky investment because it goes up and down in price day by day. The movement in the price day by day is continually sending you a reinforcing signal that reminds you that you hold something which is risky.

When you hold a debt instrument, in the good times, all that you see is the bit of the frequency distribution of possible results, which is the favorable 100 percent payout result. And what happens in the good times is that there's a systematic tendency for people to believe that the observed bit of the distribution of possible results is the whole of the distribution. They end up believing that some instruments which are inherently risky—because there is real risk out there in the economy—are in fact riskless.

As a result, the free market, left to itself, has a systematic tendency to create more debt contracts than is optimal and, as Andrei Shleifer puts it, a tendency to create many debt contracts, which, and I quote, "owe their very existence to neglected risk." We saw enormous numbers of such debt contracts before the financial crisis—debt contracts that people assumed

> Free markets have a tendency to create more debt contracts than is optimal

were triple-A, were safe, but that owed their very existence to neglected risk, which not for that partial blindness would never have seen the light of day. That's the first difference.

The **second difference** is the impact of bankruptcy and default processes. Ben Bernanke, in his essays on the Great Depression, has a phrase which says, in a complete market's world, bankruptcy would never be observed. In the world described by smooth, neoclassical economics functions, what would happen with a debt contract is, as the operating risk of the firm grew, there would be a completely smooth process of renegotiation of the debt contract to have elements of equity. It would be an entirely smooth process because most of neoclassical economics work on the basis of nice, smooth functions. But actually, in the real world, we see processes of bankruptcy and default. What happens when you foreclose on a debt contract is that you go through processes which, in themselves, destroy value; which tend to produce asset price falls; and which tend to produce knock-on effects of the sort that propagated the Great Depression.

Thirdly, debt contracts have to be rolled over. You can imagine a market economy operating for many years—let's say five years—with not a single new equity issue. It wouldn't be a perfect market economy, it would slowly get less effective in terms of the allocation of capital, but you can imagine it because at least the equity that had already been invested does not have to be repaid; that is a permanent investment. But debt typically has contractual terms of one or two or three years or so, particularly in the corporate space. So it is being continually paid, and therefore, to maintain the same level of capital support to, for instance, a business, it has to be continually rolled over. And that means that for the continued health of the new credit provision process—if you have already allowed large amounts of debt contracts to exist—you need a continual process of rolling those debt contracts over; otherwise you will have a contraction of the credit and a contraction of the real economy.

The **fourth**—and this is crucial to Michael Kumhof's paper, *The Chicago Plan Revisited* and the work of Irving Fisher and Henry Simons and company—is not just that debt is different but that banks are even more different than nonbank debt contracts. I think maybe I focus more than Michael, or some others, on the dangers that you would have even if debt contracts were provided in a nonbank fashion, but where I certainly agree is that fractional reserve banks create a whole new level of danger. Because the fundamental fact is that, when people say, "Banks take savings and intermediate it to loans," that's not true.

One of the most fundamental insights, and it's very clearly set out in the front of Michael's paper, is that banks simultaneously create new credit and new money ex nihilo. And that is one of the most fundamental, important things for people to be taught, which economics undergraduates should be taught, about the nature of how a monetary economy with banks works.

The **fifth** and final thing is that lending against assets is particularly problematic. When you have the ability of banks to create new credit and new money, and where that credit is extended against an asset such as a house or commercial real estate, which can increase in value, you have an extraordinarily strong tendency for what Hyman Minsky described, which is credit and asset price cycles. The very extension of credit helps drive up the asset price. The higher asset price makes the borrower think, "well, that was a good idea, I'll do that again. I'll borrow some more credit." The fact that the price goes up produces a period of low loan losses that swells the capital position of the banks, which can then make more loans with more capital, and it also sends a reinforcing cycle to the lending officer, which says, "Well, I lent some money to commercial real estate, and I haven't made much losses on it, so I'll do some more." You have these incredibly strong credit and asset price Minsky cycles, which have an upward spiral and then a downward spiral.

That of course can occur within banks, but it can also—I think it's crucial to understand this point in the evaluation of these radical options—it can also occur in shadow banks. Indeed, I have a fear

> Lending against assets is particularly problematic

that what happened before the crisis in the development of the shadow banking system is that we have effectively created a sort of turbocharged and hardwired version of a Minsky cycle.

What we did in the shadow banking space is that, in putting together a money market fund, which provides a money equivalent, instant-access account, it then takes a deposit and, say, lends it thirty days to an asset-backed commercial paper issuer, or lends through the repo market or enters a complicated set of systems of securities, lending, and secured financing. What happens is that, at each step in the totality of that chain is a bank made up of many chains. In order to try and make themselves safe at various steps of that chain, actors take security, mark to market the loan's affected that they've made on a daily basis, and they call collateralized collateral against change in the mark to market value. And that, I think, has the aspects of the Minsky asset and credit cycle, but turbocharged and hardwired. This is made mathematically absolutely inevitable.

So debt contracts create risks that are not created by equity contracts. Banks create even more risk because they have this limitless ability to create new credit and new money. Shadow banks can create money equivalents and can turbocharge the Minsky cycle. And the net effect of this is that banks, and I would now say shadow banks, have an inherent tendency to create excessive amounts of credit in the upswings and then to destroy it in the downswings.

As Henry Simons put it in February 1936, "In the very nature of the system banks will flood the economy with money substitute during booms and precipitate futile effects and general liquidation

> Shadow banks can create a turbo-charged Minsky cycle

afterwards[31]." And it's very interesting to think that that was said by Henry Simons, who most people think of, and indeed was, a founding father of the Chicago free-market, laissez-faire school of economics.

So here's someone who believes passionately in free markets—free markets for restaurants or hotels or automobile manufacturers or soap manufacturers or whatever—but he thinks that finance is different. He thinks that we have here something [the financial system] which is inherently unstable, which will create excessive amounts of money and money substitute during booms and precipitate future effects of liquidation thereafter. And therefore, he said, "Private initiative has been allowed too much freedom in determining the character of our financial structure and in directing changes in the quantity of money and money substitutes[32]."

So I think there should be a real pause for people to think about this—that a set of thoughtful people, who in all other aspects of the economy were passionate free marketeers, sitting amid the wreckage which had been produced by the banking crisis of 1929

---

31 Simons, Henry. 1936. *"Rules versus Authorities in Monetary Policy."* The Journal of Political Economy 44 (1):9 - 10

32 Ibid p3

to '33, end up in a radical position, where they believe that finance and debt and banks are so different that we should effectively abolish fractional-reserve banks. These insights into the special nature of banks, of debt, of shadow banks, I think fundamentally challenge precrisis economic orthodoxy, which tended to assume that increasing financial intensity was limitlessly beneficial, and it assumed that on the basis of market completion theory.

So within neoclassical economics, there is a fundamental proposition that the more contracts you have, the more markets you have; the more that we complete markets; and, therefore, the more that we head toward a sort of a nirvana of a free market equilibrium as described by Kenneth Arrow and Gerard Debreu. But in fact, I think we know that the theory of finance, debts, and banks tells us that there's no certain mechanism by which the amount of money and credit created is optimal; indeed, we have a system which is almost certain likely to take it to excess.

And increasingly I think we have empirical evidence supporting the proposition that there are levels of debt to GDP generated by, for instance, free banking systems, above which that level of debt to GDP is harmful

> Net taxpayer losses for bailouts are the most unimportant element of the total cost

to the stability of growth and to the long-term level of growth. I'm thinking here about the empirical analysis done by people like Alan Taylor or the BIS document from July last year in which Steve Cecchetti and Enisse Kharroubi argue that, when you plot private debt to GDP against long-term growth rates, you end up with a sort of inverse U function, where financial deepening at some level of debt to GDP is positive for the economy but only up to a certain level. But the level in which the developed economies currently are is beyond that and is negative for growth.

These insights are important. They were ignored precrisis, and so credit to GDP grew massively over the fifty years precrisis both in the real economy and within the financial system in itself. And the crisis created huge harm. I think it's very important for us to understand the nature of the huge harm that the crisis created. Some people try to measure that through the costs of taxpayer bank bailouts and say the crucial thing is to end "too big to fail." But actually, the cost of taxpayer bank bailouts is either in accounting terms nil; in the United States the Federal Reserve, except in the cases of Fannie Mae and Freddie Mac, in relation to all the other interventions, is highly likely to end up with a net profit at the end of the day.

And even in the U.K. where we probably face a net loss on our equity investments in RBS and Lloyd's HBOS, the total cost there is just a couple percent of GDP. That is the short change; that's the small change; it is the most unimportant element of the total cost of the crisis.

> Free banking systems can create harmful levels of debt-to-GDP

The total cost of the crisis is the macroeconomic recession into which we have been tipped. And it's that that's the way that extra credit created in the upswing, by the banking and shadow banking system, produces a downswing thereafter; that's what we ought to focus on. So, I think that was my first point. Banks are different; credit is different. Left to itself, the system will produce too many debt contracts, too high leverage.

My second point is that, when you've done that, when you allow that to occur, you then face a huge problem in the downswing. And the downswing is characterized by what Irving Fisher described as the "debt and deflation cycle" in a great and short and very accessible article. It is characterized by what Richard Koo, in his analysis of Japan over the last twenty years, described as "a balance sheet recession."

Essentially what happens in a balance sheet recession is that, once the crisis occurs, both companies and households, in a different mix in different economies according to where the leverage developed—but it could be either companies or households—suddenly become convinced that they've got too much debt. And they therefore become determined to pay back that debt, to de-leverage. In that environment, they become almost entirely **inelastic**[33] to a stimulus provided by low interest rates. You reduce the interest rates to the zero lower bound, but people don't borrow more money, because they're basically trying to pay back the debt they already have. And this is the liquidity trap in which reducing the policy rate, interest rate, fed funds rate to the zero lower bound just doesn't stimulate the economy. We end up in a trap.

Now of course, in that environment, you can then say, "Okay well we'll go beyond simply reducing the interest rate to the zero lower bound and we'll do all sorts of unconventional monetary maneuvers, such as quantitative easing, credit easing, direct credit subsidy, central bank liquidity support, **forward guidance** on interest rates." And what all of those maneuvers, which are being deployed by central banks across the world, are trying to do is influence a wider set of interest rates than the policy rate alone. They're trying to influence long-term interest rates as well as short, forward expectations of future interest rates, as well as current rates, the rates actually paid by borrowers in the real economy, as well as the Fed fund rate, which exists in wholesale money markets.

---

33   See Glossary

But there are problems with those sorts of policies that work through those mechanisms or through asset price effects—i.e. QE pushes up the price of bonds or equities, investors feel richer so they spend more money, or they go out searching for yield. The problem with that is twofold. First, if you were really in a debt overhang, in a balance sheet recession, then the fact that you are able to influence a wider set of interest rates still may not make much difference. Borrowers may still be inelastic to changes in the long-term interest rate, as well as the short-term interest rate. They may be inelastic in response to the rate that they specifically pay, as much as in relation to the policy rate. So that's one danger, that it simply isn't very effective.

The other danger is that, when we use these unconventional policy levers to restimulate the economy, we are attempting—through the mechanism of the famous hangover cure where you give another shot of alcohol to the alcoholic—we end up with a set of policies the purpose of which is to stimulate people into taking on more debt when we are faced with a crisis that has been clearly produced by too much debt! And there's a real irony.

And there are very major dangers, as Jeremy Stein of the Federal Reserve Board set out in a lecture in February, that these processes of unconventional monetary stimulus will, long before they have a really powerful effect on the real economy of households and companies, stimulate all sorts of carry trade and put option writing and leverage activity in the financial system, which will recreate forms of a financial stability risk.

That's the situation; that's the problem we've got—too much debt in the upswing and a balance sheet recession de-leveraging in the downswing.

My third point is that observing those two problems suggests the need to consider greater radicalism of public policy along two dimensions. In macroeconomic policy, it suggests that there might be circumstances of deflation and de-leveraging so deep that you have to consider the option Ben Bernanke proposed for Japan in 2003, which is helicopter money, printing money, financing an increased fiscal deficit.

> Jeremy Stein: Long before Main St. sees the benefit, Wall St. is writing put options, doing carry trade, and leveraging

Some people, the moment they hear that, say, "Oh my God. That's hyperinflation rate. That's a terrifying thing to do." But I give you another irony from the history of economic thought, along with my previous one where Henry Simons, this great laissez-faire, free market economist proposes the complete abolition of banks. The other irony is that Milton Freedman, a man who most people think is absolutely determined to fight against inflation, proposed in 1948 that not only should we *sometimes* pay for public deficits with new created money but that we should always do that—that that should be the standard form of dealing with fiscal deficits in order to produce a steady increase in the money stock, compatible with a slowly or steadily growing low inflation economy.

So in macro policy, the observation of this extreme liquidity trap can take you down the radical route of helicopter money, i.e., the creation of irredeemable fiat money to create demand. The observation of the harm that leverage has done takes us to the question of how do we have a dramatically less leveraged economy for the future? How do we manage to write down existing high levels of debt and/or to achieve fundamental changes to the financial system, for instance through the abolition of fractional-reserve banks, creating an environment in which the pace of nominal demand growth is no longer dependent on the growth of private leverage?

These two elements are closely linked—the idea of money finance of deficits and of radical change to create 100 percent reserve banks. These are logically linked; they are logically linked in Michael Kumhof and Jaromir Benes' paper, and they were logically linked in the writings of Friedman in 1948 and Irving Fisher and Henry Simons.

What do we think about these? Let me give some thoughts. Essentially, what Jaromir and Michael have done is propose a revisiting of the Chicago Plan. This would involve banks being 100 percent reserve backed; a variety

> Milton Friedman: Always use new money creation to pay for public deficits

of different possible ways to provide loans in the future, either through treasury loans or essentially equity backed, which would make them somewhat similar to Larry Kotlikoff's idea of Limited Purpose equity bank loan funds and with credit creation essentially focused on investment and real activities rather than in, as much as it is today, intertemporal consumption smoothing as between old and young or patient and impatient.

So you just understand how little of current bank credit is focused, at least in some countries, on investment in real activities. I suggest the following figures. In the United Kingdom, the sterling lending of the UK banking system is about 1.8 trillion pounds sterling. Of that about 1.3 trillion pounds is either house mortgage loans or short-term consumer credit loans. In the United Kingdom, unlike in Ireland or Spain or the United States, very few of the house mortgage loans have anything to do with the construction of new houses because we don't construct many new houses in the United Kingdom. It's almost entirely to do with the financing of an exchange of preexisting houses between old and young people or those who have houses or not.

So 1.3 trillion pounds out of the 1.8 trillion pounds has very, very little to do with the real investment process. Of the remaining 500 billion pounds, 280 billion pounds is lending to commercial real estate companies. Some of that is real investment in attractive, new commercial real estate investments. But a hell of a lot of that is also simply financing asset plays on existing commercial real estate assets.

So you're down to 220 billion pounds out of 1.8 trillion, which is actually to lending to the non-real estate companies. Indeed, if you look at the manufacturing sector in the UK, they are net depositors into the banking system, not net borrowers from it.

> Only a very small part of banking activity actually finances productive capacity

I think it's very important for us to understand how little of the present banking system actually is the sort of activity that you get iconically described, when people are arguing to keep away from the regulation, which is investment going into new companies, etc. It's a very small part of what most banking systems do.

That's the proposition, in two different ways, which Michael and Larry gave. I think there are a set of issues which might make me not fully convinced to say, "Yes, I'm going to sign up to the Benes/Kumhof Chicago Plan with Kotlikoff mutual funds."

I interchanged quite extensively with Michael by e-mail a couple of months ago. I think the new version of the paper addresses some of the issues. But there were some issues that I'm not absolutely clear on that would make this in total doable or necessarily desirable.

First of all, I think, that any system which involves a big write-off of existing debts, however hard you try, is going to, somewhere in the system, create winners and losers. I think it's almost impossible to do large debt write-offs without some distributional consequences. I think that's just very difficult politically, as well as creating some simply uncertain consequences which will result from distributional effects on wealth.

Secondly I think there's an open issue about how we should think about lending for intertemporal consumption smoothing. I think there's far too much of it, but I think there could still be an argument that some of it is valuable up to a point. The basic process of saying, "We enable younger people to borrow money to buy houses off older people, rather than all houses flowing through an inheritance process or being bought by the accumulation, first, of enough cash to buy them." I think that may have a social welfare optimality.

I think one of the most important bits of economic theory that we really haven't thought through is, what is the social optimality there? How much is socially optimal? But I think that's an unexplored bit of economic theory. Even some elements of lending from patient to impatient people may be socially welfare optimal, even though it has absolutely nothing to do with creating higher growth.

I do have some concerns about the distributional issues, about how we should think about intertemporal consumption smoothing. And I do have some concerns that any attempt to create an entirely 100 percent reserve banking system would be likely to create more shadow banking systems—i.e., near money substitutes. So I'm more doubtful than Michael is about the ability of us to prevent the creation of near money substitutes.

In relation to Larry's proposals, I'm not totally convinced that it would get rid of pro-cyclicality. Given that I

> Mark-to-market in the shadow banking system will still be pro-cyclical

think that mark-to-market systems in the shadow banking system were themselves a cause of pro-cyclicality, I can imagine that, if we have mutual loan funds in which you hold a mark-to-market investment and if we can really mark-to-market those on a day by day basis, or even a week by week, I think we may see some pretty strong pro-cyclical behavior—in self-reinforcing cycles—in response to the mark-to-market of the value of such funds.

So I do have some questions about the precise forms of radicalism. Underlying those questions, there is a fundamental issue, which is, what do we think about maturity transforming banks? Is there a useful role for maturity transformation to enable the creation of debt contracts below those which would otherwise exist?

I think Larry and Michael and others in the really radical camp have convinced themselves that there's no value in that at all— that we should simply abolish it. I don't think I'm in that space. I'm convinced that, left to itself, the system does more maturity transformation and more debt contract and money creation than is optimal. But I'm not quite in the space of believing that we should abolish it entirely.

I think it's possible that there is some role for leveraged maturity transforming banks to create a wider set of debt contractors than might otherwise exist. Walter Bagehot in *Lombard Street*[34] certainly argued that that had played some role in the superior early development of the UK economy versus, for instance, the French economy. I don't think that's an entirely fanciable concept, though it could certainly be challenged.

I certainly believe that the amount of debt contracts created by purely free markets is likely to be deeply suboptimal—i.e., they'll

---

34 Bagehot, Walter, *Lombard Street: A Description of Money Markets*, Project Gutenberg, 1873

be too much. I have strong reasons to believe that, left to itself, the amount of debt contracts will always be suboptimally large.

I'm therefore attracted to what Jaromir and Michael, in their document, set out in section I, which is compromise solutions. I hope I'm not simply being wimpish and going for the compromise solution. I note that, in that section you very carefully, very politely point out that those who go for compromise solutions are sort of intellectual wimps. They're not really going for the absolutely pure aversion.

Let's talk about what a compromise solution might be. One way forward has been suggested by Anat Admati and Martin Hellwig in their new book, *The Bankers' New Clothes*[35]. They state that the

> We are the inheritors of a 100-year policy mistake

bankers are running naked and we've not admitted that so far. They basically argue, and I entirely agree with them, that as regulators today, as policy makers today, we are the inheritors of a hundred-year policy mistake, in which we have allowed banks to operate with ludicrously high levels of leverage, which are completely unnecessary for the effective operation of a market economy.

They argue that, in a perfect world, we wouldn't be playing around with Basel III, where those of us like me spend many, many hours in windowless rooms throughout the world negotiating it. We're very proud if we manage to get the leverage for the capital ratios up from five to six to seven. They say, "Forget all that. The optimal level is something like 25 to 30 percent." I believe that. I believe that, if one were fortunate enough to be the benevolent dictator of a greenfield economy and able to simply ignore transition problems or political

---

35   Admati, Anat and Martin Hellwig, *The Bankers' New Clothes: What's Wrong with Banking and What to Do about it,* Princeton University Press, 2013

disagreements between different authorities throughout the world, I'd go for something like a 25 to 30 percent equity ratio.

I think it's then important to realize two potential problems with that Admati and Hellwig approach. First, setting capital ratios however high does not actually necessarily constrain the total level of debt contracts in society because you constrain the ratio of total bank loans to equity but you don't constrain the amount of equity that people chose to put into the banking system. If you had equity ratios of 25 to 30 percent, investments in bank equity would be very low risk. These would be your classic utilities, in which widows and orphans, the famous most iconic figures, ought to invest for dividend return. I think you might well find that there was quite a large supply of people willing to invest in bank equity as a not-far-off deposit equivalent. It wouldn't be money; it wouldn't be useable as money. But in terms of a store of value, it would be seen as a pretty safe store.

So I think you could have the Admati/Hellwig very high capital ratios but still end up with a system generating debt to GDP ratios that were suboptimally high. The fundamental problem here is that, when you constrain banks through the capital ratio, you're constraining a ratio, but you do not directly constrain what the numerator is, how much capital there is.

That is different from when you do it on the reserve asset side of the ratio, where if you have quantitative reserve asset requirements, you not only can impose a ratio but you ultimately determine how many reserves at the central bank there are. So I suspect if we really wanted to go forward with the Admati/Hellwig compromise radicalism, we might have to combine very high equity ratios with the restoration of quantitative reserve requirements and pretty high reserve requirements, which, again, is, I'm afraid, yes, the comprise solution that I see that Jaromir and Michael criticize as, indeed, did Irving Fisher. It's sort of "Well, we proposed 100 percent reserve requirements and you're coming back with X, which is quite large but not 100 percent." But that's where I might be.

The second concern I have with Admati and Hellwig is, how are we going to deal with the transition? The fact is, it would be much better if we had not created all these debt contracts in the economy. But we have. Given that we have, if we simply come along and say, "You've got to hit a much higher capital ratio," there is a danger that, left to themselves, the banking systems will choose to meet those high capital ratios through a speedy process of de-leveraging. While that de-leveraging, at one level, is required to end up in a more stable overall economy, in the short term, given the starting point that we had, it could be depressive to the economy.

Therefore, if you go with the Hellwig/Admati mechanism, I think what you've got to do is demand a higher capital ratio and demand that it is met through an increase in the numerator, not an increase in the denominator. To do that, you've

> I am very concerned with shadow banking arbitrage and avoidance

really got to backstop that requirement for a higher capital ratio with a statement that says, "If you don't manage to get that higher equity in the private equity markets, we, the public authorities, are going to subscribe that new equity."

My third concern, even with the Admati/Hellwig compromise, is shadow banking arbitrage and avoidance problems. I am very struck—one of the main things that I've looked at over the last two years is the development of the precrisis shadow banking system—and I've been very struck by the way that it is able to create alternative ways of bank credit equivalence, i.e., near money equivalence.

I think we're seeing across the world that there are a lot of arbitrage opportunities. Look at China and the major developments for shadow banking systems there. I think, essentially, the system can produce near money equivalents, which are not dependent on the underpin of deposit insurance and lender of last resort but which are created by the use of collateralization and haircut techniques, which as I said earlier, can be even more unstable and even more pro-cyclical than banking per se.

I'm interested in that intermediate solution of the Admati/Hellwig approach of very high capital ratios combined with the restoration of quantitative reserve requirements, which is heading a bit toward 100 percent reserve banking but not the whole way. But I'm aware of problems.

Let me end with one possibility of how we might head toward that—one very radical proposal, which ties together what I said earlier about radicalism in the monetary space and helicopter money drops (money finance creation) and heads toward a more stable banking system.

Suppose we made a policy commitment that required banks to increase their equity ratios to the sort of 25 or 30 percent that Admati/Hellwig had proposed. We'd combine that with a process that said, "If you ever fall below 15 percent, we'll take you into some sort of central bank conservatorship, tidy you up again, write off the existing equity, and refloat you." Therefore, we would have very strong incentives for sound bank management, which would never let the equity ratio get down to those 15 percent numbers. We require that of the banking system, and we make it clear that, if private equity is not available to meet that higher capital requirement, we will have public funds injections into the banking system.

But that fiscal injection would be paid for, if needed, entirely with new central bank reserves. You can think of this as a Bernanke helicopter money drop totally dropped into bank equity rather than into Milton Friedman's famous dollar bills lying around the ground. The political economy benefit of this is that, if the helicopter money drop is limited to this exercise only—this specific exercise of heaviness toward a less leveraged banking system—then it does not raise the political economy dangers that make people very terrified of the more generalized use of money-financed government deficits. I'm talking about the danger that once politicians realize that it's possible to finance deficits with central bank money, they'll want to do it all the time and to excess, rather than in an appropriate amount and at an appropriate time.

These measures of creating a more liquid and more capitalized banking system would, however, have to be combined with measures that directly control both borrowers and lenders. It would have to be combined with things like LTV and LTI limits in key areas such as residential housing. It would have to be combined with much more aggressive than currently planned use of countercyclical capital requirements, particularly in things like commercial real estate. And it would involve the restoration of the policy tool of quantitative, unremunerated reserve requirements to insure that new reserves created cannot limitlessly create new money constrained only by that imperfect equity ratio constraint. And this policy would have to be controlled and constrained with very tight control of shadow banking—capital liquidity requirements on money market funds, minimum haircuts in repo and secured lending and securities financing contracts, and the ability of the regulators to impose leverage and liquidity constraints on any institutions which over time became bank-like in nature.

So what I've ended up doing is agreeing with the analysis of Michael and Larry, who are saying that there's something very fundamentally wrong about too much leverage and therefore something very fundamentally skewed about

> I agree with Michael and Larry's analysis but suggest a compromise solution

fractional reserve banks. But I'm suggesting, yes, a compromise solution, which does not abolish fractional-reserve banks nor abolish, as Henry Simmons wanted, debt contracts. Here is an intermediate level of radicalism—still radical enough that they will probably get some of my erstwhile colleagues in the official center a complete shock when they read it—a process that will end up taking us toward a dramatically less leveraged banking system without that costing an increase in fiscal deficit because of the use of money financed credit. That is, I'm taking some of the insights from Michael and Larry and other's analyses, some of their radicalism, but suggesting a way forward, which would still be incredibly difficult to get political support for, but which resides in an intermediate radicalism space.

So thank you very much for listening, and I'd be happy if we can to take questions from the floor and respond to it over the next fifteen minutes. Thank you.

ULI. Thank you very, very much, Lord Turner. I really appreciate your insightful analysis. You know, we're streamed live. Half of our audience is around the world live, and half of it is right here in this room. Approximately.

Here's a question from Positive Money[36] from the UK. I know you're aware of their work. Here's their question: "Do you agree that we should not prohibit fractional reserve banking because maturity transformation is useful? If there was a way of allowing maturity transformation without the creation of private money, then would it be worth preventing private money creation via a fractional reserve banking system?"

LORD TURNER. That's interesting. Obviously, you could have the state play the monopoly role as the maturity transformer. I guess I'm a little bit wary of that. I hope I'm not just being institutionally conservative in accepting the world as it is, because I do have significant concerns about state direction of investment funds. I think there's a whole set of reasons to believe that's not very successful. So I think I'm still in the camp of believing that with very tight controls—by the sort of mechanisms that I have proposed— we can take the benefits (and I think there still are some benefits) of a free system of competitive fractional reserve banks.

Essentially, I'm saying there can be a role for fractional-reserve banks but that the fraction never needed to be anything like as small as what we allowed to develop in the precrisis period. I think we should certainly be open to a range of radical ideas. But I think I'm convinced that, with a radical enough set of regulations, we can constrain the fractional-reserve banking system to prevent it being the dangerous driver of excess credit money creation that it has been in the past.

Another question?

LARRY. Hi there, it's Larry Kotlikoff. Great presentation, very much enjoyed your remarks, agreed with a few of them. One thing on the

---

36   A British organization advocating banking and monetary reform. See http://
      www.positivemoney.org/

maturity transformation; there's this paper by Charles Jacklin[37] that shows you can achieve the same good equilibrium as you would have in the Diamond-Dybvig Model with just people buying short- and long-dated securities without having the bad equilibrium of the "bank-run equilibrium."

So that's one question for you—kind of connects to the question that was just asked—whether there's an alternative mechanism for maturity transformation. After all, it's trying to assure people that have suddenly become impatient. I think that's all fourth order, to tell you the truth, as an issue. But even so, security markets can seem to deal with that.

My other more important question is, in your entire talk there was no discussion of disclosure of transparency. If you have financial institutions, no matter how much capital they have, if nobody can see what they're actually investing in, then the market can lose faith in the value of the capital. In the case of Lehman, three days before it failed, it put out a glossy report that was approved by the SEC; it was, in effect, a stress test for Lehman Brothers.

It said that its capital ratio was 11 percent, which is higher than most US banks now have under our stress test. So I'm not sure whether capital ratios are all they are touted to be; I don't think you can be "a little bit pregnant" here. You have to have—I think we need to have—full disclosure by a government agency of the securities that are being marketed to the public. I think as soon as you introduce any leverage potential, you have this entire regulatory structure that you need to have in place.

Furthermore, on the issue of capital requirements, think about AIG

---

37   Jacklin, Charles J. 1987. Demand deposits, Trading Restrictions, and Risk
      Sharing in Contractual arrangements for Intertemporal Trade, ed. Edward
      Prescott and Neil Wallace. 26-47. Minnesota Studies in Economics, vol 1. 1

engaging in the sale of CDSs. In effect, that was leveraging because they were committing the payback in certain states of nature—huge amounts of money—and they didn't have it. It wasn't in all states of nature, but in certain states of nature, when the company they were insuring was defaulting on its debt.

So what is leverage is an open question, as is whether the capital requirements will cover everything that's leveraged and whether the companies would then buy securities or themselves become more leveraged. All these problems go away with Limited Purpose Banking but are there with your compromise.

LORD TURNER. Okay, let me pick up a couple of points. I think I'm less convinced than you are, Larry, of the mileage that we can make by transparency. Let me try and illustrate this point. I remember in the autumn of 2008 when we were right in the middle of the financial crises and people said, "What we're going to do is force the banks to tell us how bad the losses are by telling us about the quality of their assets."

The trouble is that there is no answer to that question because the value of the assets is deeply endogenous to what is about to happen to the economic cycle. If

> The value of assets are deeply endogenous to the economic cycle

there is competence in the system and they have enough money to make some more loans, the value of those assets is higher. If the system goes into a downward spiral, then the assets are worth less. There is no such thing as the value of the assets in some defined sense. It is, I think, deeply endogenous to the state of the economy, which in itself is a continually evolving process.

So I'm more wary I think than you, Larry, that disclosure will do it all. And indeed, I'm slightly worried that incredibly wide disclosure, combined with the tendency of financial markets to be subject to herd effects and rumors, can produce continued mark-to-market cycles which, in a sense, are self-fulfilling.

So my response is, what you have to do is just have enough equity capital that you have a high degree of confidence that, if the assets turn out be worth less than you thought they were, the worst that can happen is the equity holders lose. And it's up to them to have a dialogue with the managers of the bank about what they need to do. So as long as you can get yourself to a situation where the level of equity you run at in the good times is high enough, except in a hundred- or two hundred-year scenario, the worst that can happen is that the equity write-off is going to take you from 25 percent to 15 percent.

As long as you have a defining process—at that point of saying, "Okay, guys, game over. You equity guys, you haven't done your job; you're wiped out. We'll take the asset for free. And we'll tidy it up and sell it off, a process in which the state or central bank will typically make a profit—I think you can have a level of equity that is less than 100 percent, which makes the likelihood of hitting bank failure with the consequences that has for new credit supply and macroeconomic instability so low that you have reduced it to the point where every 150 years, yes, you'll have to bail out the banking system. But as long as it's every 150 years, it's probably socially optimal to accept that's what we do. So that's my aim, and I think there can be a ratio which is high enough to achieve that—certainly if we're talking about straight loans.

> The most egregious failure was that only internal value-at-risk models were required

Now your point is, how do we then deal with this proliferation of derivative accounts and securities lending and repo-secure financing, etc.—all the stuff that the investment bank trading operations did. Where you're quite right, Lehman had an equity capital ratio of say 11 percent, of course on a simple nonrisk-weighted adjusted basis, it was much less than 11 percent. I don't know what it was, but against the absolute gross value of all the contracts they were in, it was probably just 1 or 2 percent.

And that reflected the fact that the most egregious failure of our capital system, before the crisis, was the capital system that we applied to trading activities where we said, "It's up to you guys, the industry, to model your required capital on value-at-risk models. You are allowed to run those value-at-risk models by working out what's the worst loss at the 97 percent confidence interval that you think you can have over a ten-day period"—allowing them to develop their own models of "how bad could it be?"

And what they did was develop extraordinary pro-cyclical models, which said in spring 2007, "Well, volatility in the markets is way, way low, so we don't need much capital because, given the volatility in the market is low, the worst loss we can have in a ten-day period is X, so we don't need much capital." Which ended up as a total pro-cyclical machine because the very fact that you didn't then need much capital to trade made a whole load of people trade more, which has a short-term effect of driving down the volatility, until you get a crack point; and then the volatility explodes.

I think the lesson of that is that our trading book capital regime was completely wrong. I think we've taken some steps but not nearly enough to put it right. I think we should still be aiming for dramatic increases in required capital requirements against trading activities. I think the net result of that is probably, as the investment bankers will tell you, that less trading will occur. But I think some of this trading is completely unnecessary and socially useless in any case. It gets justified with iconic statements like, "market liquidity" or "the need for price discovery," which I think are rhetoric flourishes rather than things really well rooted in economic functions that we need.

Clearly, there is an important process of price discovery, but we don't need as much price discovery as we assert. So maybe I'm too optimistic, Larry. But overall, I believe there is a level of equity capital ratio sufficiently high that it would cover losses in all states of the world, provided we roll on, as we are committed to roll on, to a fundamental review and reformation of the trading book capital regime which is required.

And on disclosure I've always been in a camp that says, disclosure is like motherhood and apple pie; nobody can be against it. But I'm not convinced that markets are efficient enough or information processes are efficient enough or people are sufficiently rational for disclosure and transparency to be as powerful a lever for stability, as I know you are.

ULI. One more question.

BILL POOLE. I want to hold an asset, which we call money, that can be available, used at any time, and is the final satisfaction of a payment. It's not a debt, but it's final satisfaction—a payment for a good or service. It's also inherent in economic life that, sometimes, households or certainly firms want to be able to borrow for a certain period. And they want to borrow for a period that is not a demand note. Now in fact, of course, banks write a lot of demand notes. However there is the understanding that, provided the borrower is in good standing and provided the bank is not in deep trouble, the money would not be demanded without any notice. So it seems to me that maturity transformation is an inherent and useful function of banks, and I see no possibility of any regulation that would effectively control maturity transformation because it's easy for banks to write the terms of a contract, that is a note, saying it's a demand note, but in fact, the practice is that they don't demand it.

LORD TURNER. Yeah, well I think I agree with you. I mean I'm not suggesting an abolition of maturity transformation. But I think you highlighted something that I honestly don't think economics so far has

> It is impossible to regulate maturity transformation

provided a really good enough analysis of, which is, what is the optimal level of both debt contracts and of maturity transforming credit and money creation? And I think this is very fundamental. There is a very lovely short essay written by the mid-twentieth century Italian economist, Luigi Einaudi. And it's called simply *Debts* or in Italian, *Debiti*[38].

And Einaudi, reflecting Simons says, "Look it's obvious if we could create a world in which there were only equity contracts in both a capital finance fashion and a labor market fashion, we would have a much more stable economy." So he said if all investments in business were equity investments and if all labor market contracts took the form of shares in the profit, whatever the profit was of the firm in question, then we would not have the fluctuations that arise from the inflexibilities of wage contracts and debt contracts that led to the Great Depression. And I think that's a reasonable case.

But then he goes on to say, "But we have a whole load of debt

---

38   Einaudi, Luigi. 2006. *"Debts."* In Luigi Einaudi: Selected Economic Essays, edited by L. Einaudi, R. Faucci, and R. Marchionatti. New York: Palgrave Macmillan. (First published as *"Debiti"* in La Reforma Sociale XLI, Volume XLV (No. 1 [January] 1934.)

contracts, and we have fixed labor contracts. I fix wages, you're going to pay me thirty thousand dollars a year whether your company works or not. And you're going to pay me an interest rate of 5 percent, whether you make a profit or not." These have arisen he says, "because of a fundamentally naturally arising human desire for certainty. Human beings can't deal with the uncertainty inherent in every contract being an equity contract."

And I think that's right. So an element of debt contracts is a good thing, its wealth maximizing as a response to some needs of individuals in the way that they invest and the way the company wants certainty of what it's going to pay. But you can accept that argument and still believe that there could be too much debt contracts in aggregate in the economy.

I think maturity transformation is the same. I think the way that you have described it, which says that people want to be able to simultaneously borrow money for twenty years and have some of their wealth invested in an instant access account. You can see to a lot of people and to businesses, that's an attractive thing to do. That gives all sorts of flexibilities, and you can see why the possibility of that may have been important to businesses making entrepreneurial commitments, which is part of the wealth creation process.

So again, I think maturity transformation can be both an absolute welfare-optimizing function, even if it doesn't drive growth, and I think it may have also contributed to growth. But again, that doesn't tell us that limitless amounts of maturity transformation are good. And I think one of the really missing bits of our understanding of economic theory is that—once you've accepted that

> One of the most fundamental missing pieces of economic theory is determining the optimal level of maturity transformation

some debt contract is better than no debt contract and once you've accepted that some maturity transformation is better than no maturity transformation—we're still way short of a good theoretical understanding or an empirical understanding of how much is optimal. Given that there are very good reasons to believe that both debt contracts and maturity transformation, once unleashed, have inverse U functions, some debt contracts within society (debt to GDP) and some maturity transformation are good up to a point and then bad beyond that point.

And I think we're lacking both good theory and good empirical analysis that could help us locate that point. I believe that's one of the most fundamental missing bits of our basic theoretical understanding of optimality in a monetary economy.

LORD ADAIR TURNER

 Lord Adair Turner has combined careers in business, public policy, and academia. Since April 2013, he is senior fellow of the Institute for New Economic Thinking (INET).

From September 2008 to March 2013, Lord Turner was chairman of the UK Financial Services Authority and, from January 2008 until spring 2012, chair of the Climate Change Committee.

He became a cross-bench member of the House of Lords in 2005 and was chair of the UK Pensions Commission, 2003 to 2006, and of the Low Pay Commission, 2002 to 2006. He is the author of *Just Capital: The Liberal Economy* (Macmillan, 2001), and *Economics after the Crisis: Objectives and Means* (MIT Press, 2012).

He is a visiting professor at the London School of Economics and at Cass Business School, City University; a visiting fellow at Nuffield College Oxford; and a trustee and chair of the audit committee at the British Museum.

Prior to 2008, Lord Turner was a nonexecutive director at Standard Chartered Bank, United British Media, and Siemens UK; from 2000 to 2006, he was vice chairman of Merrill Lynch Europe, and from 1995 to 1999, he was director general of the Confederation of British Industry. He was with McKinsey & Co. from 1982 to 1995, building McKinsey's practice in Eastern Europe and Russia between 1992 and 1995. He was chair of the Overseas Development Institute (2007 to 2010).

Lord Turner studied history and economics at Caius College, Cambridge, from 1974 to 1978 and was college supervisor in economics from 1979 to 1981.

CHAPTER 9

A Free Market Perspective

DR. WILLIAM POOLE IS THE former President of the US Federal Reserve Bank of St. Louis. His presentation comes from a libertarian approach. This is an important analysis, as it demonstrates that both the left and right philosophically view our current fractional reserve banking system with suspicion and are looking for answers.

The self-stabilizing characteristics provided by the Chicago Plan and Limited Purpose Banking, leading to a major decrease in regulatory oversight, appeal to the right. The increase in social equality effected through the operations of a monetary commission (see Chapter 4: "The Chicago Plan Revisited") appeals to the left.

Dr. Poole's résumé is found at the end of this chapter.

BILL POOLE:

This reminds me—because the audience is thinning—I was in New York doing a lecture for the National Bureau of Economic Research on October 19, 1987. I suspect that everybody in here knows that date[39]. And I came down from my hotel room where I was finishing working on my remarks.

And the stock market was already down. It was 10:00 in the morning, and it was already down by 7 or 8 percent. And then it kept going down and down and the crowd, mostly financial people get thinner and thinner. By the time I spoke, I think there were probably about six people there, something like that.

And I also have vivid memory of the taxi ride out to LaGuardia. The cab driver had the radio on, and every few minutes there was another stock market report; maybe it was every five minutes or something like that. And the DOW was down another 40. And it was an astonishing day!

Okay, I'm probably going to sound like a libertarian purist, and if I do, I hope you will think about it as a measure, perhaps, of how far we've come and how far we are away from the founding principles of our country.

Now the original title that I had was *Banking Reform: A Libertarian Perspective*. [Dr. William] Dunkelberg is not here any more, but he made me change it. So it now reads *A Free Market Perspective*. But I do want to keep in mind the Libertarian perspective.

I'm not doing anything new at all. I'm trying to restate what I think

---

39   Generally referred to as Black Monday (Black Tuesday in Australia and New Zealand), because on that day stock markets globally crashed, with the Dow Jones Industrial Average loosing over 22 percent.

are some important principles. And I also want to emphasize that the libertarian principle is important to me anyway, not just because it frees up people to create products like the iPhone and all the other technological advances but because personal freedom and liberty is valuable in its own right. Our nation is what it is because people have been able to pursue their dreams. Often, these don't work out, but we can pursue our dreams in this country to an extent that people can't in most other places around the world.

So when we get to banking, we ought to want for the banking industry what we ought to want for all industries, which is the maximum liberty for parties to engage in voluntary exchange, subject to constraint, and that their activities do not endanger the welfare of third parties.

> We ought to want maximum liberty for the banking industry

And yes, financial firms do have their special characteristics, but so do auto manufacturers, hospitals, airlines, and so forth. In fact, I was involved in a debate at the University of Delaware last night and the two—I'll call them opponents or colleagues in the economics department at the University of Delaware—were insistent that supply and demand does not apply to health care, as we were debating social security and health care. So they were insistent that supply and demand does not apply to health care. And there wasn't enough time and probably wouldn't be enough time over the rest of my life to argue them out of that position. I just think that's wrong.

A sound approach to banking reform requires that we identify the special characteristics of financial firms—we've been talking a lot about that—and legislate rules appropriate to those special characteristics and beyond that keep the government role to a minimum.

So my approach is informed by two facts. First, there is a long history, certainly, of both petty financial fraud—and of course sometimes it gets very large such as in the case of Madoff—and of large financial crises that cause significant economic loss. But secondly, there's also a long history of financial regulatory failures. To understand those failures, we must adopt a public choice perspective; and public choice perspective insists that regulation in a democracy is not the disinterested process that advocates of regulation presume. How can we trust government when its actions are so often so clearly adverse to consumer interests and protective of producer interests?

> There is a long history of financial regulatory failures

I consider the last of these points first. Governments shamelessly promote state lotteries that exploit the poor and uneducated while outlawing the so-called "numbers racket" of private lotteries that provide much better odds to the players. Another example, to protect funeral directors, a number of states outlaw unlicensed sale of caskets, as discussed in a recent op-ed in *The Wall Street Journal*. And we could multiply these examples over and over and over again.

But free market perspective also emphasizes the importance of the rule of law, rather than the rule of regulators or persons. The US Congress has delegated vast powers to regulators. And US experience is not unique. Perhaps especially in financial services, much of the delegation is unnecessary from a public policy perspective. Indeed, the delegation is harmful because it strengthens producer interest and gives consumers a false sense of security.

Many claim, as in the 2011 documentary film on the financial crisis, *Inside Job*—I suppose a number of you have seen it, and if you haven't, I would recommend it as picking it up from a library or whatever—that the crisis was a failure of regulators and not of regulation. Now there is some limited truth to that argument. While I was the St. Louis Fed president from 1998 to 2008—during the years that the financial time bomb was being built and was beginning to smolder—I do not recall clear warnings within the Fed about the accumulating dangers. The 2007 FOMC [Federal Open Market Committee] transcript is now available, and no one reviewing it will find, for example, a staff presentation on just how rotten the subprime paper was and how vulnerable were the portfolios of several huge firms. The Fed did miss this problem.

The danger was there, we know, for anyone to find if he had looked. And we know that from the very readable book by Michael Lewis, *The Big Short*. Lewis chronicles the story of several hedge fund managers, especially Steve Eisman and Michael Burry. Those two came to distrust the subprime products well before the financial crisis, and the crisis of course then demonstrated they were absolutely right.

The problem they had was to keep their investors on board until the ultimate day of reckoning came. These fund managers did not have anything close to the staff resources available to the financial regulatory agencies. The Fed and the other agencies could have uncovered the same facts that Eisman and Burry did.

However, suppose that the Fed had uncovered these facts, should Alan Greenspan have criticized by name—it would have been hard to avoid at least the implication—should Alan Greenspan have criticized by name the two presidents of the United States who led administrations with an official policy of extending more mortgage credit to marginally qualified borrowers to increase the rate of home ownership? Should Greenspan have criticized by name the congressional leaders who had the same goal? As the appointed official, is that what he should have done?

Now surely, it would seem to me that it is the role of appointed officials to administer the law and not to undercut the elected officials through pointed highly visible criticism. Greenspan did, in fact, testify on several occasions that reform of Fannie Mae and Freddy Mac was needed. And he worked behind the scenes to help forge new legislation. He failed, but he was not as blind to the risks as his critics claimed.

With that said, the financial firms that accumulated large portfolios of subprime paper bear responsibility for their behavior. Bear Stearns, Lehman, Merrill Lynch, Citigroup, AIG, and all the others had ample research resources to uncover the subprime facts. The management and directors of those firms are responsible for their firms' behavior. The federal government did not make them do it. They did it themselves, and they should have known better.

The federal government and regulatory agencies should not have been trusted. They have failed in the past, as with the savings and loan mess as we know in the 1970s and 1980s. And they'll fail again. The rating agencies failed. President Reagan said it best, "Trust but verify." The large financial firms apparently trusted the rating agencies, but they certainly did not verify.

And more than that, major financial firms violated sound Banking 101 known from the nineteenth century. A portfolio of long-duration, risky assets should not be financed by short maturity liabilities with minimal capital. I had a little discussion with Larry about Lehman's capital. He had quoted a figure of 11 percent. I don't think that was correct on

> The rating agencies will fail again

a mark-to-market basis, and so the market knew that Lehman's assets were going down the tubes and that Lehman was using up whatever margin of capital it had on the statements that the SEC was willing to certify.

So my question is, what could they have been thinking? These firms were apparently enamored of a portfolio model based on the assumptions of continuous trading in both asset and liability markets. That model of continuity had broken down in the 1987 stock market crash when portfolio insurance models collapsed and again in the 1998 crisis at Long Term Capital Management. Substantial finance literature has emphasized the importance of discrete price jumps, up and down, and fat tails. The firms that failed deserved to fail. Of course, they didn't all fail, unfortunately. And the only regret ought to be that investors in those firms' liabilities lost too little.

Now investors in banks do have an information deficit, and Larry Kotlikoff emphasized that point. It's a beautiful day out here. Suppose you're walking down the street and a well-dressed man, you know with a suit and tie, approaches you and says, "I'm a bank. Please deposit a hundred dollars with me, and I'll keep it safe. And here's a little book and we'll sign you up, and you can have it back at any time." Your reaction of course is that this guy is a nut. You don't just hand over a hundred dollars to somebody walking down the street. However, if you walk past a building that has impressive pillars, iron grates over the windows, and the word *Bank* in gold letters up there somewhere, you may be quite willing to walk in and deposit your hundred dollars without much investigation at all. And of course it's FDIC insured.

> It is impossible, even for a PhD economist, to determine the safety of a bank

But the fact is that there is no possibility—no possibility—that the average PhD economist, even I think, the well, way up in the upper tail, trained PhD economist, trained in finance, can determine the safety of a bank. Of course the reason is that the publicly available information just doesn't tell you what you really need to know about the quality of the assets.

Now consumers rely on a variety of mechanisms to judge the quality and suitability of products in the markets. We cannot engage in destructive testing of toasters, but we can read consumer reports, and we can look for the Underwriters Laboratories' seal of approval. We rely on the views of friends and experts, brand names, and so forth.

And when it comes to money, I believe that the federal government certainly does have a role. Deposit insurance up to some limit—and I'm not opposed to the current limit—does make sense. We can regard the deposit insurance as the equivalent of government efforts to maintain the quality of the circulating currency, that is the hand-to-hand currency, against the risk of counterfeiting.

Currency would be far, far less useful if someone receiving payment had to examine every bill, perhaps using a special machine to look for counterfeits. The US government does such a good job maintaining the quality of the currency that it is not necessary to examine bills at all when receiving payment, except possibly, for large-denomination bills from a questionable source. And similarly, households and small businesses can trust their deposits below the insurance limit without investigating their banks. So, as I emphasize, even if they investigated their banks, they couldn't determine the safety anyway.

So the crux of the bank safety problem is to create a structure such that someone has both the incentive and the information necessary to oversee and discipline bank-lending activities—both the incentive and the information. Even large depositors above the deposit insurance limit do not have much incentive to understand a bank. I include in large depositors here all those who have claims on banks and bank holding companies. I'm just treating that as one grand enterprise.

When large depositors come to distrust a bank, it is always cheaper, simply, to move the funds to another bank than to investigate possible problems with your own bank. And of course, that's a bank run. So, given that fact, the only way—and I want to emphasize only way—to create a stable banking system is to require that banks maintain large capital positions. The capital must consist of some combination of equity and long-term debt that cannot run—long-term debt that cannot run!

Capital provides the cushion to absorb losses, and capital owners have the incentive to monitor the bank. It's important to define the capital requirement in simple terms and not

> "Risk weighted" capital is actually "politically weighted" capital

on a so-called "risk-weighted" basis. Our experience with risk-weighted capital makes clear that the proper term is "politically-weighted" capital.

For capital to be defined in statute law and not through the uncertain process of regulatory decisions, the capital should be assessed against all balance sheet liabilities, off-balance sheet guarantees, and the net value of derivatives positions. The only task for the regulators is the accounting one of adding up the data and monitoring its accuracy. Professional investors in a bank's equity and/or its bonds have the incentive and the resources to understand the behavior of the bank in very great detail. If a bank does not provide the disclosure professional investors require, then investors will go elsewhere. That's what we do all across the market economy.

As is true for so many aspects of the modern economy, we rely on specialized expertise to uncover and evaluate information. Private providers of capital will routinely do a better job of evaluation than will regulators, provided that they are forced to accept that responsibility by the risk of loss. Keep in mind that regulators don't lose anything when a bank fails, except, at most, reputation.

The banking regulator views his job as writing rules, interpreting them, and enforcing them to control bank behavior as if the regulator were approving each and every transaction. Now, if this seems exaggerated, it is only slightly so. The regulator's job, at least the way we do it now, is to stop what he views as harmful or risky behavior, and not to encourage innovation and efficiency. The mind-set is illustrated by the guidance the regulators offer from time to time, as illustrated by a recent *Wall Street Journal* headline, "Lenders Are Warned on Risk, Regulators Act to Pop a Potential Bubble Caused by Surge in Leveraged Credit." This was just a month ago, March 22—of course at the same time that the FOMC leadership is insisting that there is no bubble in place.

Peter Wallison in his fine new book, *Bad History, Worse Policy*[40], makes clear how the regulatory imperative to protect consumers under Dodd-Frank will deny them access to credit from regulated financial firms. Under Dodd-Frank, the Consumer Financial Protection Bureau is to design "plain vanilla" financial products. For all other products, lenders may have to assume responsibility for the suitability of the products for the customers.

---

40   Wallison, Peter, *Bad History, Worse Policy: How a False Narrative about the Financial Crisis Led to the Dodd-Frank Act*, AEI Press, 2013

Lenders, subject to the possibility of expensive suits, will probably forego offering products except those for which suitability is clear and the plain vanilla characteristics are approved by regulators. Dodd-Frank will do wonders for the loan-sharking business. Given regulatory experience in the United States and elsewhere, regulation of bank activities is not an adequate substitute for capital. Regulators, and apparently banks' senior management as well, can have the same difficulty private investors do in understanding what a bank is doing.

And finally, as I've already emphasized, regulators are subject to political constraints to encourage certain activities, such as housing. The actual record of regulation and the constraints we understand through the public choice literature destroy—and I don't think that's too wild a word—destroy the case for regulation as a substitute for adequate capital.

> Regulators are under political pressure to encourage certain activities

The ultimate outcome of the conflict between mandates under the Community Reinvestment Act ("CRA"), which aims to broaden access to credit and consumer protection under Dodd-Frank, is unclear. We don't know where that's going to go, but I would not be surprised if banks make more grants to affordable housing and consumer advocate nonprofit organizations to fulfill their CRA mandates. So the money goes to politically active nonprofits instead of mortgage borrowers. There are those who will welcome this outcome, but I am not among them.

So what is a bank? Certainly a financial firm that wants to offer insured deposits must be a bank and must abide by the regulatory restrictions necessary to protect the deposit insurance fund. The FDIC has a valid interest in examining banks to detect fraud and misstatement of financial accounts. As I have emphasized repeatedly, by far the most important and effective regulation is a hefty capital requirement. I would argue for a base requirement of 10 percent on liabilities up to $50 billion and 20 percent on all liabilities in excess of $50 billion. But I'm willing to discuss that; that's not the issue. It has to be hefty, though.

Besides deposit insurance, an additional, valuable feature of a bank charter should be, of course, access to the central banks' lending facility for liquidity. Central banks should only discount sound paper at a penalty rate of interest. Such paper need not be very marketable, which is why central bank support is necessary in the first place. Marketable paper can be sold into the market to raise funds.

Now, many will regard the approach that I have outlined as "unworkable and hopelessly old-fashioned." Well, so be it. Putting aside the politics of entrenched interests, which is what economists ought to do, the issue is whether a bank subject to stiff capital constraints, will find itself in competition with near banks that forego deposit insurance and access to central bank support.

The money market mutual fund is a good example. This industry grew in the early 1970s as a consequence of regulatory avoidance; the regulation was the restriction of interest rates on deposit accounts. And now we have

> The money market industry has grown to have the political muscle to maintain the $1 fiction

the problem that these firms, which as mutual funds do not require capital, have been permitted to value their liabilities at a dollar per share, even if the net asset value of a share differs. The industry has grown to the point that it has the political muscle to maintain this accounting fiction. There's really not much to say about this issue. If a government allows a bakery, for example, to sell a one-pound loaf of bread that weighs only fifteen ounces and the package label says one pound, well, there's not much hope for orderly government in a free society.

During the recent crisis, several investment banks converted to bank holding companies to obtain Fed discount window support. To create the correct incentive, a requirement that such conversion remain in force for ten years, say, might be appropriate. We don't want a financial firm to convert to get the Fed support and, when things quiet down, to go back. That's not going to work in the long run.

Nevertheless, there is a valid issue about how to deal with near banks that do not meet the legal requirements and choose to forego the privileges of firms with bank charters. In a free society, government has an important role in enforcing laws on accurate disclosure and maintaining a legal system that permits citizens to recover damages for fraud. These are traditional functions of government.

There is, however, another function of government that we would have had to discuss a hundred years ago. Government must permit bankrupt firms to fail. The liberal market system cannot function properly if firms can use their political power to gain bailouts. My close friend Allan Meltzer puts it this way, "Capitalism without failure is like religion without sin[41]." That's the way he puts it.

A banking system characterized as containing banks that are too big to fail is a terribly serious problem. The approach in Dodd-Frank is to establish a

> Capitalism without failure is like religion without sin

41   Meltzer, Allan H., *Why Capitalism?*, Oxford University Press, 2012

new agency, the Financial Stability Oversight Council, to designate specific firms as systemically important financial institutions [SIFIs], subject to enhanced oversight and an orderly liquidation procedure. Peter Wallison is convincing, I believe, in saying that this process cannot be effective. Market fears that FDIC might seize the firm and begin the resolution process will create the same sort of run that, ultimately and quickly, brought down Lehman.

Now, much larger capital is part of the solution. But more than that, though, we need to design the proper incentive structure within the capital requirements to force a large but weak bank to shrink. The only device that does what needs to be done, as far as I know, is to require banks with over, say, $50 billion in assets, to include subordinated notes in its capital structure. And the subordinated notes with a ten-year original maturity and convertible into equity at the bank's option on maturity would provide the correct market discipline. So, if the bank is running short of equity, it forces the bond holders to convert to equity at a rate that is determined at the time the bonds are sold.

Now this idea has been around for a long, long time. It dates back to the early 1980s. With these capital requirements, the mechanism would provide a market-based way of forcing a gradual liquidation of a failing, large bank. And we simply must allow a large bank to fail. I like the way Alan Greenspan put it at one point. "There are banks that are too large to liquidate quickly. But there must not be any that are too big to fail[42]."

Subordinated debt is a mechanism to accomplish what has to be done. It is a market-based mechanism that does not rely on a vision of what financial activities are appropriate for large financial institutions. If there are sound economic reasons for financial

---

42   October 15, 2009, at a speech to the Council on Foreign Relations, New York

institutions to be huge, spread across many activities in many countries, then we should not prevent entrepreneurs from building such institutions—provided, of course, that there are no monopoly concerns, which there rarely are in financial services. Provided there are no monopoly concerns, we do not block the creation of large firms in any other industry. Why should we do so in financial services?

Again, we have to set it up in a way that the large firms are stable, and that's what stiff capital requirements would do. The principal alternative to requiring much larger capital is to insist on a narrow

> Greenspan: No bank should be allowed to become too big to fail

bank of some sort and we spent a lot of time talking about that. The problem with this approach, from my point of view, is defining the permissible activities of the narrow bank. As we are currently observing with the so-called "Volcker Rule," it's extremely difficult for regulators to decide what activities are permitted and what are not.

The approach is subject to endless negotiation between regulators and firms—and lots of regulatory avoidance. But the rules can be subject to political interference. It's really not that difficult for large financial firms with substantial contributions to political campaigns to persuade some congressman or another to slip a provision in a piece of obscure legislation that goes sailing right through, and the only people that know about it are the ones who are directly interested.

A narrow bank is essentially a firm, I believe, designed in Washington, rather than through market forces. No one knows what financial services are efficiently provided in a single firm and how that firm should evolve over time. Sandy Weill created

Citigroup as a financial supermarket in the late 1990s. Now the firm is shedding activities, perhaps because the firm is too unwieldy to manage and/or the anticipated advantages of putting the disparate businesses together did not arrive. In any event, Citi is an instructive example. Although its shrinkage is partly due to regulator pressure, it is mostly a market outcome. Government mistakes are rarely corrected so quickly.

Why do we so ignore the incentive to leverage? And I agree with everything we've said today that leverage is the real killer in this whole subject. Why do we ignore the incentive to leverage in the tax system? Economists generally

> Why do we ignore the incentive to leverage in the tax system?

argue to change incentives rather than create command and control solutions. There's no reason, I believe, not to eliminate the deductibility of interest in both the personal and corporate tax code. If you did that, of course it would produce a big disadvantage to financial firms. Incidentally, I would do it in a revenue-neutral way. You could simultaneously lower the statutory corporate tax rate from something like where it is now, 35 percent, to about 15 percent in a revenue-neutral way. That's just a back of the envelope calculation that I made.

Everyone agrees, including those who advocate tighter regulation, that the evidence is overwhelming that Fannie Mae and Freddie Mac captured Congress and did so through the capture of the regulator, which was the Office of Federal Housing Enterprise Oversight, or OFHEO. Congress made sure that OFHEO never had the resources and authority to do the job correctly. This was an egregious case. Advocates of more regulation are silent as to how to correct the inherent tendency in a democracy for regulatory capture. They wish it weren't so. But it is so. When will advocates of regulation face up to the facts of regulatory capture? Why are they so willing to ignore history and economic theory? I wish I knew.

ULI KORTSCH. We have just a few minutes for questions.

BILL POOLE. I hope I provoked somebody.

QUESTIONER. The movie *Inside Job* is available from the Free Library Philadelphia; glad you made reference to it. From a libertarian perspective, the regulators, I see, are really corporations with a revolving door; that was referred to earlier, especially in the FDA. From a libertarian perspective, how do we control the revolving door so that we don't have the problems of regulators regulating their buddies? Thank you.

BILL POOLE. I think the statement of fact is correct. A lot of regulators move out into the private sector and earn three to four times their previous salary the first year out. They go to the agency, they get a lot of training, they learn how the agency works; and that's the apprenticeship. And then they go out and earn the big bucks. And that's a fact.

What I think we need to do is to put our requirements in the law, in the statute law. The requirements need to go in the statute law. I mean, there are lots of examples, here. Think about your property taxes. Your assessor doesn't have the authority just to come around and say, "You have to pay this much tax, and this guy has to pay that much tax." There are requirements in the law that determine how your property tax is set.

> Fed regulators are doing the best they can with the authority they have

And there's an appeal process. If you leave it to the regulators, the regulatory process, then this problem will continue indefinitely.

Now I know some regulators. I mean, I was employed by the Federal Reserve System for ten years; my God, I know some regulators, and they're all very nice people. And they're well aware of the pressures that they face—well aware of that. But they are often caught in a situation that is simply impossible for them to deal with. And they're stuck. They're truly stuck. But they do the best job they can, given the authority that they have. And that's where we are. So I don't think there's any way out at all without putting the rules into the statute law.

MICHAEL KUMHOF. Okay. So you made a point about regulatory capture several times. To capture somebody, to capture the regulator takes some money—although, deplorably, it seems to be pretty cheap. But even so, it takes some money. And for institutions that can print money, essentially, they can create money, that is a hell of a lot easier than for institutions that have to convince somebody to deposit money first before they can do that. And so I think some of the proposals that were floated here would make it at least harder to capture the regulator.

But I think your emphasis on regulations was throughout your talk, and I would like to go away from that a little bit. And I would like to make a distinction between regulations and institutions. Because some of what we're proposing here is to create institutions whereby the economy would be on autopilot, and it would not require the regulator to be a very ...

BILL POOLE. It would be in the law.

MICHAEL KUMHOF. It would be in the law.

For example, if it were true that these banks were basically just administering reserves of public money, that would not be very different from holding an account directly at the central bank.

I mean, it's just somebody intermediating that, essentially, and providing some computers to intermediate that.

In that case, there is nothing else to regulate than the money supply, at least, in this economy [as described by Kumhof in Chapter 4: "The Chicago Plan Revisited"], it wouldn't need a lot of regulation because the institutions would be set up correctly. There would still be issues in the credit system, but at least the money system would be safe—not because of regulation, but because of institutional structure.

BILL POOLE. I don't want to get into a review of what we've already discussed. But I just want to reemphasize—I absolutely agree—we need to put it into the law. But I also want to emphasize that we should want an end result that allows for creativity and innovation in finance. It should not so constrain financial institutions that we lose the possibility of innovation and creativity.

The dimensions of innovation and creativity in finance run in many different directions. We can think of some that have been important. During the last twenty-five years, I happen to think of the credit default swaps market. That's a very useful

> The needed banking law must allow for creativity and innovation

innovation. I think the same thing is true of interest rate swaps. I think that opening up credit to subprime borrowers was a good idea. The problem was it went to excess because the underwriting criteria went to pot for a whole variety of reasons. Read Wallison[43]. He emphasizes—and I think he's right—the enormous role of the federal government in creating those incentives, the enormous role. And the role was administered through Fannie Mae and Freddie Mac. They were forced to hold an increasing part of their portfolio

---

43   See footnote 40

in these instruments designed to achieve the affordable housing goals; that's the way it was put.

Moreover, Wallison emphasizes—I have to go back and look at his book to be sure I've got the dates exactly right—that, as their portfolios grew, they systematically concealed the fact that so much of this growth was in the subprime category. So they were out there reporting that they had, sort of, AAA conventional mortgages, but they had no such thing. Well, obviously, that was an important part of their business. And one of the ways they did it was that they would have mortgages that had an 80 percent loan-to-value, but the originator had given a second mortgage that was the other 20 percent. That exposed the borrower to default when the borrower couldn't meet those payments.

Fannie Mae was fully aware of the fact that there were these second mortgages tacked on but hid that fact. And OFHEO did not have the authority to force the disclosure. So these are government-sponsored enterprises. That part of it was not market-produced.

Where I differ from Wallison is I think the investment banks also need to be held feet to the fire because they accumulated portfolios of this crap. And they need to be held responsible for their outcome. We should not excuse them because they got sucked in by what the government was doing. You know, the government does all sorts of things, and we need to be suspicious of some of that stuff.

WILLIAM POOLE

Senior Fellow at the Cato Institute

William Poole is senior fellow at the Cato Institute, distinguished scholar in residence at the University of Delaware, senior advisor to Merk Investments, and a special advisor to Market News International.

Poole retired as president and CEO of the Federal Reserve Bank of St. Louis in March 2008. In that position, which he held from March 1998, he served on the Federal Reserve's main monetary policy body, the Federal Open Market Committee. During his ten years at the St. Louis Fed, he presented over 150 speeches on a wide variety of economic and finance topics.

Before joining the St. Louis Fed, Poole was Herbert H. Goldberger professor of economics at Brown University. He served on the Brown faculty from 1974 to 1998 and the faculty of the Johns Hopkins University from 1963 to 1969. Between these two university positions, he was senior economist at the board of governors of the Federal Reserve System in Washington. He was a member of the Council of Economic Advisers in the first Reagan administration, from 1982 to 1985.

Poole received his AB degree from Swarthmore College in 1959 and his MBA and PhD from the University of Chicago in 1963 and 1966, respectively. Swarthmore honored him with the Doctor of Laws degree in 1989. He was inducted into the Johns Hopkins Society of Scholars in 2005 and presented with the Adam Smith Award by the National Association for Business Economics in 2006. In 2007, the Global Interdependence Center presented him its Frederick Heldring Award.

Poole has engaged in a wide range of professional activities, including publishing numerous papers in professional journals. He has published two books, *Money and the Economy: A Monetaristic View* (Addison-Wesley) and *Principles of Economics* (Houghton Mifflin). In 1980 to 1981, he was a visiting economist at the Reserve Bank of Australia, and in 1991, Bank Mees and Hope visiting professor of economics at Erasmus University in Rotterdam. At various times, he served on advisory boards of the Federal Reserve Banks of Boston and New York and the Congressional Budget Office.

Poole appears frequently on the speaking circuit and is well known for his commentary on current economic and financial developments.

Poole was born and raised in Wilmington, Delaware. He has four sons.

CHAPTER 10

Social Implications

I AM THE CEO OF Global Partners Investments and the Founder of the Monetary Trust Initiative. In this talk I draw extensively on my experience internationally, especially in the developing world, to look at the social implications of our banking and monetary system. I give examples showing the human cost of the Great Recession. Income and wealth inequality are demonstrated and a brief overview given of how these are transmitted in our current system. I end with a passionate call to change, given the social cost engendered by the fractional reserve banking system.

My résumé is found at the end of this chapter.

A 3-D Prezi presentation accompanied my speech, so I'll attempt to describe the visuals.

ULI KORTSCH:

As the opening visual—depicting the above-water portion of an iceberg with the words, "Our Ideas have real Consequences"—appears, I'm going to look at social implications and then wind it down and try and talk, as Schumacher said, "economics as if people mattered."

I think we tend to forget that in our ivory tower. I often live in one of those towers, where I talk charts, graphs, and numbers, etc. And I decided, "Let's go right brain, because we've had a left brain day all day." I don't know about you, but at the end of the day, I can't handle left brain anymore. I've got to be careful of what I say here.

(Laughter.)

So, I decided—initially I started with charts and graphs—and I thought, let's do pictures and movie clips and have them help us describe what it is that we're really talking about. What are the implications of the theories, of the agreements, of the disagreements, and of what it is that happens? The world, very much, is involved in what we're doing.

(The opening slide visually morphs into a slide showing the quote read aloud.) Here's a quote by John Maynard Keynes. "The ideas of economists and political philosophers, both when they are right and sad to say when they're wrong, are more powerful than is commonly understood. Indeed, the world is ruled by little else." I wouldn't want to say that, but I think we'll let the late Mr. Keynes say that.

That's really, ultimately, what the implications are all about, right? I think we forget in our discussions the fact that the decisions that we make here, here in this building [the Fed], here in this group of people, affect the lives, well in our case, of 310 or 320 million people or however many we are today. The policy of the Fed and the United States affects policy all over the world. Jeff Sachs said that very clearly where he's saying, "Look, the decisions that we end up making have huge effects on everybody else." Well, a lot of those effects are hidden. (*The next slide shows the underwater portion of the iceberg.*) Ninety percent of what we talk about is under water; we don't tend to see it very easily. Let me speak for myself; when I sit for down for dinner and I try to explain something to somebody, the first thing I do is get a napkin out and draw some parabolic chart or something because that's how my brain thinks, but that's not what this is really all about.

> We forget...that the decisions we make here affect 320 million people

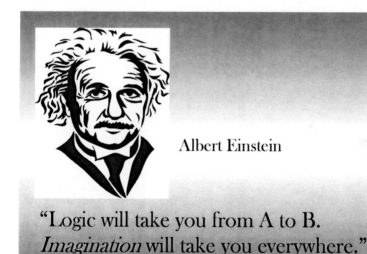

Albert Einstein

"Logic will take you from A to B.
Imagination will take you everywhere."

Figure 10.1: Albert Einstein Quote

So ladies and gentlemen, here we go. "Logic will get you from A to B"—some really famous person said that, like Albert Einstein—"but imagination will take you everywhere." And that's what I'd like to do for just a few minutes at the end of the day today. Because when we get it wrong, as John Maynard Keynes just said, the implications are phenomenal.

Figure 10.2: Image of a Riot in Greece

Figure 10.2 is a shot from Greece. I don't think I need to say anything, do I?

Figure 10.3: Bank Line in Cyprus

Figure 10.3 is a shot from Cyprus. These people are withdrawing their money, what is allowed, I think it's three hundred euros per day. Wow, can't you live off that for ever and ever? How'd you like to be a company and meet payroll on three hundred euros per day? Thank you, you're bankrupt, just like that.

You do realize we now have two different kinds of euros, don't you? There's the "normal" euro, being what we think is the euro, and there's the euro that's in Cyprus; it's not a real euro anymore because you can't take it out, can't go anywhere with it. Those are the kinds of consequences—that come from our decisions and our discussions and what it is that we talk about here—that result in bank lines; that result, sad to say, in suicides; that result in riots on the street.

What I did in that great underwater portion of the iceberg that you saw is I decided to take just a few bits and pieces of what could've been handled. (Multiple items are listed in the underwater portion of the iceberg graphic.) I probably left 80 percent out, all sorts of things that have been mentioned today. I thought, let's just have a look at a few of them.

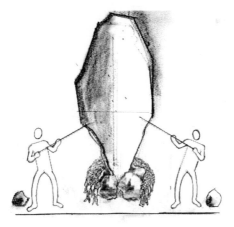

Figure 10.4: The Banking System Monolith

(*References the portion of the underwater graphic listed as "Banking Instability."*) Here's what I would say. Figure 10.4 is a rough picture of our monetary system, our banking system. So what it is, is this huge monolith, menhir, and it's standing on a point. It's very unstable. Now you will notice that we've created some really nice rocks here at the bottom; these are stability systems that are part of what it is that we've created. That's the FDIC; that's all sorts of regulatory constructions that we've created that help us stabilize this block. But we've got these big guys, and I would say this is the Fed here in the United States, working to stabilize a highly unstable system.

I am in a Fed building, and I want to praise the Federal Reserve system. I think they've done a phenomenal job for a system that I would consider as inherently unstable, and essentially everybody has said that today. We may disagree on different policies, systemic issues, whatever, but I don't think anybody has not agreed with that. We've all agreed that the system is highly unstable. So we've got these guys, and they've done a good job. This is the hundredth anniversary, as the Fed was created in 1913, right; it's the hundredth anniversary. It's not that we haven't had any problems, but by and large, I can't believe how few problems we've had considering the essential nature of what the system looks like.

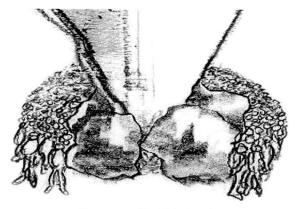

Figure 10.5: The Little People

Well, let me show you another thing about this picture. Figure 10.5 shows the bottom of the previous figure: those are the little people. Those are all human beings; those are little people down there. They actually cover everything, but then of course the whole picture wouldn't make any sense. When that big monolith falls down, it crushes those people—and that's what we're talking about today. It's a very important subject!

Let's talk about social inequality. (*Shows graphic from the underwater portion of the iceberg labeled "Inequality."*) Remember, I'm zipping through this really fast. Here's a paper[44] (*showing front page of the academic paper with pictures taken from the Occupy Wall Street movement.*) written by one of our very own, a member of the Global Interdependence Center, John Silvia, chief economist of Wells Fargo Bank. So we don't have to go very far to look at discussions of social inequality. Here's the abstract (*displays the paper's abstract*). I know we can read English, but let me read it to you:

> We study the effects and historical contribution
> of monetary policy shocks to consumption and
> income inequality in the United States.

Though Silvia said "United States," the study's findings on monetary policy and how it effects consumption and income inequality can be extended to the entire world. We continue with the abstract from the paper.

> Contractionary monetary policy actions system-
> atically increase inequality in labor earnings, total
> income, consumption and total expenditures.

---

44   John Silvia, Olivier Coibion, and Yuriy Gorodnichenko, *Monetary Policy and Economic Inequality in the United States,* (Global Interdependence Center's Society of Fellows, 2012, Banque de France, Paris), http://RealMoneyEcon. org/lev2/images/pdfs/monetary_policy.pdf.

Now let's see what part of the economy is missing from the list given; there must be something missing. No there isn't anything missing. You can clearly see that Silvia says that every part of our economy is affected, giving rise to increases in inequality throughout.

> Furthermore, monetary shocks can account for a significant component of the historical cyclical variation in income and consumption inequality. Using detailed micro level data on income and consumption, we document the different channels by which monetary policy shocks affect inequality as well as how these channels depend on the nature of the change in monetary policy.

What this says is—pardon John, I'm about to tell what it is you said in that abstract—what it says is, when people are doing everything correctly, the

> The system itself creates inequality

system inherently (the system itself) creates inequality. I could be the most wonderful, godly—whatever you want to call it—person of the human race, and yet the system itself, in the actions that I'm part of, create inequality.

We don't think about that do we? We think it's just evil people, or we think it's just somebody making a wrong decision, or we think it's just that banker who is not willing to lend me money, or that person he defaulted on his loan. No, no if everything is done correctly, the system inherent in itself creates inequality. High levels of inequality ultimately are very, very dangerous to our society. Now I'm not advocating communism; nor am I a socialist. We have strong elements of our society that are pushing strongly for redistributionism. Why are those elements of society there? Maybe because of our problem with the structure of the system. Let me run you a short video clip.

[The video can be seen at http://www.youtube.com/watch?v=
LlYojsi3Zqw]

Recording: *There's a chart I saw recently that I can't get out of my head. A
Harvard professor and business economist asked more than five thousand
Americans how they thought wealth was distributed in the United States.
This is what they said they thought it was. Dividing the country into five
rough groups of the top, bottom, and middle three 20 percent groups, they
asked people how they thought the wealth in this country was divided.
Then they asked them what they thought was the ideal distribution, and
92 percent (that's at least nine out of ten of them) said it should be more
like this—in other words, more equitable than they think it is. Now that
fact is telling admittedly, the notion that most Americans know that the
system is already skewed unfairly.*

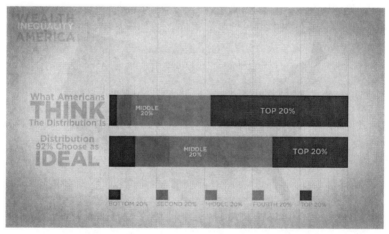

Figure 10.6: Perceived versus Ideal Wealth Distribution

What's most interesting to me is the reality compared to our perception.
The ideal is as far removed from our perception of reality as the actual
distribution is from what we think exists in this country. So ignore the
ideal for the moment; here's what we think it is again, and here is the
actual distribution.

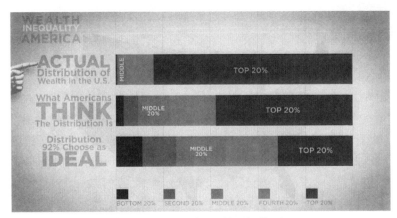

Figure 10.7: Actual Wealth Distribution

Shockingly skewed. Not only do the bottom 20 percent and the next 20 percent, the bottom 40 percent of Americans barely have any wealth, I mean it's even hard to see them on the chart, but the top 1 percent has more of the country's wealth than nine out of ten Americans believe the entire top 20 percent should have. Mind blowing!

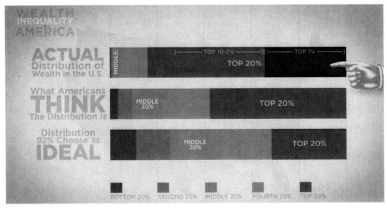

Figure 10.8: Top 1 Percent Demonstrated

Let's look at it another way because I find this chart kind of difficult to wrap my head around. Instead, let's reduce the 311 million Americans to just a representative 100 people, make it simple. Here they are teachers, coaches, firefighters, construction workers, engineers, doctors, lawyers, *some investment bankers, a CEO, and maybe a celebrity or two. Now let's line them up according to their wealth, poorest people on the left, wealthiest on the right, just a steady row of folks based on their net worth. Color code them like we did before, based on which twenty percent quintile they fit into. Now let's reduce the total wealth of the United States, which was roughly $54 trillion in 2009 to this symbolic pile of cash, and let's distribute it among our 100 Americans. Well here's socialism [see figure 10.9]—all the wealth of the country distributed equally.*

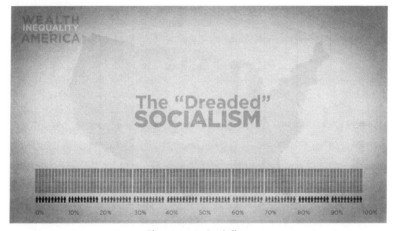

Figure 10.9: Socialism

We all know that won't work. We need to encourage people to work and work hard to achieve that good old American dream, keep our country moving forward.

So here's that ideal [see figure 10.10]we asked everyone about, something like this curve, this isn't too bad. We've got some incentive, as the wealthiest folks are now about ten to twenty times better off than the poorest Americans; but hey, even the poor folks aren't actually poor, since the poverty line stayed entirely off the chart. We have a super healthy middle class, a smooth transition into wealth, and yes, Republican and Democrats alike chose this curve. Nine out of ten people, 92 percent, said this was a nice, ideal distribution of America's wealth.

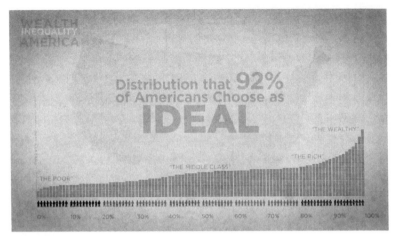

Figure 10.10: The "Ideal" Curve

Let's move on. This is what people think America's wealth distribution actually looks like [see figure 10.11] not as equitable clearly, but for me, even this looks pretty great. Yes the poorest 20 to 30 percent are starting to suffer a lot according to the ideal, and the middle class is certainly struggling more than they were, while the rich and wealthy are making roughly a hundred times more than that of the poorest Americans and about ten times that of the still healthy middle class.

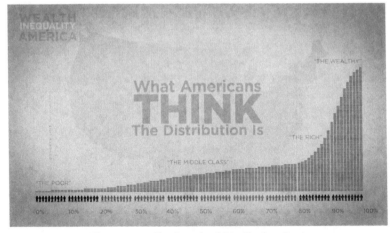

Figure 10.11: The Perceived Distribution Curve

Sadly this isn't even close to the reality. Here is the actual distribution of wealth in America [see figure 10.12]. The poorest Americans don't even register; they're down to pocket change. The middle class is barely distinguishable from the poor. In fact, even the rich between the top ten and twenty percentile are worse off. Only the top 10 percent are better off. How much better off? So much better off that the top 2 to 5 percent are actually off the chart of this scale. The top 1 percent, this guy, well his stack of money stretches ten times higher than we can show. Here's his stack of cash restacked all by itself. This is the top 1 percent we've been hearing so much about—so much green in his pockets that I have to give him a whole new column of his own because he won't fit on my chart.

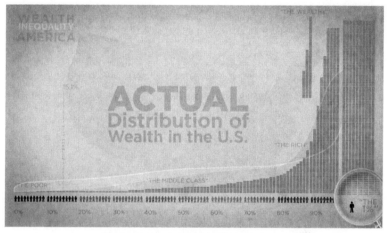

Figure 10.12: Actual Distribution Curve

One percent of Americans has 40 percent of all the nation's wealth. The bottom 80 percent—eight out of every ten people, or eighty out of these one hundred—only has 7 percent between them, and this has only gotten worse in the last twenty to thirty years, while the richest 1 percent take home almost a quarter of the national income today. In 1976, they took home only 9 percent, meaning their share of income has nearly tripled in the last thirty years. The top 1 percent owns half of the country's stocks, bonds, and mutual funds. The bottom 50 percent of Americans only own half a percent of these investments, which means they aren't investing; they're just scraping by.

I'm sure many of these wealthy people have worked very hard in their lives, but do you really believe that the CEO is working 380 times more than his average employee—not his lowest paid employee, not the janitor, but the average earner in his company? The average worker needs to work more than a month to earn what the CEO makes in one hour. We certainly don't have to go all the way to socialism to find something that is fair for hardworking Americans. We don't even have to achieve what most us of consider might be ideal. All we need to do is wake up and realize that the reality in this country is not at all what we think it is.

ULI. Now this is a conference on banking; it's not a conference on social equality. I'm not going to stand here and tell you that the banking system creates all of the inequality. I think that would be patently wrong. All I'm saying is that even our very own [GIC member John Silvia] agrees that the very banking system that we have is a significant part of a social problem that we do need to deal with.

There are a whole bunch of other things that we've talked about today, such as the application of business cycles; debt, both private and government; etc. Let's just leave those. I want to talk about banking complexity and paradigms.

I'll now entertain you for just a few minutes. Hopefully you'll enjoy this. Let's start with something very shocking. I am going to show you several short clips out of the movie *Longitude*. If you've not seen it, I strongly suggest you do see it. It's a really powerful movie. It's the true story of John Harrison and how he developed a method of developing longitude. I'm giving things away before they even start; that's terrible.

What happened is that, in the 1600s and 1700s, Britain ruled the seas, and they realized that they were losing hundreds of ships and thousands of sailors every year because they jolly well didn't know where they were. Latitude is not a problem—north/south you can tell by the sun. You know what day of the year it is, so if you know how low the sun is, you can pretty well tell where you are, north/south. Longitude, folks, it just doesn't work that easily. You haven't got a clue where in the world you are. So sailors died of scurvy; they hit reefs; they just didn't know where they were.

So in 1714, the British Parliament set up what they called the Board of Longitude, and they issued a prize of twenty thousand pounds. I can't remember exactly, but that's about $5 million today—it's a very significant prize. They asked, can anybody figure out how to do this? Along came all sorts of people who tried. The first clip shows you how serious they took this and the consequences if you diddled with it.

(*Plays a movie clip that depicts an actual event in 1707; an admiral summons the captains of his ships, as he had ordered one of the seamen hung for daring to keep a private log of what the seaman thought was the actual ship's position, which disputed the admiral's calculations.*)

Well, the nice thing is I don't think we're going to be hung by the Fed or by anybody else by looking at alternatives to the system. That's really what this sailor was attempting to do, and that's why I showed you the little clip. It was pretty deadly in those days. I think we're not quite there.

What happened is John Harrison was a simple carpenter who thought he figured this out. The solution was to create a clock that was accurate to within at least a second a day. If you could create a clock that would actually work on board a ship—they couldn't even do that on land sitting still—with all the rocking, rolling, twisting, turning, all the yawing that was going on, to do that, and then lo and behold, the ships would know where they were.

What I'm going to do, because we're running late, is I'm going to cut the next clip really short. Harrison goes before the Naval Board and asks for permission to take his clock on board ship and have it officially tested.

(*Plays a movie clip showing Harrison climbing aboard ship and then having his clock lifted by a crane.*)

There he goes. He's going onboard the ship, and there's this "tiny little clock." He's not a seaman, he's never been onboard, and he's not impressed with this at all. And that, ladies and gentlemen, is the clock.

Figure 10.13: First Version of Harrison's Clock

I want to draw an analogy. I want to say our banking system today is like John Harrison's clock. It is about a meter cubed and it takes a crane to lift this thing up on board ship because he had pendula going against springs, going against wheels, going against you name it. Every single motion needed a slightly smaller countermotion and a countermotion against that, and a countermotion against that, and a countermotion against that. It is said that he made over two hundred adjustments. Why do think this thing weighed so much? How would you like it if today you had to walk around with a wristwatch that is one cubic meter and weighs half a ton? That wouldn't work, would it?

What he needed was a paradigm shift. I want you to listen to the words of what's happening here in the next video clip. This is an analysis done in the thirties, and there's a speech given. Again this is a very short clip, and what in the world happened? This is about forty years later from the date he build his first clock.

(*Plays movie clip showing argument between John Harrison and his son. John asserts that he can make a watch that could fit into his hand and yet be more accurate than all the large clocks he's built and tested so far. An analyst from the 1930s comes on screen and states, "Harrison took a daring and lateral leap. It is as though an aeronautical engineer suddenly ceased development on a new aircraft and instead adapted the technology to make his bicycle fly to France."*)

That watch worked, and in a massive paradigm shift, he went from this one-meter machine to invent the mechanism that you and I have on our wrists today,

> We need a banking system paradigm shift

if it's not electronic. We still use—all mechanical watches today use—the very method that Harrison, this simple country carpenter, invented. It took him forty years, and you saw the things that he built before.

Why am I telling you this? I wanted to take you on a journey of our banking system and the paradigm shift I believe we need in order to move from a crane-lifted, one-ton machine to a wristwatch, because, ladies and gentleman, I believe it's possible; I really do.

(*Shows new slide from the underwater portion of the iceberg that reads,* "*Change is* not *possible.*") Oops, that's the wrong thing; it says change is *not* possible. I've been told that as I told people what this conference was all about. I had a banker say to me, "Uli, it's impossible." And every time I hear that, I go really?

Figure 10.14 shows an interesting chart.[45]

This chart goes from 1780 until essentially today and maps out the major banking regulatory changes that have occurred over the last two hundred years. It's not like we have not created major changes before. It's not like history has not seen events that demanded significant decisions.

Why is today different? Too many people believe that changing our financial system today is impossible. But I know our financial predecessors did change the system— they did so 100 years ago with the creation of the Federal Reserve Bank and again they did so fifty years ago when we went off the gold standard. And those are only two of the many changes shown in this chart.

We could do all those things then, but today that's not possible? There's something wrong with us I guess. "Todayans" can't do these things anymore.

---

45   J. R. Barth, T. Li, and W. Lu (2009), "Bank Regulation in the United States," CESifo Economic Studies, November, doi:10.1093/cesifo/ifp026.

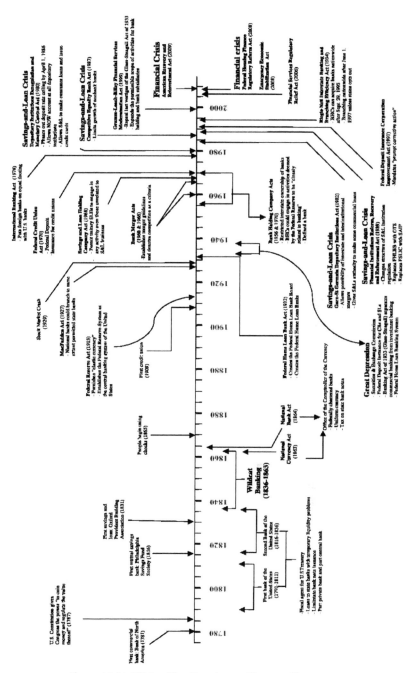

Figure 10.14: US Banking Regulatory Changes Since 1780

There is another interesting aspect to figure 1.8. If we were to draw a graph representing the number of changes over time, it would show a parabolic curve. The closer we get to today, the more changes have been created. I want to tell you we can still do it. We have a history of making good corrections. Let's keep it up.

BILL POOLE. The Harrison story is a wonderful story, but you left out something that is very interesting and relevant to our conference. I think it took about forty years from H-1, and these clocks are on display over in the Royal Observatory except I think for H-4, which is in the Clock Museum in downtown London. However, he had some opposition, and much of his prize money was denied him. Do you know who led the opposition?

> We have a history of making good corrections—let's keep it up

One of the people who led the opposition was Isaac Newton. So here you had a person who was a recognized expert in his day. Isaac Newton thought that the longitude problem, as the Brits would say, the longitude problem should be solved by using observations of the sun and moon.

Harrison had the brilliant, much, much simpler solution, but that sort of feeds into the point. I think that we need to be very careful about academics like myself—and I don't want to insult Larry because I think Larry Kotlikoff has made some great contributions—but we have to be careful about designing a system that doesn't have a lot of market input. Harrison, as you point out, was a simple country carpenter but obviously a very, very brilliant man to produce this outcome.

ULI. Thank you. Yes and it took, ultimately, the king's input. Jim, yes.

JIM. In 2009, four hundred people were responsible for paying 85 percent of all the capital gains paid in America. Conversely, those same four hundred people were also responsible for 3 percent of the GDP; this is 2009. How do you think they got that money?

[inaudible]

JIM: No, we gave it to them under bailouts. The problem with every one of these is the Italian word *sui bono*—who is going to benefit from every one of these rule changes? The same people who put the Fed in place in 1913 are the same people who are manipulating the system now. Pareto[46] tracked the tax records from Venice from 1650 or something like that; 10 percent of the population then controlled 90 percent of the wealth, at least according to the Italian model, for about eight hundred years. Nothing's changing in the world out there. You've got politics and government involved. As long as you have crooks and thieves, you're working against the system and you can't do anything about it.

ULI. Amanda, I think Larry was actually next and then Bob.

LARRY KOTLIKOFF. I have to disagree. The history of mankind is one of great progress and radical surgery. When you're driving off a cliff—you know this term *radical* is kind of pejorative, but it's actually something that I think is positive—because when you're driving off a cliff, normally it would be radically stupid to jump out of the door of a moving car, but that's the thing to do. When you have a heart patient who needs a transplant or is otherwise going to die, you want to engage in radical surgery.

We have a financial system that is radically dangerous. We've just seen that. We saw it in the thirties, and we're seeing it throughout

---

46 Unknown reference from audience member.

Europe today. We could have a twenty-year crisis the way the bureaucrats are handling it. The only real hope, I think, given the reluctance of people to think radically, is that enough of what Bill Poole and [Lord] Adair [Turner] and others are proposing, enough of the tinkering and the adding all these little features and encumbrances on banks, will lead them to go out of business and have mutual fund banking endogenously take over. If you make a big enough tax on these very dangerous entities, you will end up with something else being innovated; this connects to what you think Bill [Poole], should happen, I think.

The other thing is, Bill, just in response to this question "market tested." In 1757, a guy named Frederick II of Denmark set up the covered bond mortgage system, which is a mutual fund mortgage system, which has been operating extremely well for over two hundred years, and that's a mutual fund mortgage system. We have a mutual fund system here in the country that's extremely well-functioning and has a seventy-year history.

So, I think what I'm proposing is actually tried and true. And it has been tried by the market. It works. What's not working is this part of the banking system that has an implicit subsidy that is encouraging gambling with two public goods. And we economists know how to deal with public goods, which is, we don't screw them up. They take special care. We need to protect public goods, and there are ways to go ahead. We need a new watch [as per the John Harrison video clip analogy].

QUESTIONER. Mr. Kumhof spoke about monies being a medium of exchange. Turns out that Visa has a debit card now. I don't know if you're familiar with it, but you can put cash on it and you can carry it around. It's useful, so every time you buy a cup of coffee you don't have to fool around with the swipe. And you can also get one that is automatically loaded. You can also use it to pay salaries. If you have a debit card in my system and I pay you, it doesn't go through the bank account, not direct deposit, but right onto your little debit card.

Supposing you gave a million dollars directly instead of through the banking system. And I've got to tell you, Visa and MasterCard make the Fed look like they are bumbling fools. Billions of transactions are going on while we speak, and they track them all. They do everything. You can use it worldwide. I don't know, why isn't this a banking system? I mean, the only difference, the difference between my debit card is I have to put my cash on there. That's the deposit I make. The rest of it's all credit. And they do a fine job in deciding who gets credit and who doesn't. The problem is some people who don't get credit want it. And then you're going to have the politicians and the academics saying, "Well, it's very unfair." Get over it; unfair is the way of life.

MICHAEL KUMHOF. But I think re this last intervention just now, you have to ask yourself when they offer this service, and you put some cash on the card, what's on the other side of that transaction? It's still the debt-based system. It doesn't get away from that at all. So don't be distracted by things like this. We have a debt-based system, and solutions like that don't get us away from that.

CAROL. Uli, if you could blow up your chart again [US banking regulatory changes] and share with us, with respect to the information revolution, where some of these more heightened incidents of transfers and changes occur. One of the significant roles, of course, that the Federal Reserve has played for many years was managing the transferal of funds among banks. That role, of course, has altered with the information revolution and the capacity for us, with bits of information, to move that electronically in respect to transferals.

So, could you just share with us some of the more recent transfers and project, perhaps, about how the paradigm shifts with what our presenters today have addressed could happen? Because I think the point raised with regard to Visa and proprietary money managers and the recommendation that we separate debt management from money management that's being proposed by the two provocative suggestions that we've had for a banking system, speak to the fact that we have capacities now that heretofore we have not had.

ULI. We're already substantially over time. To do a reasonable job would, it would just take way too long. If that's okay. Anybody else? Or we will wind down. Oh. Yes?

QUESTIONER. It's just, I find it ironic that we're using the word *radical*, which in Latin means "radix", which is root structures and fundamentals. I find that interesting.

ULI. All right. Thank you very much for coming.

ULRICH (ULI) KORTSCH

Founder and President of Global Partners Investments, Ltd., and Founder of the Monetary Trust Initiative

Ulrich Kortsch is the founder and president of Global Partners Investments, Ltd. He founded the company to create financial secondary markets for the microenterprise and small-scale enterprise sectors of US inner cities and developing nations. In his capacity as president, Mr. Kortsch has written a bill for Congress, which was reviewed by the Congressional Legal Services, as well as Treasury and the Senate and House Banking Committee staffs, and conferred with approximately fifteen presidents, ministers of finance, and ministers of commerce during the course of business.

Before founding Global Partners Investments, Ltd., Mr. Kortsch served as managing partner at Kolagg Investments, LLC; executive vice president of special projects for Asset Management Associates, Inc.; chief financial officer of Dream Builders, Inc.; founder and president of Global Partners Funding (Peru); executive coordinator of the Global Dialogue Institute; and national director and CEO of Youth with a Mission (Canada), Inc.

Mr. Kortsch holds a master's in business administration from Eastern University and an honors bachelor of science in chemistry from the University of Alberta.

A native of Germany, Mr. Kortsch has held or currently holds memberships on the boards of Mercy Ships International, International Reconciliation Coalition, the University of the Nations, Dialogue Institute and Journal of Ecumenical Studies, and World Relief Canada, among others. He has held assignments in over fifty countries, is fluent in English and German, and is well-versed in French.

CHAPTER 11

Conclusions

MAY 2014

OVERVIEW

It is now more than six years since the beginning of the Great Recession and one year since the conference at the Fed. The arguments presented in this book still hold and perhaps are even more relevant as we see the lack of progress on multiple fronts, but more on that below. Economic matters appear to have entered the public consciousness to a greater degree, as the long-term effects of choices made at the highest levels trickle through. People are aware of the fact that, yes, what they personally do is definitely relevant to their lives, but they are fish swimming in a moving river. Where is that river going? And who is making decisions as to the speed, direction, and clarity of that river? There will always be those content to drift with minimal effort, but most of us want to see, understand, and take action, at least action for our own lives and those of our children.

In private meetings, senior finance and monetary staff agree that change, even radical change, is needed. Politicians voice the same interest, but there is not yet consensus as to how to structure that change. Both political and money people fear for their jobs if they are seen to espouse views generally regarded as unorthodox. It reminds me of an entry-level university course I took with over a hundred in the class. I cannot remember what the issue was, but the professor asked for a show of hands indicating which of us thought a particular solution was correct, and all put up their hands except for two brave souls. The professor responded by telling us we should let this be a life lesson, as the ninety-eight were wrong and the two were right. I had voted with the ninety-eight. I have not forgotten that lesson!

> Is the prevailing economic orthodoxy correct?

The Oxford Dictionary defines orthodox as "conforming to what is generally or traditionally accepted as right or true; established and approved." And then, most interestingly, it gives as a usage example, "the orthodox economics of today." I smiled as I read that.

Today, we think it quaint, if not downright ignorant, to contemplate orthodoxies of the past, such as the belief in a flat earth (even though a flat earth would be quite obvious to our senses), medicine's use of bleeding to treat many ailments, the right of kings to rule, or the fact of women as second-class citizens. Need I go on? The question remains: How do we overturn a shibboleth of our current times that is so much a part of the common knowledge that we don't even think about it? Our current money system is the river in which we all swim.

CURRENT STATE

The facts presented in this book were correct at the time of presentation, to the best of the authors' knowledge. What is the state of our economy today? Recessions, and most recently the Great Recession, are generally caused by credit overextensions leading to central bank interest rate increases, which then pop the asset valuation bubbles. The factors analyzed below, therefore, are those relevant to understanding the results of policies in place over the last twelve months (since the Fed conference).

On the labor market, here is a quote from the most recent missive (May 15, 2014) from Cumberland Advisors, run by David Kotok. But this is written by Bob Eisenbeis, Cumberland's vice chairman and chief monetary economist:

> Despite the marked improvement in the headline unemployment rate, a deeper look at labor

markets makes it clear that many problems still exist. The official labor force has declined, which partially explains the improvement in the headline unemployment rate, but unemployment among important labor market segments like young men and women and minorities is still high. The number of people who have been unemployed six months or more combined with those working part-time but wanting to work full-time is still much higher than in normal times. Job growth is fragmented, with most of the gains coming in low-skill, low-wage jobs. At the same time, there is a growing scarcity of highly skilled labor, hence the debate over whether the skill mismatches signify structural rather than just cyclical problems. To some, the drop in the participation rate is also a problem, although no one knows what the equilibrium participation rate should be. Finally, wage gains appear to have lagged growth in the economy. In short, those who emphasize slack in the labor market in policy discussions have plenty of arguments to work with.[47]

Figure 11.1 is a graphical representation of the latest data from the Bureau of Labor Statistics, graphed by Macrotrends. The interactive version can be found at http://www.macrotrends.net/1377/u6-unemployment-rate. Please note that, although the trend is moving in the right direction, our position today is still substantially worse than at the depth of the last recession, and this is after more than six years of supposed recovery.

---

47   Bob Eisenbeis, "Labor Market Slack and Inflation Dynamics," *Market Commentary*, Cumberland Advisors, May 15, 2014, http://www.cumber.com/commentary.aspx?file=051514.asp.

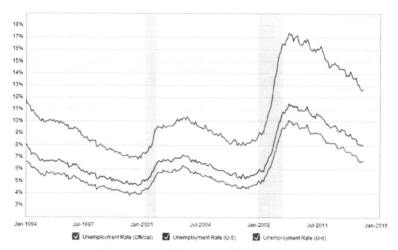

Figure 11.1: Various Unemployment Rates

I regularly hear arguments that the debt cycles are not nearly as bad as presented, as can be seen by the fact that the Troubled Asset Relief Program (TARP) funds have been 99.3 percent repaid[48] at the time of this writing and that the taxpayer has even made a profit on some of the forced investments. But that argument is deceptive, as it forgets the extent of human misery caused by the overextended credit created by our banking system. Unemployment equals human misery. This, of course, is in addition to the large increase in federal debt caused by a combination of increased transfer payments with a simultaneous decrease in tax receipts caused by this unemployment.

So where are we at with our US federal debt situation? Figures 11.2 and 11.3 are two graphs prepared from the latest data by the US Treasury site "The Debt to the Penny and Who Holds It."[49] The data set is identical, but the graphs look different because

48   http://www.treasury.gov/initiatives/financial-stability/reports/Pages/TARP-Tracker.aspx

49   http://www.treasurydirect.gov/govt/reports/pd/pd_debttothepenny.htm

the first one includes a line for "Intragovernmental Holdings," which extends the Y-axis substantially and makes it difficult to visualize. The second one only shows the "Public Debt" with identical numbers, but the Y-axis is compacted, making the visual easier to comprehend. Are we improving? It does not look like it to me. Similar graphs could be shown for EZ member countries and especially Japan.

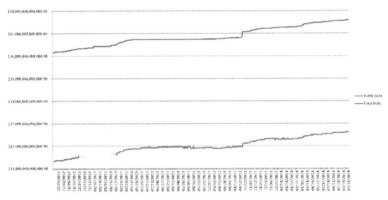

Figure 11.2: Total Federal Debt Including Intragovernmental Holdings

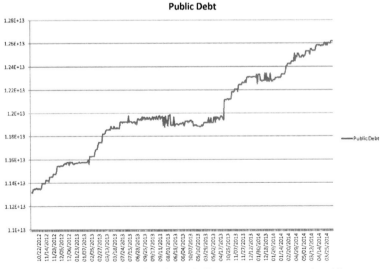

Figure 11.3: Total Federal Debt Excluding Intragovernmental Holdings

David Kotok (see Chapter 3: "Central Bank Actions"), deals with the unprecedented buildup of central bank balance sheets. The intent of these actions was clearly to stimulate the relevant economies devastated by debt overextension into bubble territory with the resultant crash. A year later, what are the observable effects?

A recent interview of the former chief economist of the Bank for International Settlements (BIS), William R. White, "I see speculative bubbles like in 2007" was reported by Mark Dittli in the prestigious Swiss business newspaper *Finanz und Wirtschaft*.[50] White is regarded as a premier expert on global financial and monetary conditions.

> I see speculative bubbles like in 2007

Somewhat into the interview Dittli asks White, "But didn't the extreme circumstances after the collapse of Lehman Brothers warrant these extreme measures?" He's referring to the unprecedented expansion of central bank balance sheets.

White replies:

> Yes, absolutely. After Lehman, many markets just seized up. Central bankers rightly tried to maintain the basic functioning of the system. That was good crisis management. But in my career I have always distinguished between crisis prevention, crisis management, and crisis resolution. Today, the Fed still acts as if it was in crisis management. But we're six years past that. They are essentially doing more than what they did right in the beginning. There

---

50   Reported on April 11, 2014 http://www.fuw.ch/
     article/i-see-speculative-bubbles-like-in-2007/

is something fundamentally wrong with that. Plus, the Fed has moved to a completely different motivation. From the attempt to get the markets going again, they suddenly and explicitly started to inflate asset prices again. The aim is to make people feel richer, make them spend more, and have it all trickle down to get the economy going again. Frankly, I don't think it works, and I think this is extremely dangerous.

Further in the interview, Dittli asks, "Where do you see the most acute negative effects of this monetary policy?"

Again, here is White's response:

> The first thing I would worry about is asset prices. Every asset price you could think of is in very odd territory. Equity prices are extremely high if you [use] ... valuation measures such as Tobin's Q or a Shiller-type normalized P/E. Risk-free bond rates are at enormously low levels, spreads are very low, you have all these funny things like covenant-lite loans again. It all looks and feels like 2007. And frankly, I think it's worse than 2007, because then it was a problem of the developed economies. But in the past five years, all the emerging economies have imported our ultra-low policy rates and have seen their debt levels rise. The emerging economies have morphed from being a part of the solution to being a part of the problem.

> The emerging economies are now part of the problem

And little further along, Dittli asks, "What about the moral hazard of all this?"

Here is White's response:

> The fact of the matter is that, if you have had 25 years of central bank and government bailout whenever there was a problem, and the bankers come to appreciate that fact, then we are back in a world where the banks get all the profits, while the government socializes all the losses. Then it just gets worse and worse. So, in terms of curbing the financial system, my own sense is that all of the stuff that has been done until now, while very useful, Basel III and all that, is not going to be sufficient to deal with the moral hazard problem. I would have liked to see a return to limited banking, a return to private ownership, a return to people going to prison when they do bad things. Moral hazard is a real issue.

Judging by these comments from the former senior economist of the BIS, the central bank for the world's central banks, the actions taken will have questionable outcomes in the long run. When analyzing asset prices of all types, it appears that we have moved from what many used to call "the Greenspan Put[51]" into a perceived global *central bank omnipotence*. This perception has grown from the fact that central banks have the power to create unlimited amounts of money and place these into the reserve accounts of banks and, thereby, create private portfolio displacements, lowering the cost

---

51   The perceived result of policy actions by former Fed chairman Greenspan whereby the possible profit upsides were not constrained, but the possible losses were. For a further explanation see http://en.wikipedia.org/wiki/Greenspan_put.

of risk and setting a floor under the value of multiple asset classes. The last few years demonstrate that every time GDP or the market drops significantly, the central banks inject liquidity. And individual investors can count on that but not fight it.

The final matter to look at in this short overview is the issue of too-big-to-fail (TBTF). The concept is based on the notion that certain financial institutions are so important to the functioning of the financial system as a whole that they cannot be allowed to fail. These institutions, therefore, receive an indirect government subsidy, as investors and managers assume a degree of protection from distress and this creates moral hazard. The results can be measured by comparing a number of parameters, such as credit default swaps, to those of institutions not granted the TBTF status. The fractional reserve banking system naturally leads to the existence of banks with TBTF status unless explicit governmental regulation exists limiting their size or increasing the incremental cost increases with growth. The whole point of creating these imputed governmental guarantees is to stop the possibility of another global meltdown caused by the implosion of one or several of these institutions. The question again remains: Have the efforts to do so been successful?

The April 2014 International Monetary Fund's *Global Financial Stability Report* devotes a major section to the TBTF factor (they call it "too important to fail" or TITF). Here is a quote from the summary of the relevant section on page 101:

> Government protection for too-important-to-fail (TITF) banks creates a variety of problems: an uneven playing field, excessive risk-taking, and large costs for the public sector. Because creditors of systemically important banks (SIBs) do not bear the full cost of failure, they are willing to provide

funding without paying sufficient attention to the banks' risk profiles, thereby encouraging leverage and risk-taking. SIBs thus enjoy a competitive advantage over banks of lesser systemic importance and may engage in riskier activities, increasing systemic risk. Required fiscal outlays to bail out SIBs in the event of distress are often substantial.

The TITF problem has likely intensified in the wake of the financial crisis. When the crisis started in 2007, and especially in the wake of the financial turmoil that followed the collapse of Lehman Brothers in September 2008, governments intervened with large amounts of funds to support distressed banks and safeguard financial stability, leaving little uncertainty about their willingness to bail out failing SIBs. These developments reinforced incentives for banks to grow larger and, together with occasional government support for bank mergers, the banking sector in many countries has, indeed, become more concentrated. [52]

Further in the report, it states that the value of these implicit government subsidies to the largest globally active banks is $15 billion to $70 billion in the United States, $25 to $110 billion in Japan,

> The banking sector has become even more concentrated

$20 to $110 billion in the United Kingdom, and $90 to $300 billion in the Eurozone. Other than the fact that this is highly unfair to banks not so designated, what is the relevance to the general population? In short, it demonstrates two facts—first, that the regulatory officials recognize that we still have institutions that are so internally unstable that they need the active support of the

---

[52]   *International Monetary Fund, Global Financial Stability Report—Moving from Liquidity- to Growth-Driven Markets (Washington, April 2014).* See complete paper at http://www.imf.org/External/Pubs/FT/GFSR/2014/01/pdf/text.pdf.

government and, second, that the very operation of the fractional reserve banking system imposes costs on the citizenry at large (costs that are hidden until catastrophe strikes).[53]

FURTHER RESEARCH NEEDED

The main tenets of this book have been well developed by a broad spectrum of economists, including the authors presented here.

The questions and criticisms from panelists and audience members addressed the real-world implications of the suggested policy changes on the table, rather than really questioning their basic frameworks; development, therefore, of the reference case described below is crucial. Before that can be accomplished, however, a number of academic aspects need to be researched under today's conditions. The first studies that should be contemplated are listed below:

1. *Banking Cost of Regulation versus Income from Indirect Seigniorage*

   Through the process of deposit creation, banks gain income from the capacity to create assets out of thin air, which are then again destroyed at the point of loan repayment. The benefit, therefore, from the seigniorage created is indirect, as the banks cannot create money for themselves but only for loan clients, from whom they can then extract interest for the term of the loan. In return for this extraordinary privilege, banks are encumbered by an increasingly complex and very costly regulatory environment. The goal

---

53   The logic here is not that the figures listed are a direct cost to the citizenry but, rather, that the managers and investors recognize these as risk-reduction cost savings because, in times of distress, the government will step in and use the tax base of the citizenry to stabilize the institution. These amounts will likely be much higher than the imputed subsidies shown.

of this study is to find the balance between this regulatory cost versus the income systemically created from the current fractional reserve banking arrangement.

2. *The Social Cost versus Benefit of the Fractional Reserve Banking System*

   Some financial experts believe that the current fractional reserve banking system allows for a greater level of liquidity in the economy, which enhances growth and thereby creates increased wealth for society as a whole. The purpose of this study is to ascertain whether this perceived benefit is greater than the cost to society of its effects of pro-cyclicality, banking collapses, high government deficits, and now also sovereign debt failures.

3. *Needed Changes in US Legislation and Regulation for Conversion into a Trust Banking System*

   The subject matter of this study is inherent in the title.

THE CREATION OF A REFERENCE CASE

OVERVIEW

Recently, I attended an economic conference where a plenary speaker from the research division of one of the regional Federal Reserve Banks referenced the monetary methodology presented in this book but said, "There is no model we can point to where this is currently working and which can be studied for effectiveness and transferability."

I spoke with him afterward to assure him that this is the next step planned.

We believe that significant change will only come after at least one successful model has been demonstrated. Further, fine-tuning of the system can occur in a smaller location more under the radar and with fewer negative consequences. Although the early adopters will be a type of national economic guinea pig, the benefits to early adoption for the banking system are substantial, as the anticipation is that large holders of cash will move theirs into these safe banking environments, thereby granting the banks significant income through fees. In order to forestall **Dutch disease** in the early adopters (for those not in currency unions), most countries will need legislation to allow banking deposits in currencies other than the native one. This will not be a necessity once the system is widely adopted.

> Where is the model to which we can point?

The strategy is for several participants to travel to the selected territory/country and induce an invitation as outlined below, unless of course that invitation comes unsolicited. The purpose is to write a consulting contract with the respective government and central bank, whereby we would bring multiple internationally recognized experts into the field in order to (1) analyze the current aggregate balance sheet, with special emphasis on the national and private debt levels and their sustainability; (2) analyze the current economy vis-à-vis business cycles, both monetary and fiscal aspects, competitiveness, and future trends; (3) analyze the changes that would result in these and other segments of society (for example, seniors, minority groups, international banks, currency movements, and so on) through both the conversion and then steady-state periods; (4) write the needed legislation to create the change; and then (5) run a conference at the respective central bank for about two days to present all the details in public.

A number of different jurisdictions could serve well for this purpose and, in turn, would be served well by the conversion. For the sake of an example, the process as it would be applicable to Puerto Rico, is described below.

PUERTO RICO

The Economist magazine has called Puerto Rico "Greece in the Caribbean"[54] due to the similarities the two face vis-à-vis their debt ratios, participation in a currency union, chronic uncompetitiveness, and inefficient public sector. Puerto Rico is a territory within the United States and not a state, meaning that many of its laws are unique and do not need to be carried across to the full union. Congress is in no mood to cover the debt of Puerto Rico, but its default would hurt the $4 trillion US municipal bond market and affect the financial affairs of every state and major city. Congress plus bond holders represent a unique alliance, which would be strong enough to overcome opposition so that the laws of Puerto Rico could be changed, thereby creating a few years of stability in order that other aspects of the territory's economy can be rationalized.

The effects of a default from Puerto Rican bonds would be felt throughout the $4 trillion US municipal bond market, irrespective of whether it is a restructuring, a missed payment, or an inability to roll the debt over as scheduled. Congress mandated that Puerto Rican debt have the same tax-free status as normal American municipal bonds irrespective of the fact that Puerto Rico is not a state. Part of the presentations during the conference described above will be the attempt to measure what that impact will be.

---

54   "Puerto Rico: Greece in the Caribbean" *The Economist*, October 26, 2013, page 17.

We believe that members of Congress will also be inclined to vote for the needed changes, as otherwise Congress would be faced with only two choices—to watch the territory collapse economically with results similar to what is being experienced in Greece or to bail Puerto Rico out. Neither is desired or likely. The measures presented in this book provide the only viable alternative at this time.

Puerto Rico is a territory and not a state, which is relevant to these efforts. First, it means that whatever is enacted for Puerto Rico does not necessarily have broad ramifications legally to the rest of the United States or to any state, therefore making the argument for change easier. All major Puerto Rican law needs to be passed by the US Congress versus state law, which is autonomous as provided in the Constitution. Secondly from an internal Puerto Rican perspective, it allows the legal changes to be viewed as being similar to those that would be needed for an autonomous state within a currency union.

Structure and Impact of Suggested Changes

The following are indicated as needed changes via legislation and action:

- » The creation of a Monetary Commission[55], to be overseen by the Federal Reserve Bank (Fed) but owned exclusively by the citizens of Puerto Rico (PR)

- » The ability of the Fed to create money and fund the Monetary Commission (MC)

- » The ability of the MC to pay its funds directly into the Treasury of PR as an accounting entry and not as debt

---

55 Please see the Chapter 4: "The Chicago Plan Revisited"

» The conversion of the PR banking system into a trust banking system

» The Fed creation of the money needed to totally cover the approximately 90 percent of the banking system's aggregate deposits not currently on reserve, move that into the MC, and have it purchase the representative banking assets with those funds

» The mutualization of these assets[56] and subsequent sale of these on the open market within sixty days of system conversion

» The movement of the resultant profits into the PR Treasury

» The sterilization of all funds moved from the banking depository window into the investment window within thirty days of conversion by use of the Fed's balance sheet

» The steady state monetization of increases in nominal GDP on a quarterly basis by the Fed for funding the MC and then the PR Treasury

> The model will have first mover advantage

Impact of these actions on the Puerto Rican economy:

» The immediate payment of all or most of the outstanding debt through the income generated by the sale of the banking assets bought by the MC and then moved into the PR Treasury

» The significant reduction, if not outright coverage, of government deficits through the steady state monetization of the change in nominal GDP by the Fed/MC

» Fiscal stability for the territory for the immediate future

---

56 Please see the Chapter 5: "Limited Purpose Banking"

Impact of these actions on the aggregate US economy:

- » Stabilization of the $4 trillion municipal bond market
- » Savings to the federal budget, as Congress will not need to bail PR out
- » Negligible impact from a monetary perspective on US Federal Reserve Bank operations as the PR economy is only about 0.5 percent of the US total

Impact of these changes for the methodologies presented in this book:

- » Allow the formulation of test legislation in general for the US legal system
- » Allow the study of the effects on a system acting within a currency union, which is highly relevant to Europe
- » Create a major impetus through enhanced credibility to move on to sovereign nations

If we want to forestall another crash similar or even worse than the Great Recession, we—from the sense of the greater community, which we really are—need to combine soul and role and take action. Perhaps you are one of those who only read the preface and then these conclusions and feel overwhelmed by the data and depth of ideas presented. Yet you also have a role to become more aware, more involved, and more proactive because the issues presented here affect each of us and will affect our children and grandchildren. If you are in the finance, banking, or political field, then the challenge is direct—use your platform, speak out, and be heard.

Glossary of Terms and Economic Concepts

ABACUS settlement. "The Securities and Exchange Commission today announced that Goldman, Sachs & Co. will pay $550 million and reform its business practices to settle SEC charges that Goldman misled investors in a subprime mortgage product just as the U.S. housing market was starting to collapse.

"In agreeing to the SEC's largest-ever penalty paid by a Wall Street firm, Goldman also acknowledged that its marketing materials for the subprime product contained incomplete information."[57]

aggregate versus micro-phenomena. Many phenomena that appear to be perfectly clear at the individual or micro level become obscure or even counterintuitive at the aggregate level. For instance, bank intermediation—which supposes that the funds used to make loans by banks come from previous deposits— appears to make sense at the micro level. (And people commonly believe this is what banks do.) But the question—immediately obvious when analyzing on the aggregate level—is where did

---

57   US Securities and Exchange Commission, "Goldman Sachs to Pay Record
      $550 Million to Settle SEC Charges Related to Subprime Mortgage CDO,"
      July 15, 2010, http://www.sec.gov/news/press/2010/2010-123.htm.

those deposits come from in the first place? The deposits obviously come from a previous bank account, which was deposited from a previous bank account, and so on. This leads to an endless circle, unless broken by a totally different action, as explained in this book. In economics, there are many examples of aggregate phenomena appearing to be counterintuitive.

arbitrage. The near simultaneous buying and selling of anything, such as securities, currency, or commodities in different markets in order to take advantage of price differentials for the same item or asset.

bail-in versus bailout. In reference to banks, bailout is the action by another party, usually the federal government, to recapitalize a bank under pressure in order to stop a bank run to forestall further economic damage. Bail-in, on the other hand, is the forced recapitalization by depositors or bond holders.

Basel III. The latest and most stringent requirements for capital adequacy, stress testing, and liquidity mandated to banks operating in countries participating under the auspices of the Bank for International Settlements, centered in Basel, Switzerland. These came about as a result of the 2008 banking crisis. Implementation is to be complete by 2018.

Basis point. One one-hundredth of a percent; therefore, 50 basis points equals 0.5 percent.

broad money versus narrow money. Broad money is the most inclusive measure of the money supply. Narrow money is the sum in circulation consisting of currency (coins and notes) plus bank reserves.

CDS (credit default swap). A derivative instrument designed to provide insurance against default in the underlying credit instrument, usually a bond or a loan[58].

Chicago Plan. Banking reform suggested by a group of economists centered around the University of Chicago coming from observed effects of the Great Depression. In essence, the Chicago Plan encompassed the division between funds in the depository or payment system and those used for investment/loan purposes. The most important element was that the deposit/payment system funds would be inviolable in a trust system within the banking structure, totally separated from the investment/loan functions of banking. The most prominent advocate was Irving Fisher, considered by many to be the most prominent economist the United States has ever produced.

Diamond-Dybvig. A bank model originally published in 1983 by Douglas Diamond of the University of Chicago and Philip Dybvig, then of Yale University, which provided the mathematical framework showing that banks issuing long-term debt funded through short-term liabilities will be unstable during times of economic stress.

Dodd-Frank Act. The Dodd-Frank Wall Street Reform and Consumer Protection Act was passed into law in July 2010. It brought significant changes to US financial regulation deemed necessary and appropriate in light of the Great Recession starting in 2007 to 2008. Dodd-Frank is the most extensive restructuring of US regulation and oversight of the finance industry since the Great Depression. Many feel that it overregulates aspects of finance that

---

58   For further information see, Wayne Pinset, "Credit Default Swaps: An Introduction," *Investopedia*, August 25, 2012, http://www.investopedia.com/articles/optioninvestor/08/cds.asp.

were not responsible for the economic downturn but does very little to stop a repeat of similar events.

DSGE (dynamic stochastic general equilibrium). A form of macroeconomic mathematical modeling explaining systems based on factors from microeconomics and allowing these to change over time.

Dutch disease. A term coined by *The Economist* magazine in 1977 to describe a situation whereby one factor of production or national income so increases the value of the currency that it leads to a significant reduction of all other economic activities not associated with the factor driving the currency higher. Historically, this has usually been a commodity such as oil, but it could also be foreign aid or, in the case developed in this book, a strengthening of the banking sector such that there would be a significant influx of deposits seeking safety. Dutch disease may develop if the country then does not allow deposits in foreign currencies.

elastic versus inelastic responses. Elasticity in economics refers to the degree of change created in a referenced factor dependent on another one. For instance, elasticity may refer to the change in goods produced depending on a change in price. An elastic response means that the degree of change is large, while an inelastic response means that the degree of change is zero or very minor.

endogenous versus exogenous. Endogenous and exogenous are commonly used adjectives in economics describing effects that originate from factors within a particular model (endogenous) or from the outside (exogenous).

eurozone (EZ) versus European Union (EU). The eurozone is an economic and monetary union consisting of those member states of the European Union that have adopted the euro as their currency; at the time of this writing, eighteen countries comprised the eurozone. EZ members are also under the direction of the European Central Bank. The European Union is a larger group consisting of twenty-eight member states, largely for the purpose of creating a single market.

excess reserves. Bank reserves consist of cash in the vault plus holdings in deposit at the relevant central bank, being the Federal Reserve Bank in the United States. Minimum reserve requirements are defined by federal regulation in conjunction with Basel limits as a percentage of bank liabilities (commonly customer deposits). Excess reserves are those held by banks in amounts larger than those mandated. This concept is deemed important by many, as the Federal Reserve Bank as well as all other **OECD** central banks have created trillions of dollars' worth of excess reserves since the Great Recession as an economic stimulus through their **QE** programs. In common economic thinking, these reserves can be very dangerous, as they could lead to large-scale inflation through the deposit multiplier. Some thinkers whose views are presented in this book dispute this.

FDIC (Federal Deposit Insurance Corporation). The FDIC is an independent US government agency that provides member banks with deposit insurance and bank oversight (for some but not all) and manages bank receiverships. It is funded through premiums paid by member banks. At the time of this writing, deposits are guaranteed to $250,000 per account category. No depositor has ever lost insured funds since the FDIC's inception.

federal funds rate. This is the interest rate at which banks trade reserves held at the Federal Reserve Bank, usually overnight and uncollateralized. It is an important benchmark for financial markets, and its value is targeted by the Fed through open market operations. The target rate is set by the **FOMC**.

FOMC (Federal Open Market Committee). The FOMC is a committee within the structure of the Federal Reserve Bank tasked with overseeing the open market operations of the Fed. It consists of twelve voting members—the seven members of the Federal Reserve Board plus five of the twelve presidents of Federal Reserve Banks. Its primary purpose is interest rate targeting through the federal funds rate in order to fulfill the Fed's dual mandate of price stability and employment maximization, both left undefined by Congress.

forward guidance. Central banks have a limited tool set with which to control aspects of the economy. Lately, forward guidance has been added to this set in order to stabilize markets by letting the public know in advance what the planned actions of the central bank will be with respect to the setting of interest rates, **QE**, and so on. In essence, forward guidance represents a greater openness in the decision making process so that market participants can make appropriate choices for the future.

Glass-Steagall. The Glass-Steagall Act, officially called the Banking Act, was passed by the US Congress in 1933. Although it encompassed a number of reforms, including the creation of the **FDIC** and the **FOMC**, it is most remembered today as creating a separation between commercial and investment banking. The act was weakened over the decades and finally repealed in 1999 during the Clinton administration. Several authors in this book believe that the Great Recession would not have occurred if this separation had been kept in place and, for the sake of banking stability, actively promote a total separation of the two functions.

intermediation (banking). The common thinking that banks—or the banking system as a whole, and it's important to make that distinction—accept nonbank deposits of savings and then lends these out to someone else who needs them. The fact that this is not what happens is one of the most important aspects to understand when it comes to banking and the monetary system as a whole.

intertemporal consumption (smoothing). In economic theories, intertemporal consumption, takes into account that people have different preferences with respect to saving and consumption over the course of their lifetimes. For example, spending tends to be high during the ages of twenty to forty, with the establishment of households and families; then there are about two decades of generalized higher savings and then again higher consumption for sixty-plus-year-olds.

Within the context of this book, questions are raised as to the efficacy of our current fractional reserve banking system vis-à-vis others proposed with respect to the role of debt in smoothing these consumption and saving patterns.

LIBOR (London Interbank Offered Rate). LIBOR is the average interest rate in London, estimated by leading banks, that they would be charged if borrowing from other banks. This is probably the most used benchmark rate globally for the setting of short-term interest rates. It is estimated that derivates and other financial products in excess of US$300 trillion are tied to it.

liquidity trap. Within the modern context, the term liquidity trap refers to the inability of monetary policy to stimulate demand; it is also known as the "pushing-on-a-string problem." The primary tools of a central bank are its control of interest rates and its ability to create excess reserves. Both of these tools depend on the transmission mechanism of (a) banks being willing to issue loans and (b) customers being willing to take them out. In de-leveraging economies, such as have been operating within **OECD** countries since 2008, neither of these two conditions exists. Therefore, no matter how low the interest rate or how much excess reserves are created, demand will not be stimulated. This effect is also measured through a low or decreasing velocity of money.

macroprudential versus macroeconomic policy. Macroprudential refers to the oversight and regulation of the financial system with respect to the health of the system overall versus that of, say, an individual bank. For example, the setting of reserve requirements for banks is macroprudential, as this affects the system as a whole.

Macroeconomic policy, on the other hand, consists of the combination of monetary and fiscal policies to control and stimulate the aggregate indicators of an economy, such as inflation, employment rate, money supply, and so on. Macroprudential could, therefore, be seen as a subset of macroeconomic.

Main Street versus Wall Street. Main Street is a "colloquial term used to refer to individual investors, employees and the overall economy. 'Main Street' is typically contrasted with 'Wall Street.' The latter refers to the financial markets, major financial institutions and big corporations, as well as the high-level employees, managers and executives of those firms. You'll often hear about Main Street vs. Wall Street in rhetoric about the differing goals, knowledge levels, interests and political power of these two groups. Some people think that what's good for one group is bad for the other. For example, high executive pay is seen to conflict with ordinary workers' pay and job security."[59]

mark-to-market accounting. Mark-to-market accounting, also known as fair value accounting, is the accounting of an asset or liability based on its most recent market value as determined by the last public price paid. This has been the accepted method of

---

59   Taken from *Investopedia* at http://www.investopedia.com/terms/m/mainstreet.asp.

the generally accepted accounting principles (GAAP) for several decades, versus accounting by historical value. The reason mark-to-market accounting is an issue is that, during times of volatility, mark-to-market is highly pro-cyclical. It is arguably the cause of the bankruptcy of Lehman Brothers, which caused the near convulsion of the global financial system.

maturity transformation. The act of using short-term funding to create long-term obligations. Maturity transformation is a service to the depositor or initial funder, but it leads to financial stress during times of low liquidity. Although an important service of the banking industry, maturity transformation has repeatedly led to bank runs. Several authors provide means of keeping this function while eliminating or greatly reducing its attendant risk.

monetary versus fiscal. Fiscal refers to the government's use of taxation, expenditures, budgets, and debts to fund itself and influence economic behavior. Monetary refers to the money supply and its affects—in other words, its creation, control, and policies used to direct it.

money multiplier or deposit multiplier. The theoretical amount by which the reserves of a commercial bank can be multiplied into loans to customers. For instance, if the reserve requirement is 9 percent, then the money multiplier would be 11.11.

In actual fact, this is a misunderstanding of how the fractional reserve banking system works, as explained in detail in this book. Over the last two years, the Federal Reserve Bank has created about $3 trillion in additional reserves. With a money multiplier of 10, this would suppose an increase in the broad money supply of $30 trillion. It is most obvious that this has not occurred, as the effective multiplier today is essentially zero.

multiple equilibria. In economics, an equilibrium exists when economic forces are balanced if external forces remain unchanged. The intent of much fiscal and monetary policy is to create such an equilibrium with benign conditions, such as low unemployment. Multiple equilibria is the condition in which an equilibrium can exist under identical conditions but with variable outcomes. For example, long-term unemployment may be stable at multiple levels, such as 4, 6, or 8 percent due to structural issues. It may have increased from 4 to 6 percent due to an external shock and then remain there. The role of monetary and fiscal policy is to find a catalyst (a short-term external force) to move it back to the 4 percent equilibrium level.

near money or money substitute. Highly liquid assets that can be easily converted into cash or used for barter. One of the substantial differences is that near money or money substitutes are always valued in terms of money but never the other way around.

nominal versus real value. Nominal value is expressed in terms of the current money; real value is expressed taking into account other factors, usually inflation. For example, a dollar in the year 1950 has the same nominal value as a dollar today, but the real value would be about nine dollars today.

OECD (Organisation for Economic Co-operation and Development). A club of the highly developed countries, today consisting of thirty-four, committed to democracy and the development of a market economy. The OECD uses peer pressure to stimulate and improve policies in the areas of economics, the environment, and social issues. It is headquartered in Paris, France.

PCE (Personal Consumption Expenditure) deflator. The PCE deflator measures the average change in price over time and is, thus, similar to the consumer price index (CPI) in measuring inflation. It measures the actual and imputed expenditures of individuals for all durable and nondurable goods and services, including substitionary choices made as relative prices change (called chain-type).

Phillips curve. The Phillips curve represents a relationship between the rate of inflation and that of unemployment, found by Phillips to be a curving, inverse one. Continuing work by economists came to show that the relationship was only stable in a condition of a stable rate of inflation. From this came the "nonaccelerating inflation rate of unemployment" (NAIRU)[60].

pro-cyclicality. Pro-cyclicality refers to items of policy or regulation that tend to accentuate the ups and downs of the business cycle. One of the policy items mentioned in this book is **mark-to-market accounting**. Generally speaking, countercyclical policy is to be recommended, as it would lead to a more stable economic environment. Automatic buffers can be created which expand or contract as needed for countercyclicality e.,g, unemployment insurance.

QE (quantitative Easing). QE is the purchasing of assets by central banks in an attempt to stimulate economic activity. It is an aspect of monetary policy that used to be considered unconventional but appears to have become the norm of late.

QE is misunderstood by the general public, who consider it to be a case of printing money into circulation. In the United States, the Fed started by purchasing Treasury securities only but then also added GSE agency debt (Fanny Mae, Freddie Mac, and Ginnie Mae). The funds from these purchases end in the reserve accounts of

---

60   For a more in depth discussion of this topic, see Kevin D. Hoover, "The Concise Encyclopedia of Economics," *Library of Economics and Liberty*, http://www.econlib.org/library/Enc/PhillipsCurve.html.

banks and not in general circulation and are, thus, noninflationary while on account with the Fed.

QE has not been shown to increase lending by private banks, which is totally contrary to what Economics 101 would teach in university courses. The transmission mechanism is in reducing risk premia on the securities bought. The intent is that this would spill over into the private market and, thereby, create portfolio rebalancing, which would lower borrowing costs for corporations and thus lead to greater supply and demand in the general economy.

regulatory capture. Regulatory capture is a form of government failure. It occurs when the industry to be regulated is able to undermine or even direct the very regulatory agency that ought to be overseeing that industry. This can come about through various forms of corruption or having a revolving door between management in the industry and the regulatory agency.

seigniorage. The difference between the face value of a piece of money and the cost of creating it. For example, if a one-dollar bill costs one cent to produce, then the seigniorage would be ninety-nine cents. In the fractional reserve banking system, it is the commercial banks that accrue an indirect seigniorage, as money is created through debt contracts (loans to clients) but then eliminated when those debts are paid off. In the interim, the bank receives interest on the funds created, which is why the seigniorage is only indirect.

SIFI (systemically important financial institution). Financial market utilities deemed important to the overall health of the US economy. These include the largest banks, insurance companies, hedge funds, and others. Once an organization is deemed to be an SIFI by the US government, it is subject to extra stringent regulation and oversight.

sovereign debt. The amount of money a central government has borrowed, usually in the form of bonds issued. This does not include obligations the government may have taken on—usually called unfunded liabilities in the United States—but for which it has not yet issued debt securities.

subprime real estate mortgages. Those mortgages issued to borrowers who were not able to qualify for a prime rate mortgage. The reason this classification is important is that the US government mandated that the percentage of home ownership be increased, and so numerous methods were developed to create mortgages for which these clients could qualify, including adjustable rate mortgages (ARMs), nondocumented mortgages (to become known as liar loans), etc. In the process, the regulatory oversight, as well as the incentive structures for issuing agents, became perverse. Hundreds of billions of dollars of these loans were issued (over $600 billion in 2006 alone), and then most were securitized into structures often rated as AAA[61]. When ARMs started resetting and the real estate market flattened, making refinancing impossible, the derived securities collapsed causing strain to many banks and investment companies globally and, ultimately, initiating the Great Recession.

SWIFT (Society for Worldwide Interbank Financial Telecommunication). Among other services, SWIFT provides a method of secure communications globally between financial institutions, the most important effect of which is institutions' ability to facilitate funds transfers securely by communicating payment orders through participating banks.

tapering. A recently coined term referring to the slow reduction in the monthly amount of securities bought by the Fed as part of its **QE** program.

---

61   The highest and most secure rating possible for a security. The ratings are issued by credit rating agencies.

TARP (Troubled Asset Relief Program). "A group of programs created and run by the U.S. Treasury to stabilize the country's financial system, restore economic growth and prevent foreclosures in the wake of the 2008 financial crisis through purchasing troubled companies' assets and equity. The Troubled Asset Relief Program initially gave the Treasury purchasing power of $700 billion to buy illiquid mortgage-backed securities and other assets from key institutions in an attempt to restore liquidity to the money markets. The fund was created on October 3, 2008 with the passage of the Emergency Economic Stabilization Act. The Dodd-Frank Act later reduced the $700 billion authorization to $475 billion."[62]

tontine. A tontine is an arrangement whereby a group of participants pay an equal amount into a fund and draw a lifetime annuity from this fund for each participant based on dividends from the invested capital. As a participant dies, the remaining participants gain increased annuity shares through the redistribution of the deceased participant's shares and, thus, increased annuity payouts for the survivors. At the death of the final participant, the capital reverts to the government or corporate body that organized the scheme. A variation paid the capital to the final survivor. Due to the lottery nature of the scheme and to abuses such as underestimating the longevity of participants, tontines we outlawed in the United States and Great Britain over a century ago.

transmission mechanism. "The monetary transmission mechanism describes how policy-induced changes in the nominal money stock or the short-term nominal interest rate impact real variables such as aggregate output and employment. Specific channels of monetary transmission operate through the effects that monetary policy has on interest rates, exchange rates, equity and real estate prices, bank lending, and firm balance sheets. Recent

---

62   http://www.investopedia.com/terms/t/troubled-asset-relief-program-tarp.asp

research on the transmission mechanism seeks to understand how these channels work in the context of **dynamic stochastic general equilibrium** models."[63]

U3 versus U6 unemployment rates. U3 is the official unemployment rate—the percentage of those unemployed in the civilian labor force. The Bureau of Labor Statistics Web site explains U6 as follows: "Total unemployed, plus all persons marginally attached to the labor force, plus total employed part time for economic reasons, as a percent of the civilian labor force plus all persons marginally attached to the labor force." It adds, "NOTE: Persons marginally attached to the labor force are those who currently are neither working nor looking for work but indicate that they want and are available for a job and have looked for work sometime in the past 12 months. Discouraged workers, a subset of the marginally attached, have given a job-market related reason for not currently looking for work. Persons employed part time for economic reasons are those who want and are available for full-time work but have had to settle for a part-time schedule. Updated population controls are introduced annually with the release of January data."[64] The reason this definition is included here is that many believe that the real number used publicly should be U6, which is always substantially higher than U3 but shows the true percentage of those who would like to work even if they are not currently on the rolls of those actively looking for a job.

Volcker Rule. Named after former Federal Reserve Bank chairman Paul Volcker, the Volcker Rule disallows banks from trading on their own books for short-term securities, as these trades do not profit a bank's own customers. Banks may continue to offer all

---

63   The New Palgrave Dictionary of Economics: http://www. dictionaryofeconomics.com/article?id=pde2008_M000214.

64   Found at http://www.bls.gov/news.release/empsit.t15.htm.

these services to their customers on the customers' accounts and make profits on those activities. In effect, it is a sort of Glass-Steagall lite.

ZIF (zero interest rate floor). ZIF refers to the fact that central banks cannot lower interest rates (federal funds rates) below zero, as, otherwise, investors, institutional as well as individual, would simply park their funds "under the mattress." In fact, negative interest rates have been used historically and are advocated by some for certain types of holdings in order to increase the velocity of money. Under both the **Chicago Plan** and Limited Purpose Banking (see Chapter 5), negative rates would exist under the payment/deposit windows of banks, as these would offer no interest income but charge fees for holdings.

ZIRP (zero interest-rate policy). The financial policy by which a central bank lowers the policy rate (the federal funds rate in the United States) to zero or close to it. The reason for doing this is to stimulate the economy by motivating loan creation through commercial banks. The negative effect tends to be financial repression whereby savers are forced to fund the investments of those able to borrow at super low rates or to take advantage of the international carry trade, whereby funds are borrowed low and invested high. This policy is a major inducement to further financial inequality.

Bibliography

Benes, Jaromir and Michael Kumhof. *The Chicago Plan Revisited: Revised Draft of February 12, 2013.*

Buchanan, Mark. *Ubiquity: Why Catastrophes Happen.* New York: Broadway Books, 2002.

Evans-Pritchard, Ambrose. "IMF's Epic Plan to Conjure Away Debt and Dethrone

Bankers." The Telegraph, October 21, 2012. Available at http://www.telegraph.co.uk/finance/comment/9623863/IMFs-epic-plan-to-conjure-away-debt-and-dethrone-bankers.html

Ferguson, Niall. *The Ascent of Money.* Penguin Books, New York, 2008.

Fisher, Irving. *100% Money: Designed to keep checking banks 100% liquid; to prevent inflation and deflation; largely to cure or prevent depressions; and to wipe out much of the National Debt.* New York: The Adelphi Company, 1935.

———. *100% Money and the Public Debt.* Economic Forum, Spring Number, April–June 1936, 406–420.

Friedman, Milton. "The Monetary Theory and Policy of Henry Simons." *The Journal of Law and Economics,* 10, (1967).

—. *A Program for Monetary Stability.* New York: Fordham University Press, 1960.

Friedman, Milton and A. Schwartz. *A Monetary History of the United States, 1867–1960.* Washington, DC: National Bureau of Economic Research, 1963.

Graeber, David. *Debt: The First 5000 Years.* Melville House Publishers, New York, 2011.

Kucinich, Dennis and John Conyers (Sponsors, US House of Representatives). "H.R. 2990 (112th): National Emergency Employment Defense Act of 2011," https://www.govtrack.us/congress/bills/112/hr2990/text.

Huber, Joseph. *Monetäre Modernisierung.* Marburg: Metropolis Verlag, 2011.

Jackson, Andrew and Ben Dyson. *Modernising Money; Why Our Monetary System is Broken and How It Can Be Fixed.* Positive Money, 2012.

Kindleberger, Charles. *Manias, Panics, and Crashes: A History of Financial Crises.* John Wiley & Sons, 2000.

Kotlikoff, Laurence J. *Jimmy Stewart Is Dead: Ending the World's Ongoing Financial Plague with Limited Purpose Banking.* Wiley, 2011.

—. *The Economic Consequences of the Vickers Commission,*

Civitas:74 Institute for the Study of Civil Society, London, June 30, 2012.

Kumhof, Michael and R. Rancière. *Inequality, Leverage and Crises,* IMF Working Paper WP/10/268, 2010.

Mauldin, John and Jonathon Tepper. *Code Red: How to Protect Your Savings from the Coming Crisis.* Wiley, 2014.

Reinhart, Carmen. and Kenneth Rogoff. *This Time Is Different: Eight Centuries of Financial Folly.* Princeton and Oxford: Princeton University Press, 2009.

Silvia, John, Olivier Coibion, and Yuriy Gorodnichenko .*Monetary Policy and Economic Inequality in the United States,* (Global Interdependence Center's Society of Fellows, Banque de France, Paris, 2012 http://RealMoneyEcon.org/lev2/images/pdfs/monetary_policy.pdf.

Tainter, Joseph. *The Collapse of Complex Societies, New Studies in Archeology.* Cambridge University Press, 1988.

Zarlenga, Stephen. *The Lost Science of Money.* Valatie, NY: American Monetary Institute, 2002.

Global Interdependence Center

The Global Interdependence Center (GIC) is a Philadelphia-based nonprofit organization with a global reach.

Our mission is to encourage the expansion of global dialogue and free trade in order to improve cooperation and understanding among nations, with the goal of reducing international conflicts and improving worldwide living standards.

With that focus driving our work, GIC provides a forum for the exchange of divergent perspectives. We engage experts to identify emerging economic, social and political issues vital to the interdependent global community. GIC organizes country and region-specific meetings, conferences and briefings for educational and networking opportunities. We promote global partnerships among governments, non-governmental organizations, corporations, businesses and academic and research institutions. GIC also prides itself on sharing its findings with policymakers and the press worldwide.

http://www.interdependence.org/

The views expressed in this book are those of the
authors and do not necessarily represent those
of the Global Interdependence Center.

Open Book Editions
A Berrett-Koehler Partner

Open Book Editions is a joint venture between Berrett-Koehler Publishers and Author Solutions, the market leader in self-publishing. There are many more aspiring authors who share Berrett-Koehler's mission than we can sustainably publish. To serve these authors, Open Book Editions offers a comprehensive self-publishing opportunity.

A Shared Mission

Open Book Editions welcomes authors who share the Berrett-Koehler mission—Creating a World That Works for All. We believe that to truly create a better world, action is needed at all levels—individual, organizational, and societal. At the individual level, our publications help people align their lives with their values and with their aspirations for a better world. At the organizational level, we promote progressive leadership and management practices, socially responsible approaches to business, and humane and effective organizations. At the societal level, we publish content that advances social and economic justice, shared prosperity, sustainability, and new solutions to national and global issues.

Open Book Editions represents a new way to further the BK mission and expand our community. We look forward to helping more authors challenge conventional thinking, introduce new ideas, and foster positive change.

For more information, see the Open Book Editions website:
http://www.iuniverse.com/Packages/OpenBookEditions.aspx

Join the BK Community! See exclusive author videos, join discussion groups, find out about upcoming events, read author blogs, and much more! http://bkcommunity.com/

CPSIA information can be obtained at www.ICGtesting.com
Printed in the USA
BVOW07s1230250914

368124BV00001B/192/P